W9-BYE-110

SILVER
BULLETS

SILVER BULLETS

A Soldier's Story of How Coors Bombed in the Beer Wars

Robert J. Burgess

St. Martin's Press New York

Editor: George Witte
Production Editor: Eric C. Meyer
Copyedited by Miranda Spencer
Design by Judith A. Stagnitto

ISBN 0-312-09251-2

First Edition: May 1993

10 9 8 7 6 5 4 3 2 1

For all the dreamers who've had the
courage to ask, "Why not?"

Contents

Acknowledgments

From the very first time I escaped the boredom of grade school by immersing myself in a book, I've dreamed of seeing my name, as author, on a book cover. At last, that dream has been realized. But while my name will grace the cover, this dream would not have been possible without the help of many others.

Silver Bullets would never have happened without the experienced publishing professionals at St. Martin's Press. In particular, I wish to thank my editor at St. Martin's, George Witte, and his assistant, Ann McKay Farrell, who shared and shaped my vision of this project. Eric Meyer and Miranda Spencer also provided valuable insights and expertise in editing this manuscript.

Special thanks to Peter Miller, my agent, and Jennifer Robinson, his associate at PMA Literary and Film Management, Inc. Your patience and diligence on my behalf will never be fully repaid.

A number of family members and friends provided much needed encouragement and constructive criticism during the writing of this book. Of note, Deborah Walker of Sterling Heights, Michigan, believed in me, and this book, from the start, before anyone else recognized its potential. My brother, Patrick Burgess, tirelessly offered research assistance and feedback on the manuscript from his perspective as a professional marketer. Finally, my mother, Doris Keating Burgess, was a veritable font of wisdom and encouragement during the eighteen months I spent writing *Silver Bullets*. My mother's constant reminders that "writing is in my blood," and honest reviews of my manuscript were more valuable than she will ever know. Thanks Mom.

Space constraints preclude me from thanking every one who had a hand in shaping *Silver Bullets*. But I would be remiss if didn't say thanks to my comrades-at-arms in the trenches at Coors. We fought the good fight, and can hold our heads high. To borrow a phrase from another brewer, this one's for you.

Author's Note

This is the true story of my years as a research analyst for Adolph Coors Company. Pseudonyms or nicknames have been used for many of the people depicted in the book. Throughout the book, dialogue has been reconstructed from meeting notes, my recollection of the events, and the recollections of others who were present.

Through the Looking Glass

Colorado Chiller . . . the new adult drink that's
lighter than beer, more refreshing than wine,
and naturally flavored for a crisp, clean taste
that you can stay with.

—Announcer in Colorado Chiller Ad

It seemed like a typical summer
morning in Colorado: full of bright sunshine, deep blue skies,
and a cool, crisp breeze that would eventually give way to
scorching afternoon heat. I drove north on Denver's Valley
Highway, through the rush-hour traffic, toward Golden, where
the Adolph Coors Company brewed its world-famous beer. I
had joined Coors just three weeks earlier, in July 1985, as a
market research analyst; but it was the anticipation surrounding
the day's special events, rather than my new work routine,
which kept me wide awake during the early-morning commute.
For this was "Colorado Chiller Launch Day," the birth of the
"new" Adolph Coors Company.

Colorado Chiller was Coors entry in the burgeoning wine
cooler business. Wine coolers were the hottest new consumer
product of the 1980s, and the largest beverage companies, from
Gallo to Anheuser–Busch to Coca-Cola, wanted a piece of this

profitable new market. According to newspaper accounts, Colorado Chiller was a malt-based (beer-like, with a frothy head) flavored alcohol product, what Europeans and Australians referred to as a "shandy." Backed by millions of dollars in advertising, Colorado Chiller was meant to herald a new, modern era at the Coors Brewing Company. Henceforth, according to industry pundits, Coors would no longer be a feisty family business, but an international conglomerate managed by professional marketing executives, competing on equal footing with giants like Coca-Cola, Anheuser–Busch, and Seagram's.

When I reached the outskirts of Golden, I glimpsed the smokestacks from the Coors Brewing complex in the mountain valley below. Against the deep blue sky, the billowy white steam from the smokestacks rose like cathedral spires. Indeed, the Coors complex was a cathedral of sorts: It was a shrine to the growing American conservative movement, and a symbol of both the glorious past and the tempestuous future of American industry.

Like many American businesses founded in the late nineteenth century, Coors had been family-owned and operated for several generations, growing to the sixth-largest brewery in the United States. Founder Adolph Coors struck gold by manufacturing and selling a *quality* American product: in this case, a lighter, smoother, American-style beer that was dramatically different from the darker, heavier English and European brews.

But while the other American companies evolved and matured, the Coors family business clung to the tenets of its hallowed past well into the 1980s. As executive management of diversified conglomerates became the norm, Coors remained a family-owned and -operated brewery. Though unions were a major force throughout most of industrial America, Coors stubbornly waged open warfare with them after a strike in the late 1970s. While many companies invested millions on marketing to spur their businesses' growth, Coors steadfastly refused to embrace Madison Avenue. And while the Civil Rights Act and other social legislation promoted equality and countered workplace discrimination, Coors freely administered lie-detector tests, sometimes probing the applicant's political affiliations.

The Coors family firmly believed that stewardship of their empire entitled them to public advocacy of the family's traditionally conservative social agenda. Management at companies like IBM, Georgia–Pacific, and Kraft scrupulously protected their firms' image and avoided public controversy. But Coors family philanthropy sponsored everything from the "right to life" movement to the Nicaraguan Contras.

Still, as I drove through the gates of the Coors plant on Colorado Chiller Launch Day, I thought that Coors might be changing. Colorado Chiller represented a radical departure from the company's troubled past. Pete Coors, supposedly less conservative than his father, Joe, had been placed in charge of marketing, and would officially "launch" Chiller. Pete had hired scores of professional managers to run Coors, and the company planned to raise its profile and boost sales with an aggressive marketing campaign behind Colorado Chiller.

At 7:30 A.M., I walked into an elevator at Coors main office building. The lobby was empty. A few hours later, tourists would crowd Coors main entrance, eager to soak up every morsel of information about the company and its founder, but mostly eager to soak up the free beer provided at the end of the tour. I pushed the button for the sixth floor, and, as the doors closed, I rose toward the company auditorium and my first launch party!

When the doors opened, it was as if I had stumbled into a roving carnival. Colorado Chiller balloons floated through the air, undisturbed by crowds of employees wearing everything from T-shirts with work overalls to suits, who had taken the idea of a launch "party" quite literally. Inflated penguins, the mascot for Colorado Chiller, lined the hallway in their permanently formal attire, like a receiving line of beaked bridegrooms. Scores of people gathered at booths to receive gifts from the company, including buttons, bumper stickers, T-shirts, and six-packs of the new drink, all emblazoned with the blue and silver "Colorado Chiller" logo. In the auditorium, Colorado Chiller's new television commercials were played, interrupted occasionally by loud bursts of laughter—or, I hoped, applause—from the audience. But what really reminded me of a carnival was the smell!

No, not the smell of soiled hay, burnt hot dogs, or fresh popcorn, but the caustic, unforgettable odor of stale beer foam tinged with lemon or lime. As I moved closer to the front of the tasting line, I realized that the new product, Colorado Chiller, caused certain sensory overload for anyone within twenty yards of an opened bottle. I hoped that Colorado Chiller tasted better than it smelled.

Nearing the front of the tasting line, I licked my lips in anticipation, until I *saw* Colorado Chiller. It was a neon greenish-yellow liquid, with a thick, foamy head. Sort of like mint juleps served at a college frat party. It looked either refreshing or sickening, depending upon how many times I blinked. I stepped out of the line, remembering my breakfast of just forty-five minutes ago; it was too early in the day to drink a fruity beer. Instead of sampling the product, I decided to view the new commercials for Colorado Chiller. Even if Coors ancient brewmasters had let me down, Madison Avenue wouldn't.

As I made my way to the auditorium, I passed a number of graveyard-shift workers from the brewery who had already slammed down their complimentary six-pack of Colorado Chiller. After a long night on the bottling lines, maybe even neon, greenish-yellow beer was refreshing.

I took a seat near the back of the large auditorium, ready to be entertained and inspired by advertising from some of Madison Avenue's brightest talents. Pete Coors, labeled a vibrant young marketing executive by industry analysts, introduced the ads. Like most Coors family members, Pete was tall and extremely lean, resembling a character from an El Greco painting. He was dressed in a V-neck sweater and open shirt, folksy attire that belied his millionaire status. Staring briefly at his feet and then at the audience, I heard Pete mumble, "And." Gulp. "Colorado Chiller represents part of our bright future." Gulp. "We're very excited with its potential." Gulp. "We'll be testing the product over the next year—" Gulp. "—and we're sure that it will allow us to compete with Anheuser–Busch." Pete's hesitant manner and halting speech were hardly inspiring. Oddly, he seemed uncomfortable playing the role of master of ceremonies at Colorado Chiller's "coming out" party.

"So, without further ado, welcome to the world—" Gulp. "—of Colorado Chiller." As the crowd's applause died down, and the screen crackled with the opening to the first commercial, I leaned forward in my plush seat, gripped by anticipation and sorely tempted to pinch myself to prove that the moment was real. This was what the "new" Coors was all about.

The three new commercials for Colorado Chiller took place, appropriately enough, in a wintry, wooden tavern. This dark, South Pole version of "Cheers" was staffed and patronized by stiff, mechanized penguins, all of whom drank . . . Colorado Chiller. Many of the penguins wore hard hats and ball caps, no doubt to appeal to the blue-collar males who usually drank beer. But weren't coolers, like the Bartles & Jaymes and Seagram's brands, usually targeted at young women? Like Pete Coors, I gulped nervously. The Chiller ads looked like typical beer ads, except that penguins (rather than young, male, working-class humans) were going for the "gusto." I gulped again.

The penguins promoted Colorado Chiller with rousing song and dance, uttering through their mechanical beaks such original lines as "More chilling . . . tastes great," "I'm going to drink my cooler on the rocks," and "Chill out." (Get it?) The penguins weren't so much cute as obnoxious, attempting to be funny when they were really caustic, corny, or even pathetic.

Was it just me, or would other people have trouble relating to the cool, dark, almost foreboding setting in which Chiller was quaffed? The wintry tavern fit with the Chiller name, but I felt like offering the penguins a hot toddy to brighten their dark, dank existence.

The commercials gave way to a short promotional film intended to stir up excitement for Colorado Chiller among Coors beer distributors. Considerably longer than the commercials, the film contained two memorable moments. In the first, we learned that the soundstage for the commercial was custom designed, as were the obnoxious penguins. These weren't rented penguins; they had been created specifically for these commercials, at considerable expense.

In the only other memorable scene of the film, a towering senior marketing executive in charge of new products for Coors argued with one of the short, mechanical penguins about how refreshing the product was, or something of equal importance. I don't remember who won their debate, but their matching tuxedos sure looked great. (I always wondered what the executive had told his family at dinner the day he shot the film. "It was a tough day, honey. I had a helluvan argument with this mouthy penguin about one of our new products.")

I stumbled out of "Coors Theatre of the Absurd" while Pete Coors asked, rhetorically, what the audience thought about the commercials. Numb, I expected a loud chorus of boos, but was surprised to hear muted, polite applause.

"What do you think? Are we ready for battle?" Startled, I looked up to see Bob Rechholtz, Coors senior executive vice president of marketing, the only marketing executive who reported directly to Pete Coors. Rechholtz was responsible for Colorado Chiller, and, ultimately, everything else in the Coors Marketing Department. I looked around to see who he was talking to, and was surprised to learn it was . . . me.

"Cat got your tongue?" he boomed again in his loud baritone. This second question was fired at me with nary a trace of a smile. Now I knew why Bob had earned the nickname "Herr" Rechholtz: He had a booming voice, a commanding presence, an intense, almost wild look in his eyes, innate aggression, and firm devotion to a vision that Coors was fighting a war of some sort.

"Great stuff," I stammered, caught off guard and uncomfortable with this chance meeting.

"Warriors don't use words like 'great' and 'stuff,' " Rechholtz huffed as he walked away.

Nothing at the launch party had made sense: not the product, not the advertising, not the promotional film, not the smell, and certainly not Herr Rechholtz. But maybe it was just me. I was new to the world of Madison Avenue marketing, and to Coors. Perhaps this was par for the course. After all, the hundreds of brewery employees enjoying the party didn't seem to mind.

Modern companies, I reminded myself, marketed their products *by the book*, carefully planning, researching, and implementing their winning marketing plans. There was no time for turf battles, politics, greed, lack of foresight, pettiness, gross incompetence, and all of the other qualities that plagued the "old" Coors and other ill-fated American businesses.

Confused, I walked out of the launch party, down a long hallway and a set of stairs, to my desk on the fifth floor in Coors old, tattered office building. In my tiny office, staring out the window at the stark, gray cement walls of the main bottling lines, I searched for inspiration. In a few minutes, I convinced myself that the Colorado Chiller launch party was simply a matter of perspective. When you're thirsty, Colorado Chiller probably *does* taste good. I'm sure the penguins are *cute* on TV. And the product doesn't smell *that* bad.

I continued to daydream, gradually recovering from the caustic fumes of Colorado Chiller's indelicate "bouquet" at the party. The more I daydreamed, the less the nightmare of Colorado Chiller's launch seemed to matter. But the launch party *should* have mattered. It was a harbinger of things to come.

For when I had joined Coors, I had unknowingly signed up to go to war. The stakes were billions of dollars, the loyalty and patronage of 80 million American beer drinkers, and career glory to the winning warriors. This wasn't a war of bombs, trenches, and field rations. This was a different sort of warfare— marketing warfare—known to its soldiers as, simply, The Beer Wars.

The front lines weren't enforced trenches, but offices and conference rooms in cities like Milwaukee, St. Louis, Detroit, and Golden. The generals weren't the mythical heros of past wars, but high-powered executives who often succumbed to earthly, mortal temptations. And the troops weren't comprised of Marines, tank brigades, or artillery batteries, but of modern marketing and sales managers, the white-collar warriors of the 1980s. In this war, brains, budgets, and common-sense strategies took a back seat to office politics, fear of the enemy, and a warped sense of "tradition" that was invoked in the name of the ancient beer barons.

I ignored the alarm bells on that warm summer day. Only in the aftermath of battle would I realize that the "new" Coors really was the same old Coors, despite the best efforts of Madison Avenue; that the quest for profits and the Coors family agenda superseded the tenets of corporate responsibility and good citizenship; and that even in a large, bureaucratic corporation, the political and social beliefs of the company and its managers cast a large shadow of public mistrust over *every* employee.

Later, when the smoke cleared from the battlefields, weary participants would realize that The Beer Wars epitomized both the best and the worst of times in modern American business. Many of us would grow to value camaraderie and teamwork, and realize the potential of imagination and sheer force of will in triumphing over ineptitude. Alas, we would also witness the permanent damage caused by sacrificing product quality for a fatter bottom line; the folly in selling sizzle, without the steak; how greed, pettiness, and other human frailties too often triumph over sound ethics and good business judgment. Most of all, we would learn that even the most talented troops cannot win when strong leadership and creativity are lacking in officers whose sole quest is for personal profit.

But these painful lessons were far off in the future. On Colorado Chiller Launch Day, the first major battle had just begun.

2

Joining Bill and Joe's Excellent Misadventure

We are shaped and fashioned by what we love.

—Goethe

Working for Coors was a little like playing football for the Los Angeles Raiders. The Raiders, one of pro football's most successful teams, are loathed by the majority of fans. But players love the challenge and notoriety of becoming a part of the Raiders mystique. The Raiders always have their "pick of the litter" when it comes time to sign players.

Similarly, hundreds of marketing executives and managers joined Coors in the 1980s, viewing the company's (and the family's) ugly reputation not as a deterrent, but as an incentive. As the ultimate warrior, Herr Rechholtz once said (somewhat facetiously) during a meeting, "If we can market watery beer brewed by right-wing weirdos who, according to the critics, are responsible for every plague and pox known to mankind, then we're doing one helluva job at marketing." He was right. The challenge was too much to ignore for any marketer worth his or her salt. Besides, I had no choice but to work for Coors. It appears to have been my destiny.

I'm not sure when I chose marketing as a career, but it was my choice for as long as I can remember. Like many Baby Boomers, TV was a major influence on the development of my value system. It was a conduit between escapist childhood fantasies and the realities of the sedate, middle-class suburban lifestyle in which many of us were reared during the sixties.

Among all the TV characters of the era, I was most fascinated by Darrin Stevens and his career at the fictitious advertising agency McMahon & Tate, as chronicled on "Bewitched." I was hooked by Darrin's ability to create advertising amidst the peculiar cast of witches, warlocks, and historical characters that regularly entered his life. As a practical child, I never expected to duplicate the magic and excitement of Darrin's supernatural world. But I always maintained the hope that I could have an exciting, challenging career, despite being relegated to the boring white-collar world, *if* I became an advertising or marketing man. (I only wish I had paid more attention to the Larry Tate character, the spineless advertising agency manager who would do or say almost *anything* to please a client. Later in life I would learn that Larry Tates were the norm, and Darrin Stevens's life was the fantastic creation of an inspired TV writer.)

Darrin Stevens's impact on my life continued long after the show went off the air. As if by magic (perhaps witchcraft), fate intervened, steering me on a path to a career in marketing.

In the fall of 1982, I signed up for a college class called "The Principles of Advertising." At each session, a project team of three to four students presented a solution to a marketing case. After the very first presentation, the floor was opened to questions. In the quest for an "A," the best strategy was to ask a basic but intelligent question, so that the professor, former L.A. adman Chuck Patti, would think you were at least *mildly* interested in his dull class. I plunged in with, "Have you considered the ramifications of a discounting strategy on your product's image?"

The silence following my question was eerie. Time stood still, as if I had spoken in tongues, or questioned the ancestry of the presenters. I knew the question was basic, but I didn't think it was *that* stupid. I prayed for a quick answer, or a swift move to the next question, or even for Samantha, Darrin's bewitching TV wife, to conjure me out of the room. Surely, the professor had noted my blunder. Finally, the silence was broken, about a minute after the question.

"We never really thought about that," stammered Karen, the project leader. "But if we'd had more time, we *would* have," she added indignantly. Her penetrating stare spoke volumes, and I quickly averted my gaze.

To Karen, I was a chump, the prick who had purposely embarrassed her and her project team. To the class, I became the Clint Eastwood of questioners, an intimidating presence. And to my professor, I became an automatic "A," a student who had mastered the thrust of the course. A legend had been born.

Thereafter, project teams tried to bribe me to refrain from asking questions, with offers of free beers and food. Classmates would pick my brain before tests, trying to find out what I thought was important, as if I was omniscient. For the rest of the quarter, I tried to plead dumb luck, and explained that I really *wasn't* capable of asking unanswerable, "stump the panel" questions on a routine basis. I wanted to be *liked*, not feared. But it was futile to protest. This was the 1980s, the "me" decade of greed and selfishness, and assholes were admired.

And so I rode The Question, as it came to be known by classmates, all the way to graduation, through a year of graduate school, where I picked up an MBA, and into my first job as a market research analyst. Eventually, even I began to believe that Madison Avenue marketing really was my destiny.

The Gilded Age of the eighties was also the dawning of the

Era of the Analyst. Self-help books, TV talk shows, even "The Today Show," provided information on how to cope, succeed, change, build relationships, cook, know your erogenous zones, and other "basic" skills. The fact that civilization had coped without this sage advice for the better part of a few million years didn't stop an industry and profession from sprouting up. Analysts were like football coaches. They didn't actually play the game, but they studied facts, observed success and failure, and became industry experts who could make predictions and sell advice. There were stock market analysts, political analysts, media analysts, Hollywood analysts, even N.F.L. draft analysts. Studying information and spouting "informed," expert opinions became a major growth industry. (There may even have been "analyst analysts" who monitored the growth of this fledgling industry.)

Marketing analysis was, and is, no different. Like movie critics, market reseach analysts are paid to critique advertising campaigns, new products ideas, and other marketing programs, based upon the results of consumer research, such as surveys. The insight and guidance provided by marketing analysts can make the difference between a dismal failure, like the Edsel automobile (a new product in the 1950s which cost Ford Motor Company more than $2 billion in losses), and a stunning success, like Chrysler's Cordoba and its ad campaign featuring Ricardo "Rich Corinthian Leather" Montalban.[1]

I plunged into the Era of the Analyst in the summer of 1984, taking a job as a market research analyst with the largest bank in Colorado. My job was to study the marketing effectiveness of the bank's advertising campaigns and new banking products, like debit and ATM cards.

---

1 Marketing expert William H. Reynolds estimated Ford's loss at $350 million in late 1950s dollars in his article, "The Edsel Ten Years Later," which was first published in the fall, 1967 edition of *Business Horizons*. In 1991 dollars, this would be well over $2 billion, even allowing for a "guesstimate" of the original loss.

Traditional bankers, with their spit-polished wing tips, blue three-piece suits, and immaculately groomed hair (what was left of it), treated marketing with disdain. To these commercial lenders, who made million-dollar loan deals with big businesses, marketing was "women's work," the "artsy" type of thing that English majors and secretaries did to earn their keep. If I really wanted to become a banker, I was told, I would have to become a commercial lender. As one lender said to me, "You can find anybody to paint pretty brochures, but *real* men are out pounding the pavement making the big loans."

These bankers didn't yet view marketing as a respectable occupation, and felt it was superfluous to the operation of the bank. (In retrospect, they may have been right.) Of course, as an analyst, I knew that some of the commercial lenders had made bad loan deals that would some day place the bank in a precarious financial position. I also knew that few lenders "pounded the pavement"; instead, they usually trudged around golf courses.

Once again, the hand of fate intervened to save me, just as it always had for Darrin Stevens on "Bewitched"; this time, it was from a long, stifling career in banking. In May 1985, I attended a training seminar held in Cincinnati. Companies from all over the country were represented. But oddly enough, Laurie, the person sitting to my immediate right, was a marketing analyst at Coors, located just west of downtown Denver. We hit it off immediately. And, though the seminar was—like most research seminars—dreadfully dull and forgettable, it changed my life.

Laurie resigned from her job on the second day of the seminar to move to New York with her fiancé. She offered to give my business card to her boss, if I was interested in working for Coors. Coors? Though I had lived in Denver for several years, I didn't know much about the company. As I would soon discover, there was a lot to know.

The beer business is big business. By 1985, Americans were consuming almost 185 million barrels of beer per year, worth more than $40 billion at retail.[2] To put that in perspective, that's about two-thirds of a barrel, or twenty gallons of beer, for *every* man, woman, and child in the United States. American beer companies were spending more than $600 million on beer advertising in 1985, enough to pay the interest on the federal government's debt for a few minutes.

The beer business started innocently enough, when German families immigrated to America and, naturally, brewed the beverage of their native homeland. Most of the breweries were small, family-owned companies that sold beer primarily in their own neighborhoods and hometowns, as was the custom in Germany.

Localization persisted in the beer industry until World War II. Many of the serviceman who fought the war returned to the United States as hardened beer drinkers, having developed a taste for their favorite malt beverages in Germany, England, and other beer capitals of the world. A revolution had been started.

Tantalized by German beers and the East and West Coast brews that they had sampled during their tours of military duty, vets soon eschewed their favorite local brands and began to drink quality national beers, such as Schlitz, Budweiser, and Miller High Life. Beer executives figured out that drinkers in Boston were not terribly different from those in Mason City, Iowa. Plus, there were economies of scale in marketing national brands. Advertising was purchased on national radio and TV, or in national magazines, like *Look* and *Life*. National distributor networks were established, reducing costs, and the ever-mobile American consumer was retained as a customer, even when he moved from New York to San Francisco. Big national brewers enticed drinkers to switch to their products by reducing prices and offering discounts, another benefit of the economies of scale.

2 *The IMPACT of American Beer Market Review and Forecast,* M. Shanken Communications, 1984, p. 5.

But Coors was different. While the Budweisers, Schlitzes, and Pabsts of the world bludgeoned each other in the battle for national supremacy, Coors continued to enjoy its own peculiar version of a Rocky Mountain high, secure and content in its own little section of the country.

Coors was founded in 1873 by Adolph Coors, who started with five thousand dollars, as recounted in the epic film *Nothing by Halves*, mandatory viewing for new employees of the company.[3] Adolph located his brewery in the tiny hamlet of Golden, Colorado, just west of Denver, because of the crisp, clear, Rocky Mountain springs that bubbled to the surface there. These springs provided perfect water for making beer, and Adolph peddled his brew to mine workers throughout Colorado, using horse-drawn wagons to tote the heavy beer barrels and bottles.

The Coors Company resisted the dramatic changes in the beer industry after World War II, at least for a while. Adolph Coors's grandsons, Bill and Joe Coors, had inherited the job of managing the brewery, and continued to brew a lighter-tasting beer using Rocky Mountain spring water. Coors was sold in just fourteen Western states, and during the 1960s and early 1970s, the company turned the limited availability of the product into a distinct marketing advantage. Visitors to Colorado often smuggled home one or two cases of "Colorado Kool-Aid," as Coors was called, giving Easterners and Midwesterners a rare chance to sample the beer made in the upper reaches of the Rockies. Coors brewed only one beer, so all of the company's efforts were focused on just one product. It was a profitable business, but it wouldn't last forever.

3 The actor who portrayed Adolph Coors in this film later went on to stardom in a commercial for Masters III Beer, again portraying the original Adolph Coors. Fortunately for his career, demand for Adolph Coors look-alikes ceased before he could be typecast, as Masters Beer was cancelled just nine months after Coors first started brewing it. See Chapter 4.

In the mid-1970s, the tide turned against Coors. After almost one hundred years of uninterrupted tranquility and prosperity, Bill and Joe Coors, and the company that their grandfather had entrusted to them, came under fire on several different fronts. It was the company's archaic management philosophy that first brought the viability of the brewery into question.

Following Adolph's lead, the frugal, conservative Coors family refused to borrow money. This fiscal conservatism limited growth and made expansion east of the Mississippi River little more than a dream. Other companies developed new products, spent lavishly on advertising, and increased their sales and profits, but Coors operated on a "pay as you go" basis. Today's profits didn't buy much future success in the increasingly competitive beer industry.

Further, the company refused to market their products actively. To traditional beer barons like the Coors family, marketing was anathema, something competitors, like Anheuser–Busch and Miller Brewing, used to cover up the poor quality of their product.

However, the real challenge for Coors came in 1975, when Miller Brewing, owned by the marketing-savvy Philip Morris Corporation, introduced Miller Lite. For years, Coors had brewed a light-tasting, drinkable product, Coors Banquet Beer, billed as "America's Fine Light Beer." While Coors invested in new bottling lines and copper brewing kettles, Miller had done its marketing homework, and figured out that a lower-calorie beer that was less filling, but still tasted like a regular beer, would be a big seller. True, Coors brewed a lighter beer, but it still had plenty of calories. Besides, Miller was available in all fifty states, but Coors was only available out West. "America's Fine Light Beer" was being phased out by a *finer* light beer, Miller Lite. Miller's lavish advertising campaign, featuring famous ex-athletes such as Ray Nitschke, Bob Uecker, and Boog Powell, helped assure that. Sales of Coors Banquet Beer dropped by 0.5 pecent per year from 1975 through 1980, while sales of Miller Lite increased by an average of 36 percent per year.[4]

While Golden burned, emperors Bill and Joe Coors fiddled. Instead of taking bold action to reverse a decline, the brothers set out on a series of public-relations blunders that dogged their grandpa Adolph's company for years, and accelerated the company's decline.

These public-relations blunders began when Coors encountered labor troubles at the Golden brewery. Burdened by heavy inflation and stagnant wages, Coors workers struck in a salary dispute in 1977. The impasse became heated, and Bill Coors vowed never to hire union workers at Coors. Striking line workers were fired and replaced by non-union employees, and the brewery continued to brew and sell Coors Banquet Beer in the western United States. However, labor unions nationwide vowed to fight the "union busters" at Coors by instituting a national boycott of Coors beer. Sales continued to plummet.[5]

Once Bill Coors's rigid anti-union stance had been publicized, it became fashionable to bash the Coors Company's conservative "philanthropic" endeavors. In 1984, Bill was quoted in a *Rocky Mountain News* account as attributing the difficulties of Zimbabwe's economy to the blacks lacking "the intellectual capacity to succeed." Bill Coors sued *The Rocky Mountain News* for libel, and asked for $150 million in damages. The case was settled out of court in 1987, and *The News* printed an apology stating that "the headline and certain references in the article could have been more precisely prepared and worded to avoid any misrepresentation." Joe's wife, Holly, topped Bill by an-

---

4 *The IMPACT American Beer Market Review and Forecast*, M. Shanken Communications, 1984, p. 30.

5 This boycott lasted until 1989, when brewery workers finally voted against unionizing in an election sanctioned, or at least tolerated, by Coors management. The circumstances behind this change in policy are discussed in Chapter 9.

nouncing that she was considering running for governor of Colorado, suggesting that she could redecorate the governor's mansion, far from the highest priority for Colorado voters. Not wanting to be left out, Joe Coors, as a card-carrying conservative and member of President Reagan's informal kitchen cabinet of advisors, decided to buy Oliver North, of Iran–Contra fame, a $65,000 plane to be used by the Contras in the Nicaraguan civil war.[6]

And the troubles didn't stop there. Appearing to be bigoted, ultraconservative, and anti-union, the Coors brothers and the company were also rumored to be supporting almost every "right wing" cause known to mankind. Large constituencies of consumers, including gays, blacks, Catholics, Jews, Teamsters, women, and environmentalists, charged that the Coors Brewery was socially irresponsible.

Several years after I joined the company, Pete Coors told me during a beer taste test, "It's not easy to take stands. Sometimes we're [the Coors family] portrayed unfairly. But that comes with the territory."

Despite Pete Coors's charge of unfairness, thousands of consumers felt that they had a reason to avoid drinking Coors beer. After all, the Coors family ran the company, their name was on the label, and their wealth had been amassed in the beer industry. A manager in the Human Resources Department dramatized Coors problems by telling me, "We used to be the top-selling beer in Colorado, but we turn down about forty thousand people a year for jobs, and a lot of them fail the polygraph test. [Polygraph testing at Coors is discussed later in this chapter.] That's a lot of people running around hating Coors." In combination with the introduction of Miller Lite, the public-relations furor drove down sales of Coors Banquet Beer by 11 percent to 13 percent *per year* from 1980 through 1983, which

6 Bob Woodward, *Veil: The Secret Wars of the CIA 1981–1987* (New York: Simon & Schuster), 1987, p. 400.

cost the company more than $360 million in lost sales revenue.[7]

Bill Coors and his family were now caught in a vise. Their product was no longer unique, and to the drinker with a conscience, drinking a Coors was like buying a share in a Contra plane, or supporting union-busting. (When I worked at Coors, employees regularly joked during sales updates about how many Contra gunboats sales and profits could buy. This gave new meaning to the term "Beer Wars.") To remedy the situation, Bill decided to turn day-to-day management of the company over to his nephews, Jeff and Pete Coors. (Bill remained as chairman of the board, and his brother Joe as vice chairman.) He also made the momentous decision to hire beer marketing veteran Bob Rechholtz, and to invest in marketing.

In the 1950s and 1960s, Schlitz was the Budweiser of American beers: the top-selling product in the United States, the kind of beer that every Joe Palooka drank. As late as 1975, Schlitz Beer was still the second-most popular brand in America, accounting for nearly $1.8 billion in annual sales at retail.[8] However, after a series of marketing and production mishaps which alienated loyal Schlitz drinkers, a weakened Joseph Schlitz Company, based in Milwaukee, was sold to Stroh in 1982.

Unemployed beer executives found a savior in Bill Coors. And in Bob Rechholtz, a former Schlitz executive, Bill thought he had found the marketing man to lead his company out of the darkness.

Bob Rechholtz looked, sounded, and even acted like a Coors family member. Tall, lean, and El Grecoesque, he was a

7 This estimate of lost revenue is based on lost sales volume of 6.2 million barrels between 1980 and 1983. Assuming that Coors charged $60 a barrel to distributors, this sales decline would result in lost revenue of more than $360 million. The volume numbers used to calculate lost revenue were obtained from *The IMPACT American Beer Market Review and Forecast,* M. Shanken Communications, 1985, p. 30.

8 *The IMPACT American Beer Market Review and Forecast,* M. Shanken Communications, 1984, p. 43.

staunchly conservative and frugal executive, with a booming voice and a commanding presence. A fastidious exerciser, he also believed in tidy offices, clean desks, and a lean (in actual body weight) office staff. Rechholtz often conducted desk checks on Friday nights, not only to see who, if anyone, was working late, but also to learn who had left a messy desk, and who had breached "security." (He must have marveled at my desk, once dubbed the sloppiest in the North Office Building in the company newsletter.) "A tight office is a good office," Rechholtz once remarked to me in the locker room at the Coors Wellness Center.

A classic "Type A" personality, Rechholtz couldn't help but dispense free advice to many of the people he passed in the hallway. Coors employees were sure to get his attention if they were just the slightest bit overweight or less than perfectly neat in appearance. And when Herr Rechholtz taunted, he used his loud, deep voice, which amplified the embarrassment. "Why don't you quit smoking and get rid of that paunch?" he would bellow to a red-faced executive at the elevators to the Coors marketing offices.

Beyond clean offices and neat appearances, Rechholtz was most obsessed with war. Herr Rechholtz thought nothing of interrupting meetings to hector participants, "We're at war, goddamnit." Nobody quite knew what that meant, or how they were supposed to respond, but it sounded dramatic. Most meetings were silent for several moments after Rechholtz had sounded the air-raid siren, but I always wondered how many others besides myself had the almost irresistible urge to dig a trench, or plan some sort of commando raid, in response to Rechholtz's apocalyptic pronouncements. After all, isn't that what people at war did?

On one occasion, Rechholtz even went so far as to belittle a manager of Irish ancestry, Lori Sheehan, by pointing out that the Irish hadn't won any wars lately. "Why should I listen to you?" he taunted. "How many wars have *your* people won?"

A fiery redhead, Lori retorted, "The Irish are the best terrorists, and have done a better job of battling the English," than Herr Rechholtz's Germans had.

Ironically, both Lori Sheehan and Herr Rechholtz were instrumental in my joining the Coors army. Having given my card to the fellow Denverite at the market-research seminar in Cincinnati in May 1985, I never actually expected to hear from Coors. It is a standard practice for businesspeople to ask for your business card as a matter of courtesy, only to discard it later. This business practice works on the same principle as a visit from long-lost or rarely seen relatives. At the end of the visit, everyone makes plans to see one another again soon, knowing full well that a millennium will pass before another visit actually takes place.

Still, in June 1985, I was surprised to receive a phone call from Lori Sheehan. She asked me to send her a résumé, and in mid-June I was invited up to Golden to interview for a position in the Market Research Department at Coors.

The interviewing took place on a beastly hot day, both inside and outside the brewery's offices, as Coors air conditioning system had broken down. This accentuated the stale smell of malt that seeped into every crevice of the building, and into my clothes. The interviews were conducted in the small cubicles that passed for offices. As interviews go, they were relatively uneventful, full of questions about marketing research, new-product development, and the standard lines about goals and objectives. (Interviewing is an art form, like dating. The key is to be aggressive enough to make the company want to hire you, without making interviewers feel threatened or intimidated, using lines like, "I want to be president of the company . . . some day, but not right away.")

The most enticing part of this Coors marketing job was clearly the challenge. According to Lori Sheehan, the Coors family was changing radically. She spoke approvingly of Herr Rechholtz's plans to stem the tide against Coors by introducing new beverage products and "revving up" Coors advertising.

Several weeks later, Lori called to make a conditional offer on a job as a marketing research analyst at Coors. In career terms, it was a parallel move (same title and responsibilities), with a mere two-thousand-dollar annual raise from my salary at the bank. But given the meager role of marketing in my current field, American banking, it was an offer worth considering. I told Lori I would think over the offer for a few days and then get back to her. She said that was fine.

And then, offhandedly, I asked, "What's conditional about the offer?"

"Oh, nothing much," Lori said soothingly. "All of our employees are required to take, and pass, a lie detector, er, polygraph test," she continued. "It's no big deal. Coors just wants to make sure that you're the right person to be working here. If I can pass it, anyone can."[9]

Right type? What, blood type? Size and weight? Personality? Weird, but not the end of the world. Though no choirboy, I'm not a hardened criminal, either. Maybe this is standard practice for Madison Avenue marketing companies.

Lori finished the conversation by giving me the phone number of a manager in the Coors Human Resources Department who would coordinate the polygraph test and give me more details about what it would entail. I thanked her, figured I'd wait to take the test, and then make a decision about accepting the Coors offer.

The human-resources staffer I contacted told me that the test was given to all prospective employees because one of the heirs to the Coors family fortune (Adolph Coors III) had been kidnapped and murdered in the 1950s. During the test, she told me, "every prospective employee is asked if they would ever harm any of the Coors family members." (If anybody said "yes," I wondered if they were then asked *how* or *when* they wanted to harm the Coors family member, or if those details were saved for the police.)

---

9 The 1988 Employee Polygraph Protection Act later outlawed the use of such tests in hiring and firing employees.

Additionally, the human-resources manager told me that employees were asked "whether they had a criminal record, had ever stolen anything before, used illegal drugs, and, from time to time, whether they were a Communist." *This is weird. Even though it's supposed to be a security measure, it seems as if the polygraph test is being used to weed out "undesirables" from the work force.*

Like my prospective new boss, Lori Sheehan, the human-resources staffer told me to relax, that I would probably "sail through" the test. "Almost half of the people who take the test pass it," she said, attempting to reassure me, but in reality pressing my personal panic button. *Half? Almost* half?

I am a born worrier, and now I was worried. Not because I was an "undesirable" as defined by Coors, but because I am a nervous person, given to extreme variations in blood pressure. And that's how polygraph tests work. After a question is asked, the respondent answers while hooked to a sensor that measures changes in blood pressure and pulse. Supposedly, when you lie, the pressure and pulse fluctuate wildly, betraying the lie. I had seen pictures of polygraph test results in *The National Enquirer,* and knew that when a respondent lied, the sensor drew squiggly lines on a piece of paper. But this could happen to *me* even if I was telling the truth. If I got nervous, I would fail. (Or so I thought.) So I devised "The Nerves Strategy."

The Nerves Strategy was simple. I'd work myself into a frenzy and elevate my blood pressure, through worry and angst, to something like 200/150, before the test even started. And then my pulse and pressure would be steady throughout the test, because they couldn't possibly go any higher. Plus, I could certainly never relax *during* the test, which would send the pulse and blood pressure readings lower. I might die of a stroke, but at least I'd pass the test.

Finally, test day arrived. I put The Nerves Strategy into play, and by the time I arrived at the testing center in the western Denver suburb of Lakewood, I had a headache and my ears were beet red. If my blood pressure had jumped any higher, blood would have burst through vessels and gushed out my ears.

Taking the test was like facing the biblical Judgment Day. As the tester hooked me up to the machine, all past transgressions from my relatively short life passed before my eyes. *Stole a pack of baseball cards when I was ten. ("I knew it. He's a thief.") Drank to excess occasionally in high school and college. ("A druggie if ever there was one.") Read* Playboy *and* Penthouse *from time to time. ("A sexual deviant. Bet he even enjoyed that pornographic trash.") Had studied* The Communist Manifesto *in high school and college. ("No," I'd plead. "Lennon was one of the Beatles. When I said I was a fan of his, it had nothing to do with communism.")* Judgment Day had arrived, all right, though I was far from dead.

"Okay, now I'm going to read you a series of questions. Please answer them truthfully," instructed the test administrator. He looked just like a tester *should* look, with wild, uncombed hair, several days of facial stubble, and thick, horn-rimmed glasses, accented by a sparkling plastic pocket protector filled with Bic pens, and the latest in plaid polyester slacks.

"Sure," I replied, as calmly as I could. *Bump-bump, bump-bump. Good. The old ticker is still beating furiously. The Nerves Strategy has a chance.*

"Have you ever stolen anything of value before?" The inquisition had begun.

My mind raced. *Are baseball cards considered valuable? I've never placed a value on mine before. Honus Wagner cards can fetch upwards of six figures. I only stole one pack, when I was ten years old, and there wasn't a Honus Wagner card in it. Quick, answer, before this guy thinks you're lying.*

"Just baseball cards when I was ten," I blurted. The honesty approach. I'll charm him with my honesty, I thought, as a knowing smile creased my face.

"I said of *value*," he scolded. Points had been lost. He hadn't heard of Honus Wagner.

"Oh, then no," I stammered, staring at the floor as my proud smile gave way to a sheepish grin.

The interrogation continued, like a scene from *The Great Escape*. I began to loathe the test administrator. *Who the hell is this guy to ask me about my political philosophy? I'm a registered Republican, but I once voted for Ted Kennedy in the 1980 Illinois presidential primary. That's probably close to being Communist for the conservative Coors family. Who made this tester a judge of good character? Despite his nerdy profile, he could be a major pervert, the kind of person who exposes himself in crowded subways in New York City. I'll bet he probably gets some cheap thrill out of this whole testing process.*

Finally, and mercifully, the questions ended. I let out an audible sigh, and tried to smile cheerfully. "All finished?" I wondered pleadingly.

"We're going to ask you several questions over again, if you don't mind," the tester said.

"Sure," I said.

What choice do I have? I want to pass the test. But I've probably failed, or am borderline, or else they wouldn't be starting all over again. This is becoming ludicrous. Do kidnappers really get screened out with this test? "Sure, I plan to kidnap Pete Coors on Monday, November twenty-fourth, at 7:30 P.M." Ding-ding-ding, the machine would flash. "We caught one of them!" a proud tester would scream. What about pathological liars? Does Coors really think that exposing Communists makes the work place safer for everyone named Coors? What if a Coors family member is Communist? Is he excommunicated from the family, or fired from his job at the brewery?

As Round Two started, I remembered The Nerves Strategy. *Does hatred elevate the blood pressure? If so, I'm in good shape, because I hate the test administrator. Deeply.*

I answered the second set of questions the same way as the first, and finally Judgment Day had ended.

"How'd I do?" I chirped with mock cheerfulness.

"Oh, we don't have the results for at least a week," the tester said as he casually rearranged his number-two pencils and Bic pens in the pocket protector.

Now, I did feel like kidnapping and terrorizing somebody: the tester. A week? What were they going to do with the test? Send it to the FBI crime labs in Washington, D.C.?

"Our analyst is on vacation this week," the test administrator continued. "As soon as she gets back, she'll get right to work on this. In the meantime, relax until we get back in touch with you."

Easy for you to say, Mr. Pocket Protector. You haven't been humiliated taking this test. And your future doesn't hang by a thread, depending upon how some analyst interprets a bunch of wavy lines. Another damn analyst!

"Well, thank you," I said, quickly sprinting to the door to get the hell out of the office, and get my blood pressure below the stroke level. Stopping by my local church to make a confession also raced through my mind.

I left the reception area at the testing center, and started walking down the hallway to the parking lot. About ten yards outside the door was a twenty-dollar bill, lying in the middle of the floor, unmarked, and apparently unwanted. *A trap. I must have tested borderline, and they want to see how honest I really am. If I just pick up the twenty-dollar bill and go home, I'll fail the test for sure.* So I picked it up and headed back to the reception area of the testing company.

"I found this in the hallway," I told the receptionist, while flashing a twenty-four-karat grin to show her that I was onto their "game." I was met with a blank stare, which I figured was staged. *She's no doubt a veteran of the old "Twenty-dollar Test," probably surprised I'm even back here. Thought you could pull one over on me, didn't you? Well, you have to get up pretty early in the morning to fool this analyst.*

"Oh, well, we'll keep it here in the reception area," she assured me. "And if no one claims it within a month, we'll mail it to you."

Sure you will. And I'm the Dalai Lama.

As I walked back to my car, I kept looking for other treasures lining the pavement. Since I had passed the "Twenty-dollar Test," maybe there was a diamond necklace, a gold bar, or a Rolex watch on the sidewalk. But there were no more tests. The humiliation of Judgment Day had ended. I made it to my car without further temptation, and drove home.

A week later, I received my test results over the telehone. Surprisingly, I passed! The Nerves Strategy had worked. Now all I had to do was figure out if this was the right job for me.

I had been humiliated on Judgment Day, and the quest to root out "undesirables" had left a bad taste in my mouth. But banking was boring, and beer marketing at Coors seemed the ultimate challenge for an aspiring marketer. Certainly there had to be career opportunities at Coors, even for someone who had once voted for Teddy Kennedy. I was leaning toward accepting.

The next morning, I scanned the business section of *The Denver Post*. Coors had announced plans to bring out a new product, Colorado Chiller. As a new-products analyst, I reasoned that I would be working in a key area for the company. Besides, I had slithered through Judgment Day, despite its trials and tribulations. Evidently, Coors wanted me to be a part of their future. Figuring it was fate, I accepted the job.

About a month later, an unmarked envelope arrived in the mail. The note inside said simply, "Enjoy!" Also enclosed was a twenty-dollar bill, the same one I had found in the hallway at the testing company. Fate had been kind to me one more time. Or maybe the money was a reward for passing the test, recognition that I was a "desirable" employee, at least to the Coors family.

3

The Empire Strikes Out

We are growth- and profit-oriented, developing
new businesses from internally generated tech-
nology and synergistic acquisitions.

— *Coors Company Vision, excerpted
from its* **1990 Annual Report.**

"Every great commander has a
plan," Bob Rechholtz relentlessly reminded himself, his staff,
and Coors Chairman Bill Coors, who had hired Rechholtz in
1981. After being named to the Coors Board of Directors in
1983, Herr Rechholtz devised a battle plan to turn Coors around
that was both simple and logical.

In Phase One of the "Rechholtz Plan," Coors was to expand
its distribution area. If the company wanted to compete on equal
footing with Anheuser-Busch, Philip Morris (which owned
Miller), Stroh, and G. Heileman Brewing, then the company
would have to battle them "toe-to-toe," in fifty states rather
than fourteen. "There's no reason we shouldn't be sold from
coast to coast," Rechholtz pleaded to Bill Coors. "If you think
you make a fine beer, then shouldn't everybody have a chance
to taste and enjoy it?" Plus, by selling Coors nationally, Rech-

holtz reasoned that the company would reap huge discounts on media purchases (purchasing advertising on national television networks, for instance, instead of on a market-by-market basis) and strengthen its distribution network.

Phase Two of the Rechholtz Plan probably caused frugal Bill Coors's heart to skip a beat. According to Rechholtz, Coors would have to increase dramatically the amount of money invested in marketing and advertising. In 1982, Rechholtz pointed out, Coors had spent one-sixth as much as Anheuser–Busch, and one-fourth as much as Miller Brewing on advertising. "An army that isn't well supplied can't triumph," Rechholtz had told the Coors board in pressing the case for abandoning frugality for investments in marketing.

The Board of Directors, primarily made up of Jeff, Pete, Bill, and Joe Coors, showed their faith in the Rechholtz Plan by approving both geographic expansion and increased advertising spending. Over a four-year period, Coors was introduced into the Midwest, Southeast, and New England areas, as well as to Canada and Japan. Advertising spending surged 65 percent in Rechholtz's first year on the Coors board, and continued upward throughout the 1980s.

In response, Coors total sales grew by 15 percent in 1983, as curious beer drinkers in new markets like Boston and Chicago sampled Coors Banquet and Coors Light for the first time. Unfortunately, most of these drinkers, according to Coors own research, would try Coors once, and never purchase it again, since they usually returned to buying their long-time favorite brands, like Budweiser, Miller Lite, or Stroh. Therefore, the Coors sales increase in 1983 was a mirage.

As a veteran commander in The Beer Wars, Rechholtz also knew that even the temporary sales increase from consumer sampling in expansion markets couldn't hide the fact that the Coors Banquet brand, which accounted for more than 70 percent of the company's sales, was continuing its free fall downward. Despite the geographic expansion to new markets and increased advertising expenditures, Coors Banquet sales plunged 13 percent in 1984, and the Rechholtz Plan stalled. It was time for Phase Three.

"A winning army has to have a variety of high-impact weapons in its arsenal," he told his staff. "We can't compete with Busch, when they've got a dozen brands to sell, and we've got only two. Let's get our weapons program going." In Phase Three, Rechholtz wanted to spur growth by developing and introducing a variety of new alcoholic beverage products. In the 1980s, American businesses called this the "lottery" strategy.

The United States developed a "throw-away" mentality during that decade. While past generations had labored over time, and built and invested for the long term, American managers in the 1980s worked for immediate, lucrative returns. Resources that didn't generate fast profits were quickly cast aside. When budgets were squeezed, long-time employees were fired. Non-renewable natural resources were consumed at a record pace. Recycling, considered far from cost effective, was relegated to the bottom of the priority list. And companies were bought and sold not because of their potential for future profits, but to make profits *now*.

Madison Avenue marketing was no different. Following World War II, American companies invested millions of advertising dollars over several decades to build quality brand names like Oreo, Tide, and Prell. But in the 1980s, the emphasis in marketing shifted away from long-term investing, called "brand building," to short-term "trials" for new products. If a consumer product, like Colorado Chiller, was not immediately successful, then companies like Coors would simply pull it from store shelves, and move on to *another* new product. This was the "lottery" strategy, as more and more American businesses kept introducing new products until they hit a jackpot. Unfortunately, as Coors soon learned, the strategy was expensive, time-consuming, and alienated customers. Worst of all, the "lottery" strategy encouraged companies like Coors to introduce as many new products as possible, with little consideration given to the *quality* of the products. The "lottery" strategy was a triumph of quantity over quality.[1]

The new-products arena was still a frontier for Coors in 1985. Until 1978, Coors had made only one product, Coors Banquet. Seven years later, 99 percent of the company's annual sales and all of its profit were produced by the original Coors Banquet and Coors Light, two mainstream beers. Rechholtz knew that Phase Three would require the expertise of beer executives from outside the Coors family. To lead the Coors troops into Phase Three of his battle plan, Rechholtz hired Gary Truitt.

Like most of Herr Rechholtz's senior staff, Gary Truitt was a hardened beer-industry veteran. Bright, energetic, and outgoing, Truitt had first risen to fame as a field sales representative at Schlitz, and later as the brand manager for Schlitz Malt Liquor, known in the trade as "The Bull." Truitt caught Rechholtz's eye at Schlitz because of his hard-charging, aggressive management style. "Let's kick their ass," was one of his favorite phrases, and he was famous for his profane, intimidating outbursts. It was an act that the hopelessly Type A Rechholtz couldn't help but love. Truitt wasn't always right, but he was a man of action. Rechholtz placed far more emphasis on the latter quality.

The Beer Wars provided a haven for men of action like Truitt, street smart executives full of bravado and machismo. After all, the beer business was traditionally a man's business, and beer was a man's drink. Therefore, the executives were "real" men. The typical beer executive chased women, drove fast cars, ate and drank to excess, partied to sunrise, wore wide belt buckles and flashy rings, and made piles of money. Successful beer marketers were like Texas oil men. They told tall tales, took risks, and worried about tomorrow only when it arrived.

---

1 According to *Gorman's New Product News*, the number of new consumer products introduced by American businesses more than tripled between 1982 and 1991, and increased each year during this period.

Gary Truitt was a very talented beer executive. "He [Truitt] could talk a retailer into stocking specimen jars full of urine," a Schlitz colleague of Truitt's once said in admiration. With a firm handshake, deep laugh, and imposing nature, Truitt commanded respect and inspired action. Beer industry machismo was in his blood. He often bragged about driving eighty mph to work, showered beautiful women with compliments, unhesitatingly vowed to "kick A–B's (Anheuser–Busch's) ass," and worked the longest hours of anyone on Rechholtz's staff.

Unfortunately, Truitt knew very little about the wine cooler business, a key component of Rechholtz's Phase Three. While at Schlitz, Truitt was famous for motivating field sales reps and using aggressive price discounting (coupons and cents-off sales) to sell The Bull. His reputation was for street smarts, not for strategic, long-term thinking. Nevertheless, Truitt guided Coors through the initial phases of development for Colorado Chiller.

For several years in the early 1980s, Coors conducted experimental research into flavored malt beverages. Fruit flavoring was an emerging trend in the beverage business at this time, from Cherry Coke to flavored vodka. Some beer drinkers, especially women, expressed a desire to drink a flavored beer. Coors research indicated that flavored beers, or shandies, already were popular in Europe and Australia. The company continued to develop the concept of a flavored malt beverage at a leisurely pace in 1983 and early 1984.

But a couple of former California beach bums shook up the beverage world and changed Coors plans to market a flavored beer. In the early 1980s, Stewart Bewley and Michael Crete bottled a fruity, wine-based beverage they called "California Cooler," after years of testing at beach parties. Finding a receptive market of younger, upscale women, the entrepreneurs created a new category of beverages, to the envy of wine and beer companies. The cooler business was born, and Coors, like other beverage companies, decided in the fall of 1984 to accelerate the development of their own flavored alcohol product.

According to a secret task force headed up by Truitt, the keys to Coors successfully competing in the cooler business were:

1. Adequate advertising spending (dollars).
2. Creating a refreshing, good-tasting product.
3. Convincing Coors distributors to stock and sell a cooler product.
4. Creating persuasive advertising that would convince women drinkers to try a Coors cooler.

Pursuing the "lottery" strategy, Rechholtz and the Coors Board of Directors made tentative plans to enter the wine cooler business in the summer of 1985, the peak of the cooler-selling season. It was at this point that Truitt decided to hire a product manager, who would ensure that Herr Rechholtz's timetable was met, an executive who had no trouble fitting into the military style chain-of-command at Coors. Gary Truitt hired "The General."

I had first become aware of The General while riding the elevators at work in the summer of 1985, frequently hearing the adjective "that asshole" used before his name. A wide cross section of the Coors Marketing Department, from sales reps to market researchers, even his own management, liked to describe him that way. For a while, we thought "That" and "Asshole" were his first and middle names.

The General's profile rose still higher in the fall of 1985, when he had a blowout over the telephone with tempestuous Lori Sheehan (my first boss at Coors). The entire Market Research Department enjoyed listening in over the short partitions that walled the Coors office cubicles, as The General and Lori traded pleasantries. I later learned that The General had objected to Lori's conducting a meeting without inviting him, and called her a "conniving, red-headed bitch."

Truitt had lured The General away from Miller Brewing in March 1985 to serve as the brand manager for Colorado Chiller.

(There was considerable speculation around Coors that Miller probably listed his defection as a "marketing highlight" in its annual report that year.) The General was a short, stocky executive with a Confederate-style droopy moustache, straight dark hair, and horn-rimmed glasses. He resembled a handsome Wally Cox—the 1970s "Hollywood Squares" star—on steroids. In his late thirties at the time of Chiller's introduction, The General spoke in a slow Southern drawl that betrayed his Texas roots, which hardly endeared him to the native Coloradans at Coors. (Texans are to Coloradans what Liberals are to Reaganites.)

What endeared The General even less to the Coors rank and file was his unwillingness to cooperate—with *anybody*. As a former Army officer, The General was a devoted follower of the military custom of chain of command. The General treated sales-promotion specialists, market researchers, sales managers, and others working on his product as enlisted men and women, there to serve *him*. When The General gave an order, those around him were supposed to jump, without argument, even if the order was imbecilic. As one sales manager summed up, "That asshole has made a lifetime full of enemies in six months."

His military mode was exacerbated by a grating, caustic personality. The General was sarcastic, bombastic, crude, and prone to using obscenities. He especially made sport of women (whom he felt were inferior and called "broads" and "bitches") and any employee with an obvious physical imperfection, such as nearsightedness or a few extra pounds. (The former were referred to as "four-eyes" while the latter were "lard-asses.") If ever there was a marketing manager at Coors whom the rank and file wanted to see fail, it was The General. To paraphrase a Green Bay Packer's description of coach Vince Lombardi, The General treated everybody equally—like dogs.

Of course, beneath any successful military officer is a loyal second-in-command. For The General, second-in-command was Igor, a well-educated, Northwestern University MBA. Like

The General, Igor came from a military background, having served a tour of duty as a naval officer in the Persian Gulf. Short and stoop-shouldered, with high cheekbones, dark circles under his eyes, and a white, chalky, corpse-like pallor, Igor looked as if he could crash a Halloween party, without a costume, any day of the week. In contrast to The General, Igor was usually genial, rarely abusive. But like his mentor, he was unprepared for the challenge of marketing Colorado Chiller in the burgeoning wine cooler business.

The first indication that Colorado Chiller was in trouble came in the summer of 1985, shortly after its introduction. "Man, I hear that Colorado Chiller project is *really* a mess," I heard one marketing manager say to another while riding up the elevator at Coors.

"Yeah, a distributor I was talking to in Dayton said that he's moved [sold] only a couple of cases of product the last few weeks. Can you believe that?" responded his coworker. "Only a couple of cases?"

"I'm just thankful that I'm not working on *that* product," concluded the marketing manager.

Or that he hadn't *volunteered* to work on that product.

In July 1985, two analysts at Coors were assigned to new-product development and market expansion. I was one of them, and my first new-product assignment was Masters III, a beer which was due to be introduced in October (and which will be discussed in the following chapter). But October was a long way off and, until then, I had very little to do around the office. So I read periodicals, trade journals, and new-products magazines in order to prepare myself for the looming battle. In reality, I was bored out of my mind.

"Hey pardner, what are you working on?" Cowboy, the other new-products analyst, asked me at least once a week. Cowboy was usually charming and affable, one of the more popular officers in the Coors marketing military. But when he asked me this question, I wasn't sure if I was more perturbed by him, the question, or his mock "accent." (The closest Cowboy had ever come to the Wild West were K-Mart blue jeans and cowboy boots, because he was an Easterner by birth and had gone to school in Wisconsin. Yet, perhaps inspired by the Western surroundings, he persisted in calling me, and a lot of other colleagues, "pardner.")

The inactivity became unbearable when I ran into Mumbles, Cowboy's boss, one day at the beer trailer (where employees could buy Coors products at significant discounts). Because no one could completely understand anything he said, Mumbles wasn't considered one of the rising stars in the Coors Marketing Department.

"Hi, you . . . today," he said as he greeted me.

Having no idea what Mumbles had just uttered, I responded with a generic, "Yeah, that's true."

"You must be getting . . . pro . . . hah," Mumbles continued while we waited in line to purchase beer.

Before responding, I stared at Mumbles, searching for subtitles beneath his round face, so that I could understand the translation from "Mumblese" to English. I laughed politely, hoping he would repeat the line, or else end the conversation altogether. But I was saved by Cowboy, who stood in front of me in the checkout line.

Cowboy whispered, "He said you must be getting bored, pardner, writing all those research proposals, while never having anything *real* to work on."

That was it. When a synthetic cowboy *and* a guy who couldn't even speak in complete English sentences were able to get under my skin, I'd had enough. As an astute analyst (at least that's what I told myself I was), I noted that Cowboy was working on three projects (Colorado Chiller, Coors Extra Gold, and the company's geographic expansion) to my lone project (Masters III). It was time to pry one away from him: Colorado Chiller.

I *wanted* to work on Colorado Chiller because it appeared to be the ultimate challenge. The initial reports on Coors Extra Gold, the other new Coors product at the time, were encouraging, in stark contrast to the rumors about Chiller. Extra Gold beer was a darker (gold), heavier-tasting version of Coors Banquet, designed to compete against the "King" of beers, Budweiser. "Pardner, it's really riding the range," Cowboy told me. This was practically unheard of for a new product at Coors.

My wish was granted by Lori Sheehan, and my first meeting about Colorado Chiller was scheduled for an afternoon in October, in one of the spacious conference rooms in the new Coors office building. I was scheduled to present the results of the latest sales-tracking data, which would lead to a discussion of future promotion strategies. In addition to Igor and The General, who were Colorado Chiller's marketing managers, Herr Rechholtz and Gary Truitt were in attendance, along with several other members of the Market Research and Promotion Departments.

When my watch hit two o'clock, I jumped up to present, and asked Rechholtz, "Should we start?" I was eager to show him that my vocabulary included more than just "great" and "stuff."

"Gary, you ready?" Rechholtz asked Truitt.

Turning to The General, Truitt asked, "Ready?" I guessed that this was what military planners called "chain of command," though I was somewhat worried that it took three executives just to start the meeting.

The General nodded at Truitt, and drawled, "Burgess, hold off a minute." He cleared his throat and announced that Colorado Chiller was being "discontinued effective immediately, in its test markets of Dayton, Lubbock, Spokane, Charlotte, San Diego, and Orlando." I hadn't felt such sadness and loss since "The Brady Bunch" had been canceled. Discontinued? *Immediately?*

Colorado Chiller had far underperformed expectations, holding a market share in test markets of only 2 percent of the cooler business, a figure which was financially unpalatable for Coors. (As a result, I'm sure that I set some sort of record for shortest tenure on a product marketing team, when Chiller was canceled on the day of my first official meeting.)

Now, my "glamour" assignment was gone. With one announcement, my job had shifted from that of general practitioner to forensic pathologist. My new assignment was to analyze *why* Colorado Chiller had failed, which was like performing an autopsy on a very mangled corpse: the patient was obviously dead, and there were so many potential causes of death, it was hard to isolate just one. Mumbles suggested that the reason for failure was that "Bartles and Jaymes, and then . . . California Cooler went . . . down . . . Chiller," whatever that meant. Cowboy offered that "the filly just had too much range to ride." I didn't quite understand that theory, either. Fortunately, research conducted before and after the product's death confirmed what most of us at Coors already suspected: There were multiple causes of Chiller's demise, each of equal importance.

First, Colorado Chiller didn't taste as good as the other leading coolers, Bartles & Jaymes and California Cooler. In fact, after just a few minutes in bright light, the product turned, in technical brewing terms, "skunky." (Try to imagine what "skunky" tastes like.) That is, Colorado Chiller spoiled quite easily. One Coors executive served the "skunky" drink at an outdoor barbecue, much to his embarrassment. As he later put it, "The penguins in the ad should say, 'Less chilling . . . tastes like shit.' " Colorado Chiller was the only Coors product sold in a green bottle, which, the brewmasters said, allowed dangerous ultraviolet light into the bottle, tainting the liquid.

Second, the advertising was ineffective, confusing at best, and corny at worst. Consumers didn't appreciate the penguins' lame attempts at humor. Colorado Chiller's "spokespenguins" weren't perceived to be cute or lovable, but obnoxious. Plus, cooler drinkers found it difficult to relate to the mechanical penguins in their dark, dank bar. One woman interviewed as part of the Colorado Chiller postmortem research told us,

"They're [the penguins] cold, slimy, and probably smell fishy."[2]

Many cooler drinkers thought Colorado Chiller ads looked like beer advertisements. A creative director from Tatham, Laird, and Kudner, the Chicago-based agency that created the Chiller ad, told me, "We were pressured, not very subtly, to make this thing look like a beer ad, by the Coors Board [of Directors, consisting primarily of Coors family members]." In effect, the advertising gave cooler drinkers a reason to *avoid* drinking the product.

The product was also the wrong type of beverage for the cooler business. In marketing terms, Colorado Chiller was a bad "fit" with cooler drinkers' expectations. According to research, wine cooler drinkers in 1985 were primarily young, upscale women who were searching for an alternative to drinking beer. Yet, when they tried Colorado Chiller, cooler drinkers tasted flavored beer, not wine. As one Chiller drinker said, "It's as if a beer company tried to pull one over on us . . . calling it a cooler, and then serving beer." Now, why would a beer company do something like that?[3]

The brand name, "Colorado Chiller," was also a mistake, often confused with California Cooler. Consumers in the test markets marched out to stores after seeing a Colorado Chiller advertisement and bought . . . California Cooler. Being confused with the industry leader was a major disadvantage for the new cooler on the block.

Finally, the project's managers, The General and Igor, deserved a share of the blame for Chiller's demise. The General

2 The custom-designed penguins, which Coors had purchased for several hundred thousand dollars, were later sold to a children's amusement park in California.

3 Coors was not alone in marketing a malt-based cooler product, as opposed to the wine-based products that dominated the market: Stroh marketed White Mountain Cooler; Iron City came out with I.C. Cooler; Heileman introduced LaCroix Sparkling Cooler.

and Igor, like many other businesspeople managing during a decade marked by its emphasis on immediate gratification, preferred bold, often misguided actions (in the hope of instant success) over lengthy, well-conceived marketing campaigns. In marketing parlance, The General and Igor were "instinct marketers," using intuition and gut feelings as the basis for taking immediate action, rather than concrete research data or specific information on customer tastes and preferences.

Typical of the duo's style was that first, fateful meeting, at which Colorado Chiller was officially pronounced dead. After The General's stunning announcement, I delivered my scheduled sales presentation to a discouraged audience. As I did so, Gary Truitt (a wily debater, as shown by his celebrated argument with the pesky penguin in Chiller's promotional film) kept asking The General and Igor questions about the report.

"Do we know why White Mountain Cooler is doing so well in Los Angeles?" Truitt asked.

"No. Not yet,' The General drawled in his Texas twang. "But I have a couple of ideas, I guess."

"Do you have any idea how our distributors are going to feel about pulling Chiller from the marketplace?" Truitt later inquired.

"No, Gary, but we're certainly going to get to it in the future," The General replied.

Still later, Truitt wondered, "How is California Cooler's new orange flavor doing?"

"Beats me," Igor offered.

The meeting continued at this pace for a few more minutes, until Gary exploded, "Is there any fucking thing you *do* know? What am I paying you for? Get on the goddamned phone to our sales office and get some answers . . . instead of just guessing."

The General's impetuous "shoot first, ask questions later" style had impressed Rechholtz and Truitt for a time, but ultimately it cost Coors millions of dollars in losses (even after they sold off the mechanical penguins). While The General and Igor had met Colorado Chiller's introduction deadline (the summer of 1985, as promised by Rechholtz to the Coors Board of Directors), the management duo cut corners and skipped key product-development steps.

Product research was skipped "because we didn't have time," according to The General, and Colorado Chiller's vulnerability to sunlight hadn't been detected prior to the product's introduction. The name "Colorado Chiller" had been selected with minimal research, because The General, managing on instinct, liked it. (As a rule, whatever he liked, most everybody else disliked.) And the penguin advertising hadn't been thoroughly tested. The General was so mesmerized by the artistry of the mechanical penguins that it never occurred to him that cooler drinkers wouldn't get the point of the commercial.

Most importantly, simulated test marketing had been skipped. Marketers use this research technique to forecast sales volume in advance of a product's actual marketplace introduction; simulated test marketing is to Madison Avenue what dress rehearsals are to Broadway. Using hundreds of consumer interviews and sophisticated forecasting formulas, marketers can screen out bad products (like Colorado Chiller) and avoid costly losses. The General had called the simulated test market proposed Colorado Chiller "bullshit," and objected to the research's steep pricetag. But an investment of $60,000–$100,000, as well as two to three months of time to conduct proposed research, could have prevented a huge mistake.

In early fall of 1985, The General told Lori Sheehan, "If I listened to you research people, I wouldn't have introduced the product on time." From Bill Coors on down, everybody wished The General and Igor *had* listened to the research people, or to anybody who would have advised them to rework, or cancel, Colorado Chiller.

Ultimately, no one at Coors disagreed with the decision to pull Colorado Chiller off store shelves; the real mystery was how it had gotten on them in the first place. New-product successes are crafted by selling the right product to the right group of satisfied customers. By focusing on the calendar, instead of on customers, Coors failed to achieve even one of the four critical success factors identified by Truitt's committee in 1984. Or, as Herr Rechholtz later asked The General and Igor, "Is there anything you did *right* on Colorado Chiller?" (A failure is thought of as "your" product by senior marketing managers, while a success becomes "our" product.)

The "lottery" strategy dictated that, after the demise of Colorado Chiller, it was time to buy another lottery ticket; that is, it was time to develop and introduce another new product. Truitt favored another try at the cooler business. "It's a business we have to get into," he reasoned in an early December assessment; Chiller was dead, but a replacement was needed.

Truitt knew that the beer business was only growing about 1 percent to 2 percent per year. Though much smaller in size, the cooler market was growing at about 75 percent per year.[4] It was hard to see how a company like Coors could fail to introduce a successful new product when a category was growing that fast. If Coors was to survive, an "easy" opportunity like the cooler business couldn't be passed up, despite the company's track record with Chiller.

Incredibly, neither The General nor Igor were fired, as is the custom for big losers in the marketing game. Though they had exercised poor judgment and cost the company millions, Gary Truitt and Herr Rechholtz apparently applauded their hard-charging styles. Or else Truitt and Rechholtz reasoned that the best punishment, and the best example to give to other would-be gamblers with Coors money, was to make The General and Igor develop *another* cooler product (which, for a time, we dubbed "Son of Chiller.")

However, Truitt was wary of making the same mistakes twice (especially since Colorado Chiller was originally his project). Acknowledging The General's track record, or lack thereof,

---

4 *The IMPACT American Cooler Market Review and Forecast,* M. Shanken Communications, 1986, p. 3.

Truitt told him to hire a new-products consultant to assist in developing the next Coors cooler product.

The General didn't quite warm up to the assignment, as he didn't want to share command of this, or any other project, with a consultant. "Fuck Truitt," The General told Igor. "We can do this one on our own. We learned from our mistakes, and we don't need anybody looking over our shoulder." The General argued to Truitt that a consultant would be too costly, and that Coors should take a "long, hard look before spending any more money on coolers."

In December 1985, a little more than a month after the plug had been pulled on Colorado Chiller, Truitt brushed aside The General's objection, and called a meeting to set the agenda for future cooler product development. Ostensibly, The General, Igor, other new product development managers, and the Market Research Department would huddle and come to some collective agreement on how to proceed with the development of a cooler in terms of timing, resources, budgets, and the hiring of a consultant.

Meeting day was on a Friday, "Poker Night" for the Marketing Department. I went to lunch with The General and several other people from the department at a cheap Mexican restaurant in the foothills of the Rockies. This was the type of restaurant that featured "real" Tostitos chips from a grocery store, "authentic" recipes from *Parade* magazine, and ambiance that made diners feel as if they were a thousand miles from Mexico, which they were. It was as close to a good Mexican restaurant as Colorado Chiller had been to a good wine cooler.

Yet, the lunch conversation was even worse than the restaurant in which it took place. Soon after we arrived, I learned that The General and one of his poker partners had chosen this particular restaurant in order to prep themselves for a farting contest, to be held during the key cooler planning meeting, as a warm-up for the Friday night poker game. "Order anything with beans," The General told his opponent.

"You've got to be kidding," I said, though I knew he wasn't

joking about the contest. The General, Igor, and some of their poker buddies seemed to be anally fixated. In addition to passing gas, they frequently referred to being "reamed" by senior management, of "reaming" Colonel Khadafy and Libya, to "bending over" in meetings, and even created a "Bloody Asshole" award for their Poker Club. (I was always puzzled why they never talked about reaming the competition.) The General and another brand manager frequently ran into each other's office to pass gas, a sort of running joke. Once, The General broke wind in his competitor's office and yelled "Gotcha," only to find a female account executive from Foote, Cone, and Belding, one of Coors ad agencies, borrowing the office for the day. As the account executive stared at The General with a bemused expression, he quickly shuffled out of the office, more to avoid the impending aroma than because he was embarrassed. The General was a true goodwill ambassador for Coors.

"Do I look like I'm kidding?" The General responded to my question about the contest. "Ahm ordering two plates of refried beans. I may be a lousy marketing manager, but ahm gonna win this contest," he drawled, in one of his rare candid admissions.

When I entered the crucial planning meeting, held in one of the large conference rooms near Truitt's office, The General and his competitor in the farting contest were seated on one side of the table, prepping for battle. I took this threat seriously enough to sit as far away as I could, in the back of the room, on the other side of the large conference table.

"Let's get started," Truitt advised as he entered the room.

And they did. Soon, The General and his opponent fired their opening salvoes, silent, but very lethal, just as Betsy, another brand marketing manager, asked if she could sit between the contestants.

"Is this seat taken?" Betsy asked innocently.

"No, feel free," The General responded. "You're just in time," he added deviously, giggling like a bobby-soxer at her first pajama party.

As Betsy sat down, her nose wrinkled like freshly lit newspaper in a fireplace, and I knew the contest was for real. Clearly, Betsy wanted Scotty to "beam her up" to somewhere less noxious. The contest continued throughout the listless meeting, the contestants' pungent aroma bearing silent witness to their prowess. No consensus was reached on the future of wine coolers at Coors, and the project was tabled until after the holidays.

The contest winner was never announced. But the cooler project was the big loser. With minds more focused on farting than on marketing a new cooler product, the meeting failed to serve its purpose. What's more, I never ate at that Mexican restaurant again, and Coors never did hire a consultant.

As 1985 waned, Coors was definitely out of the cooler business, perhaps forever. The General had ensured that the first major battle in The Beer Wars was a losing one. Fortunately, the Coors marketing warriors didn't yet know that The General would eventually rise from the dead, grow in power, and plague Coors new-product development program, as Moby Dick dogged Captain Ahab, for years to come. If we had known, we might have surrendered then and there.

4

When Bad Things Happen to Good Ideas

No one would ever have crossed the ocean if
he could have gotten off the ship in the storm.

— Sign in C. F. Kettering's Office

Losing that first battle did not mean that Coors had lost the war. While Colorado Chiller was failing, plans were being finalized to launch another new beer product. In October 1985, Coors—in conjunction with Molson of Canada and the Kaltenberg Castle of Germany—introduced Masters III. The product was, in marketing parlance, a "brilliant concept."

For years, imported beers had made inroads into the U.S. beer market at the hands of domestic brewers. In 1960, just 0.4 percent of U.S. beer sales were of imported beers. By 1980, that figure had jumped to 2.6 percent, and, by 1983, to 3.4 percent of the U.S. beer market.[1] Corona, Heineken, Beck's, and other imported brands were grabbing an increasing share of the mar-

---

1 *Coors Brewing Industry Overview*, 1985 Edition.

ket, even among "Joe Six-Packs" in middle America, the "shot-and-a-beer" segment.

The solution seemed simple. Like U.S. automakers, themselves threatened from overseas, domestic brewers had to brew an import-quality product in the United States. Yet, oddly enough, this idea didn't come from one of the major U.S. brewers, but from an import brewer, Canada's Molson.

Hollis Brace, a stern, statesmanlike, no-nonsense Molson executive, had observed the rise of imports, especially European brands. While Molson sold well in the U.S., Hollis felt that the company could make greater inroads by brewing an import-quality product with the blessings of a domestic marketing giant, such as Miller or Anheuser–Busch. But these brewers were busy with other projects, and declined to join forces with Molson.

After spending hundreds of thousands of dollars researching and developing this idea, Brace and Molson finally found their partner: Coors. The companies were kindred spirits, of sorts.

Molson of Canada was founded by Eric Molson in the late eighteenth century. Like Coors, Molson was proud of its dedication to quality and touted the purity and clarity of the mountain spring water used to brew its beers. Molson had been popular for years along the Eastern Seaboard of the United States, but had failed to keep pace with the sales gains made by Corona, Heineken, and other imports in the rest of the nation.

Bob Rechholtz and his staff also realized that imports were eating away at Coors share of the beer market. With industry growth slowing and the strong dollar increasing the affordability of imports for downscale beer drinkers, Rechholtz figured that, over time, the threat of import brewers would only grow more severe. Plus, Coors had already failed, and failed miserably, in trying to launch its own higher-end, or "super premium" domestic brand, Herman Joseph's. (This product is covered in Chapter 6.) Pete Coors especially was enthusiastic about producing a thicker, heavier beer. "Great-grandpa Adolph would never have stood for this talk of 'watery' beer. I think he'd approve of us brewing something like Masters, instead of Banquet and Light."

And, so, Masters Beer was born, combining the affordability and smoothness of a domestic beer (Coors) with the perceived quality (Molson) and brewing know-how (Kaltenberg Castle) associated with foreign brewers. The product appeared to boast several benefits, with no apparent weaknesses. Coors would brew the beer, Molson would split the marketing costs and overhead of this new joint-venture company, and Kaltenberg Castle would loan its name and German brewing heritage in return for a small royalty. Hollis Brace's dream was about to become a reality.

Both Molson and Coors contributed senior executives to the new company, which, reflecting its hoped-for international stature, was headquartered in suburban Washington, D.C., in Alexandria, Virginia. Hollis Brace was president of the company. A portly, ex-Schlitz executive and Captain Kangaroo lookalike served as vice president of marketing. The director of marketing was Dan Roman, a former J. Walter Thompson adman who was as genial, refined, and bright as The General was crude and rude. And a German baron named Prince Leopold, whose family owned Kaltenberg, made promotional appearances on behalf of the new company. (To me, "Prince Leopold" sounded like a character out of the vampire film *Fright Night*.) After the company was launched, I joined this management team as the market-research analyst.

Before launching Masters Beer, several key marketing decisions were made by the new management team. First, the name "Masters" was changed to "Masters III," to avoid legal problems with the Masters golf tournament.

Second, television advertisements for the new beer were developed by the New York-based Dancer, Fitzgerald, and Sample (DFS) advertising agency. The ad's theme was "Together Is

Better," and explained how the three companies had come together to brew the world's "best" beer.

Two more key decisions were made prior to the product's launch. First, Masters III, as an independent company, would build its own distribution and sales network, bypassing Coors and Molson. Second, a prototype product would be tested and developed in the Coors R&D department, in consultation with Molson. These two decisions quickly turned Hollis Brace's dream into a nightmare.

After a high-profile product launch in October 1985, it was my job to analyze the product's performance in its four test markets: Washington, D.C., Columbus, Boston, and Miami. These markets had been chosen primarily because of the popularity of imported beers among beer drinkers in these areas. Conspicuously, West Coast markets were excluded, despite the popularity of imported beers in cities like Seattle and San Francisco. (This omission would also haunt the new company.)

From the start, Masters III was in trouble, despite a hefty advertising budget that, in national advertising dollars, would have equated to $30 million in spending. Nielsen sales reports indicated that the strong dollar continued to narrow the pricing gap between imports, like Corona and Heineken, and domestic "super premiums," like Michelob and Lowenbrau. Consumers reasoned that if they had a choice between the *real* Molson and the Coors version of Molson (Masters III) for about the same price, why not buy the real Molson? Masters III accounted for just 0.3 percent of all beer sales in its four test markets in November and December 1985.[2]

To compound the pricing problem, some of Coors own sales force sabotaged distribution efforts. Despite the fact that Coors was a major partner in the new company, these salesmen reasoned that if Masters new, upstart sales force could successfully sell Masters to grocery and liquor stores, then its own reputation

2 Based upon estimates provided by the A. C. Nielsen Company.

would be tarnished. The friction was summed up by one Coors regional sales manager, who eloquently stated, "Fuck them [Masters]. It's my city, the they'll have to kiss my ass before I'll let them shit in my outhouse." And apparently the Masters sales force did neither, because Masters occupied less than 1 percent of all beer shelf space in grocery and liquor stores, half the space of Michelob and Lowenbrau, three months after its introduction.[3]

With sales significantly below expectations (the actual market share of 0.3 percent was one-sixth the planned market share of 2 percent), Masters Brewing Company decided to conduct focus-group research to analyze what drinkers thought of the new product and its new advertising campaign. Focus groups are discussions convened with consumers, and moderated by a professional facilitator, in order to understand consumers' perceptions, attitudes, and opinions about products and services. Focus groups are conducted around conference tables with eight to twelve consumers who have been recruited by research companies. Marketing managers observe the groups through two-way mirrors which allow them to watch the discussion without allowing the focus group participants to see back into the observation room; it's a kind of organized voyeurism. Focus groups lack the numerical precision of surveys, but can be helpful in discovering what consumers are thinking.

The first focus groups for Masters III were held in Columbus, Ohio, several weeks shy of Christmas 1985. The weather was beastly, with torrential downpours accentuating the bitter, forty-degree temperatures. The Sheraton Inn that housed the Masters III project team provided little protection from the cold. The heaters in many of the rooms were broken, some rooms contained plastic "patch" over broken windows, and cold air poured beneath the flimsy room doors, most of which had been kicked in at least five or six times. I found little consolation at the recommendation from the front desk clerk to "prop a chair

---

3 Based upon estimates from the A. C. Nielsen Company.

against the door to make sure no one breaks in." The Ritz, it wasn't.

However, creature comforts weren't our goal; we needed answers to the mystery of why consumers weren't buying Masters III. The key finding from these focus groups was that some Masters III drinkers said that they felt the product was a little too light, smooth, and drinkable to be like an imported beer. In other words, the product tasted more like Coors than like Heineken. But this kernel of wisdom, a clear warning about the product, was almost completely overlooked in the "back room" observation area where the marketing managers watched the proceedings.

In order to watch the focus groups, we sat in a small, darkened chamber adjacent to the focus group room. This observation room was cramped, with poor ventilation, making us feel as if we were riding in a submarine. Once the door to the observation room was closed, the observers tended to get cranky at being shut off from the real world and consigned to watching strangers gab for two hours.

When the lights were dimmed and the "hatch" closed, the six or seven observers from Masters III and DFS (the ad agency) wanted to do anything *but* watch the focus groups. First, some observers were too busy arguing over who was in charge of the M&M's candy bowl and the cracker tray, containing snacks provided by the research company staging the groups. This dispute was settled when a creative director from the ad agency yelled that "this is my fucking M&M's bowl. Anyone who wants to take it away [from me] can step outside."

After the preliminary snacks, observers tussled over what kind of Italian food they wanted for dinner. Lasagna was more popular than tortellini, but the lasagna was in short supply. Finally, a "draft" of the available meals was conducted, based on the observers' titles.

Once the meal "draft" had been finalized, a full hour into the focus group, an argument raged over whether the right questions were being asked by the focus group moderator. Captain Kangaroo, vice president of marketing for Masters III, implored, "What the hell are we here for again?"

I was beginning to wonder myself. (For just a brief moment, I was tempted to tell him that we were here to choose between lasagna and tortellini.) I placated him by pointing out diplomatically that "we are trying to find out how to increase Masters sales." And they paid me for such wisdom?

After dinner, one of the Masters III promotion managers spent the evening pounding down bottles of Michelob (not Masters III; apparently, even *he* didn't like the taste). He spent the rest of the evening providing sage, slurred, loud commentary on the proceedings. "Noww, tha . . . that was a brrrilliant fffucking comment," he remarked, time and time again, sounding a lot like Foster Brooks from TV's "Dean Martin Celebrity Roasts."

This promotion manager, known as Cue Ball because of his stylish coif (or lack thereof), endeared himself to a female researcher from Dancer, Fitzgerald, and Sample when he opined that a hostess at the focus group facility had, "the . . . the biggest jugs I've . . . ever sss . . . ssseen."

As the lights went up after the final focus group, around 10 P.M., a discussion in the observation room ensued. Due to the "back room" activities, any insight provided by the focus group participants had been obscured.

"I sure didn't hear anything memorable," concluded Captain Kangaroo.

"Me neither," chimed in the ad agency's creative director, still cradling his M&M bowl (as no one had challenged him).

While I would have the ability to listen to an audio tape of the proceedings later on, most of the key managers in attendance would derive no benefit from the proceedings. During the "debrief" discussion after the groups, I was having what I thought was a serious discussion with Cue Ball, when he tipped over in his chair, and then couldn't stop laughing. This signalled the few remaining interested observers that the discussion was over, and most returned to their rooms at the Sheraton.

Still, the most memorable drinker of the evening was a truck driver in the first group who said he drank three to four cases of beer per day while driving his truck. He claimed to like Masters III better than his usual brand, Pabst Blue Ribbon, which was generally not considered to be a premium beer. But then, after the first case of beer, how could he tell the difference? Or, as this model of safe driving and good citizenship put it, Masters III allowed him "to piss better."

A light bulb went on in my head. *Why not seek the endorsements of urologists the world over? Urinating contests could replace taste tests in ads. The advertisements would proclaim, "Masters III—The Better Bladder Beer." Nah, it wouldn't play in Peoria.*

The Columbus focus groups provided little help, and the Masters III mystery went largely unsolved through Christmas 1985. In January, I was slated to conduct a major analysis, my first since joining Coors, of a telephone survey of four hundred beer drinkers in Masters III test markets. My hope was that I could provide some insights that *could* solve the Masters III mystery and help turn the brand around.

After eight weeks of work the survey was finally analyzed, and in March I flew to Washington, D.C. to present the results to the Masters Brewing Company's Board of Directors. This was the "big time" of marketing research, the moment I had been waiting for since driving through the gates of the Coors plant for the first time nine months before. Unfortunately, I had bad news to deliver, and I realized that angry beer executives sometimes "shoot the messenger."

Nervous about delivering this bad news, I forgot to check in at the gate before boarding my flight at Denver's Stapleton International Airport. The plane was scheduled to leave around noon, Mountain time, and the Board was going to convene at 6 P.M., Eastern time. There was no margin for error, and if the flight had been overbooked, my seat would have been given away, and the Board would have met without me. As we lifted off, I couldn't help but think that, once I had delivered my news, they would wish that they *had* met without me.

Things only got worse. It was dusk in Washington, D.C. when the flight touched down at Dulles Airport, and I was soon lost driving my rental car in the Virginia countryside, trying to find Alexandria. Once I had navigated the monuments ("Take a right at the Pentagon," one gas station attendant had told me) and found Alexandria, I proceeded directly to the Board Room. It was already 7 P.M.

But the presentation was delayed just a little longer when, upon taking my presentation slides out of my briefcase, I dropped them in a garbled heap on the floor. Two months of work down the drain, I thought. However, in about fifteen minutes, which seemed like fifteen weeks to me, the slides had been sorted back into workable order, and the funeral finally started.

Since it was Hollis Brace's dream that was being killed, the once and future Molson executive glared at me as I presented, as if I was questioning his manhood or ancestry. *He doesn't seem to be enjoying this. But, then, why should he?* He wasn't alone, though.

Captain Kangaroo peppered me with question after question, clearly distressed and agitated, in a state of disbelief. "Are you *sure* about this?" he asked over and over.

Cue Ball, the promotion manager who had gotten drunk in Columbus, stared longingly at a six-pack of Masters III in the middle of the table, hoping for temporary relief from the "hanging judge," as Captain Kangaroo later called me.

There was plenty of evidence to convict, and then hang, the accused. My research indicated that:

- Only 74 percent of beer drinkers in the test market areas were aware of Masters III beer, despite the heavy advertising expenditures. In comparison, 98 percent of the four hundred drinkers were aware of Michelob and Molson.
- Of those aware of the product, only 23 percent had actually had the urge to try Masters III. Test results showed that the "Together Is Better" campaign did not clearly

communicate to beer drinkers *why* they should drink Masters III.

- Of those who had tried the product, only 27 percent said they would drink it again in the future, indicating high levels of dissatisfaction with the taste of the product.
- Sure enough, drinkers tended to rate the product as not being full-bodied enough (thick and dark), when full-bodied was what the advertising had conditioned them to expect. In effect, Masters III wasn't much like the imports it was trying to compete against, despite the advertising claims. Masters III was too smooth and light, more like an American beer. (Or, as one consumer had said in the Columbus research before Christmas, "Masters III tasted like Coors had brewed it." For this sage insight, we later anointed this drinker the winner of the "Master of the Obvious Award.")
- Adding all the numbers together, only 4 percent of the drinkers in the test markets liked the new product.

To a trained analyst, the answer to the Masters III problem seemed obvious. To save Masters III, three things had to be done, and done quickly. I recommended to Masters Brewing's Board of Directors that:

1. The advertising had to do a better job of communicating the key benefit of the product to beer drinkers—that they could have an import quality beer at a domestic beer price. In effect, this meant that Masters III could provide the best value to drinkers of imported beer.
2. The product would have to be made darker and heartier. The advertising promised an import-style beer, but drinkers rated the beer too light, too smooth, not hearty enough; that is, just like an American beer. This was one time when Coors shouldn't have brewed a Coors-type beer.
3. The price would have to be lowered, to increase the

spread between imports, like Molson, and this Molson "clone." Otherwise, what was the point of this product, if not greater value to the drinker of import-style beers?

But the Masters Brewing Company Board of Directors wasn't buying any of it. Hollis Brace said it all: "We already tested the product, and it was rated very highly. Your research must be wrong."

Captain Kangaroo chimed in with, "It *can't* be the product. We know we're brewing a good beer."

Cue Ball just belched, after taking a big-league swig of a Masters III. I interpreted that to mean that he agreed with Hollis and Captain Kangaroo.

And, sure, they probably were brewing a good beer. But that wasn't the point. They weren't brewing a bad product, just the wrong product.

The product development team had tested the product on a "blind" basis, not telling consumers what they were drinking. Once consumers had seen the advertising, they were conditioned to expect a certain kind of beer, and Masters III wasn't it. Marketing successes are created by satisfying an unmet need with the right product. In this case, the right product needed to be darker, heavier, and stronger tasting, more like an imported beer. In effect, Masters III was selling the sizzle, but not the steak. The product simply didn't live up to what the advertising promised.

The meeting finally broke up after four grueling hours, with the Board deciding that nothing really needed to be changed. Either they didn't get the point of the presentation, or they just didn't want to own up to making any mistakes. But now was the time to correct mistakes, while Masters III was still in the test marketing stage (before full national distribution).

As Hollis got up to leave, he walked toward me. I was sure he was going to ask me about one or more of my recommendations.

"Are you staying at the Ramada tonight?" he wondered.

"Uh, yes. What did you think of the recommendations?" I countered.

"It's a nice hotel. A little cramped, but not bad for the money."

Here I am telling Hollis that his dream isn't working, and all he can do is ask me about my hotel accommodations. We're definitely operating on two different wavelengths.

The next day, Dan Roman, the classy marketing director for Masters III, and I flew to New York to present the results of the research to the advertising account team at Dancer, Fitzgerald, and Sample. "You're going to be a really popular guy at the agency," Dan teased, as we took off on the Eastern Shuttle out of Washington's National Airport. This was my first time on the shuttle, and as we walked down the aisle, to the only empty seats in the last row, I was nearly giddy. A small-town kid from Wisconsin was taking the Eastern Shuttle with world "power brokers" (or so I imagined), flying the New York/Washington "power" corridor. I kept looking around the cabin for a famous face, but failed to spot one. Soon, I would be in the Big Apple, making a presentation to one of the world's biggest advertising agencies. This was even better than I had dreamed of while watching "Bewitched" as a child.

However, the delusions of grandeur ended soon enough, and with a splash. The gentleman seated next to me spilled his morning coffee on my white shirt. No problem, I thought, since I was wearing a brand-new, double-breasted suit, which I could wear throughout the presentation to cover the coffee stains. Wrong.

After we landed, I reached up to get my briefcase out of the overhead bin. "Pop" went the buttons, and open flew my double-breasted coat.

It only got better when we arrived at DFS's offices in the Chrysler Building, in midtown Manhattan. The presentation criticized the effectiveness of the Masters III advertising, which was created by DFS. Advertising agencies usually don't like to hear this type of criticism, since negative research can cost them millions of dollars in future media placement and management fees. The gang at DFS was no different. Only this time, I knew when they were starting to get angry.

Dan Roman told me that DFS's creative director (who had once written a famous book on techniques for picking up women) would get a twitch in his eye whenever he became nervous. "If you see him twitch, don't get rattled," Dan instructed. "They've got to see this presentation, even if they don't like the results." After Dan told me this, I immediately began to wonder whether women found this twitching trait attractive. They must, I thought, or else the creative director wouldn't have written his famous book.

So, coffee-stained shirt and all, I began the rehash of the bleak research results. "Good morning. Today we're going to talk about how we can improve sales of Masters III beer," I started. So far, so good; there was no immediate twitching. About fifteen minutes into the presentation, though, when the problems with Masters III advertising were summarized, The Winker began his eyelid semaphore. I was glad Dan had warned me, or else I would have worried that this guy was "coming on" to me. It was hard to look him in the eye when he asked a question, but then it came to me. *His involuntary winking must be the residual effect of years of winking at girls in an effort to "score." Either that, or he just likes to practice his pick-up routines a lot.*

Of course, if The Winker wasn't enough to rattle a presenter, Wiggy, an ad agency planner with a Pee-Wee Herman voice, was. Sitting across from The Winker, Wiggy squeaked, "Do we know which demographic groups reacted most positively to Masters III ads?" I could barely contain myself, and had to pace the room in order to avoid a burst of laughter. *Just the kind of guy I'd want working on a macho beer account.*

Finally, in an attempt to save my composure, I settled on a compromise strategy. I stared down the middle of the conference table, only to lock eyes, at the end of the table, with a creative director who had the largest head I had ever seen. If my big head was a size $7\frac{3}{8}$, this guy had to have at least a size

9 or 10. With a head *that* big, I figured he *had* to be creative.

Great. I'm giving the biggest presentation of my life with a coffee-stained shirt, a coat that won't button, the worst possible news, and, to top it all off, I'm presenting to a group that looks like movie extras from the Star Wars *cantina.*

But I survived the theatrics at DFS intact, having finished the presentation by staring mostly at the presentation screen. As I flew home from New York, I knew Masters III was doomed. It was only a matter of time, given the Board's reluctance to take drastic action.

Sure enough, three months later, in June 1986, the Board of Directors of Coors and Molson simultaneously voted to shut down Masters III, lock, stock, and barrel. According to Captain Kangaroo, who phoned with the news, "We thought they'd give us another chance, but they just pulled the plug." Rechholtz compared it to "having your supply lines cut in the middle of battle." There would be no expansion to the West Coast, no change in the advertising or product. Nine months after losing millions on Colorado Chiller, Coors had combined with Molson to lose millions more on Masters III. In the "throw-away" era of marketing, another product had been cast on the scrap heap.

In retrospect, Masters III was a briliant marketing concept that was fouled up somewhere between the drawing board and store shelves, and that lacked long-term management vision and support. In quickly pulling the plug, Coors and Molson passed their ultimate judgment on the project: The dismal sales picture could never be turned around, and the initial invest-ments could never be recouped. If the Masters Board of Direc-tors had made the significant changes that were recommended, the original consumer research conducted by Molson indicates that Masters could have thrived as the biggest innovation in the beer business since the invention of Lite beer. Instead, Coors resisted the notion of investing to build a long-term business.

Coors had lost the first two major battles of The Beer Wars, had lost millions of dollars, had disappointed millions of drinkers, and had failed to increase the company's overall sales. Having witnessed this carnage, we beer warriors were left to wonder how the rest of the company was faring. Was Coors always plagued by the indecision that cost Masters III and its Board of Directors the success their idea had merited? Had other marketing groups made the same mistake of turning a good idea into a bad one by brewing the wrong product? If Coors wasn't going to invest in Masters III, or in a wine cooler product, what were they going to do to encourage the growth of business? The answers were far from clear. I was just glad I didn't have a nervous tick in *my* eye. I would have been winking and blinking uncontrollably.

5

The Enemy within Central Command

Our work life is exciting, challenging, and
rewarding in a friendly atmosphere of teamwork and mutual respect.

*—Coors Company Vision, excerpted
from its 1990 Annual Report.*

The key to winning any war is
the quality of the troops," Herr Rechholtz announced at the
Coors Sales and Marketing Department Annual Picnic in 1986.
In retrospect, I belive that the quality of leadership from Coors
"High Command" was just as important as the quality of the
troops.

To fight The Beer Wars, Rechholtz recruited a senior staff,
or High Command, of hardened beer industry veterans. Many
in the Coors Command had started their careers in the beer
industry, and most would finish there. Because so many of
Rechholtz's marketing executives had served with him at
Schlitz, his inner circle at Coors was nicknamed the "Schlitz
Mafia." Unfortunately, by the 1980s, their vaunted experience
was of little value, as their management philosophy was hopelessly outdated.

Prior to Philip Morris's acquisition of Miller Brewing Company in 1974, the brewing industry was in a sales-driven business, largely dependent upon personal relationships and local marketing programs (such as sponsorships and highway billboards). Brewers usually marketed beer brands in one particular area, or region of the country, allowing managers to focus their sales efforts. Marketing managers developed close, personal ties with their customers (the distributors and buyers for grocery and liquor stores), whom they wined, dined, and entertained each week. Sales to these middlemen were usually sealed with a handshake and the tippling of beers.

But the beer business changed radically after Philip Morris, the international food and tobacco conglomerate famous for its lavish consumer marketing campaigns, bought Miller. The new Miller management team, comprised of Philip Morris veterans, didn't just focus on local marketing programs, but used Madison Avenue advertising and network TV to reach beer drinkers from coast to coast. Following Miller's lead, beer marketing executives became much less reliant on personal relationships with distributors, and used high-tech, consumer-oriented marketing weapons, including advertising, target marketing, and flashy new products, to fight The Beer Wars in the late 1970s and early 1980s.

Unfortunately, Rechholtz and his Schlitz Mafia knew only one way (the pre-Philip Morris, or old-fashioned way) to manage the beer business, which didn't work very well in the 1970s, much less the 1980s. Utilizing a vast distributor network, deep price discounts, and local sponsorship and publicity programs (like the sponsorship of county fairs, and billiards and softball tournaments), the Schlitz Mafia presided over the demise of the Schlitz Brewing Company in the late 1970s. Under their stewardship, sales of Schlitz Beer plummeted spectacularly, from 12.4 million barrels in 1975, to just 3.8 million barrels in 1982. Similarly, sales of Schlitz Light and Old Milwaukee plummeted from 1975 to 1982, and the company was eventually sold to

Stroh's.[1] Undaunted, Rechholtz and his High Command set about to revive the Coors Brewing Company.

As his vice president of sales, Herr Rechholtz hired Big Wig, an obese, crude, hard-charging Texan who wore a full black wig, which brought him instant recognition, though little aesthetic appeal. If you asked someone at Coors if they knew Big Wig, and they were puzzled as to whom you meant, you had only to remind them that he was "the guy with the wig," and a light bulb of recognition would instantly blink on. "Oh, *Big Wig*," they would say.

Big Wig also exhibited a peculiar style reminiscent of Lyndon Johnson's "Texas Hill Country" mannerisms. Big Wig was far from polished, and thought nothing of questioning someone's ancestry or sexual proclivities, in the crudest of terms, during meetings. He frequently described his own biological functions in vivid detail, hinging his happiness or success in business to the quantity he urinated, or the size of his stool that day. Big Wig was an equal-opportunity verbal abuser, regularly castigating both his male sales staff and female support staff. To top it off, Big Wig shouted obscenities so loudly that inhabitants of nearby cubicles and offices often would complain about his unprofessional behavior and vocabulary, which resonated through his office walls.

To Big Wig, selling beer was a macho act, in which the hardest-working and most truthless salespersons were successful. Big Wig abhorred cerebral sales representatives, for, as he

1 Market share for Schlitz Light peaked at its introduction in 1975, and declined steadily thereafter, according to both *IMPACT* and Coors internal estimates. By 1985, the brand sold only fifty thousand barrels per year, 0.1 percent of total light-beer sales in the United States. According to *IMPACT*, sales of Old Milwaukee declined at an annual rate of 2.2 percent between 1975 and 1980. The story of Schlitz's demise is documented by George S. Day and Liam Fahey in "Putting Strategy Into Shareholder Value Analysis," *Harvard Business Review*, March-April 1990, pp. 156–162.

put it, "You don't have to think when you put your dick in her, do you?" Selling beer was the same way: all it took was instinct. Seize the initiative and push, push, push. Sooner or later, the customer would give in.

As if to underscore this approach to sales, Big Wig rarely attended briefings on sales activity provided by the A.C. Nielsen Company (which were coordinated by the Market Research Department). "I already know all this bullshit," he would drawl, when asked if he were going to attend. Only "pussies" needed to go; on presentation days, the Sales Department was usually absent. Unfortunately, they were supposed to be the primary beneficiaries of these reports.

Big Wig's counterpoint was Rob "Rain Man" Klugman, a cerebral, Harvard-educated marketing executive from Philadelphia. Rain Man was the vice president in charge of marketing for Coors and Coors Light, the company's established brands.

A lithe, dark-haired, mustachioed executive, Rain Man was fond of wearing cowboy boots and Western belt buckles, in part to dispel his Eastern "elite" image. But, like Dustin Hoffman's autistic savant in the movie *Rain Man,* what really drew attention to Klugman was his odd combination of brilliance and eccentricity. Like Hoffman's character, he often seemed to be managing in his own private world.

For starters, Rain Man had a propensity to "hold the floor" in staff meetings while he organized his thoughts. After Big Wig had drawled on about "bullshit" and such, Rainman would respond with, "Thaaaaaaaaaaaaaaaaaaaaat would seem to indicaaaaaaaaaate . . ." or "IIIIIIIII thiiiiiiiiiiiink thaaaaaat weeeeeeee . . ." Rain Man would draw out his first few words, often for ten to fifteen seconds, while thinking about what he really wanted to say. Unfortunately, most listeners in the Coors far-from-cerebral marketing offices were unable to follow Rain Man's train of thought.

Rain Man would often get up from a conference table to pace the room in the middle of a meeting, like a caged lion in the zoo, oblivious to the effect of his pacing on others and the fact that no one ever paced with him. I sometimes felt as if I had burned off a few calories just watching Rain Man walk around.

On one occasion, Rain Man, in the middle of observing a focus group, suddenly got up from his chair, lay down on the floor, and closed his eyes, as if deep in thought. While others in the room asked if he was having a heart attack, or sick, he merely stared at the ceiling.

Somewhere between Big Wig and Rain Man in obnoxiousness was Gary Truitt, who was in charge of new-product development for Coors. Gary was bright, and sometimes articulate. But having been groomed in Rechholtz's Schlitz system, he would occasionally rely on the Schlitz Mafia's favorite management tool: verbal intimidation. But this was understandable, given the pressure of the responsibility resting on Truitt's shoulders.

Having presided over the Colorado Chiller and Masters III failures, Truitt knew he was under the management microscope of the Coors family. It was no secret around the brewery that, while frugal company Chairman Bill Coors had grudgingly embraced marketing as a necessity if Coors were to stay afloat, he was still loathe to embrace marketing executives who lost millions of dollars with one roll of the new-products dice. Understandably, Truitt sometimes lost his temper under pressure. Working with The General was reason enough to snap. In one meeting, after I had made a presentation, Truitt became so enraged by The General that he picked up my presentation pointer and paced the room while wildly waving the instrument and threatening to whip The General. Fortunately, Truitt calmed down before giving in to this impulse.

At other times, Truitt and Big Wig hurled verbal obscenities at *each other* in the heat of High Command staff meetings, in a sort of "I'm a bigger potty-mouth than you are" contest. At one sales meeting, I witnessed an exchange something like the following:

BIG WIG: "Gary, that's bullshit. You fuckers in Development don't know what the hell you're talking about."

GARY TRUITT: "Oh yeah? Well, if it wasn't for you assholes [in sales], we'd have scored with Colorado Chiller."

BIG WIG: "Bullshit. Bullshit. Bullshit. Goddamn it, no one in their right fucking mind would drink that piss water, unless we rammed it up their asses, and gave 'em a Chiller enema. Why don't you candy asses leave the beer business to us?"

GARY TRUITT: "So you pricks can ruin the company? I was selling goddamned beer before you motherfuckers in sales were toilet trained, and don't fucking forget it."

BIG WIG: "Bullshit. Why don't you fuck off, asshole?"

GARY TRUITT: "Fuck you, fatass."

BIG WIG: "Fuck you, you motherfucker."

Shakespearean prose? (As Wayne and Garth would say, "Not!") Rechholtz's secretary later told me that the language at some of the staff meetings was so coarse that she thought she was listening to a demonic possession of the High Command, straight out of *The Exorcist*.

A notch below Rechholtz's High Command was the Coors headquarters marketing staff, the Central Command. Far from a homogeneous, unified group, Central Command was comprised of several different branches of the marketing military, factions with distinctly different functions.

One group, Big Wig's Sales Department, was nicknamed The Force, short for "Field Sales Force." While claiming to be a veteran beer salesman might seem like the act of a desperate braggart to most of the world, at Coors it was a badge of honor. The Force were the Marines of the Coors military, the frontline troops (and spiritual descendants of the Schlitz Mafia), charged with fighting The Beer Wars in the trenches, which, in this case, meant selling beer to Coors wholesalers, or distributors. Any time a wholesaler bought from one of Coors competitors, Coors was losing ground in The Beer Wars, like territory lost in a ground war. The Force relentlessly peddled Coors beer products, hoping not only to withstand attacks by Anheuser–Busch or Miller, but to seize market share from these formidable competitors.

As Marines use brute force, so, too, did The Force use the most rudimentary of marketing tools to fight The Beer Wars: price discounting. To gain ground at the expense of Miller, Stroh, Anheuser–Busch, or any other major competitor, The Force simply lowered the price of Coors beer until wholesalers could no longer resist buying it. Like Marines razing the battle landscape until the area is no longer habitable, The Force's price discounting had the potential to inflict severe damage on Coors. Frequent price discounting not only sacrificed profits in the short term, but had the potential to mortgage Coors future as wholesalers and consumers alike would slowly be conditioned to buy Coors *only* when it was on sale (which, by the end of the 1980s, was most of the time). Eventually, Coors beer would be perceived to be "cheap" beer by many consumers, and for Coors itself, perhaps this was too steep a price to pay to close a few sales in 1986.[2]

Since Rechholtz had promised to boost Coors sales through expansion to new markets, members of The Force, who sold the beer in these markets, were considered essential to the company's future. Accordingly, these sales reps and managers were usually richly compensated, became candidates for the executive fast track, and were considered heroes by the Coors High Command.

By some odd twist of fate, most of The Force hailed from the South, and their rich, "good-old-boy" drawls often made the Coors office building sound more like the state capitol of Mississippi than the corporate headquarters of a Colorado brewery. (Though I was born in New Orleans, years of schooling in the

---

2 Many members of The Force joked that their promotion calendars lasted fifty-six weeks, a reference to their need to discount Coors beer as many weeks as possible each year.

Midwest had largely eliminated my own Southern twang.) Plus, The Force couldn't break their ingrained sales-call habit of giving *everybody*, from clients to customers to secretaries, a folksy nickname, often ending in "y" or "ie".

Following a member of The Force down a hallway, you might hear, "Hey darlin', what's happening?" Seconds later, "Smitty, how's the biz look in Charlotte? Alright, you keep it up, ya hear?" And a bit later, "Sweetie, that's a right nice dress y'all are wearin' today."

Even the staid Coors family couldn't escape The Force's nicknaming habit, though they probably preferred being called "Billie" and "Petey" to "sweetheart" or "sugar," as members of The Force often called their secretaries and female sales representatives.

Beyond selling and drinking beer, what male members of The Force liked best to do was chase women. As fast-track executives, many were considered "catches" by secretaries and lower-level managers, and weren't lacking for offers. Two senior force members had an ongoing contest to see who could get the first date from any attractive new hires. Bash was less creative, if more discreet. He preyed on women only while he traveled, until his (now ex-) wife unpacked a pair of panties from his suitcase after a long road trip. Crazy Horse preferred romantic afternoons at a pay-by-the-hour motel up the street from Coors. Valentino bragged to anyone who would listen that, in spite of the fierce Beer Wars, he was "a lover, not a fighter." And Sting Ray simply used his brand-new, "can't afford the payments" car as his lure, until one jealous member of The Force kicked in one of the car's doors at lunch hour.

The most prominent officer on the Coors Force, besides Big Wig, was Pepe, then working in pricing and training. A former phone company executive, Pepe had designs on eventually becoming an officer in the High Command, where he would have the privilege of reporting directly to Herr Rechholtz.

Pepe was best known for his simple sales philosophy. "To sell more beer, you just need to get to know your customer.

You know, gladhand him, kiss his ass, the works," he would lecture young sales executives. Pepe showed off his "talent" for this approach during his coffee break. Using a time-tested technique, Pepe would join one group of workers in the office cafeteria for coffee break in the morning, usually bragging about his latest romantic conquest or financial windfall in the commodities market. Then, as this first group finished their break, Pepe might sidle over to a new group and start all over again.

The Marketeers, brand marketing managers charged with actually managing Coors beer brands on a day-to-day basis, were the Coors Air Force in The Beer Wars. The Marketeers were professional marketing managers who planned to win the war by luring beer drinkers with advertisements, promotional strategies, coupons, contests, giveaways, and the like. While The Force focused on pushing beer through to distributors (who, in turn, would peddle beer to consumers), Marketeers hoped to create demand (called "pull," in the marketing business) by bombarding beer drinkers with marketing campaigns. Like Air Force pilots dropping smart bombs at thirty thousand feet, Marketeers created commercials, bought advertising time, and designed promotions from the safety of their cubicles in Golden. And, like wars waged by the Air Force, the war waged on beer drinkers by The Marketeers was one of attrition. Over time, they argued, Coors could win over beer drinkers with "on-target," effective advertising campaigns, as well as increased spending on these ads (or, in airman's terms, "bomb tonnage").

The General and Igor were Marketeers, as was Cue Ball, once he rejoined Coors after the cancellation of Masters III. But more typical of The Marketeers was Rod Sterling, a former marketing executive for Gallo Wines, who had signed on to develop new products for Coors. I gave him his moniker because of his resemblance to the "Twilight Zone" host, and his frequent boast that part of his anatomy was "sterling." Sterling was a bright, well-trained, and well-mannered marketing manager, a natural counterpoint to beer veterans like The General and the Schlitz Mafia. Though I didn't know it in 1985, Rod Sterling would become my most important ally in The Beer Wars, commanding several battles that had the potential to tilt the balance of power in favor of Coors.

Caught between The Force (Marines) and the Marketeers (Air Force) was my battalion, The Crunchers, short for "number crunchers." We were the intelligence-gathering and bomb-damage assessment (BDA) unit of the Coors military, and worked for both The Force and The Marketeers. The Crunchers, including Cowboy, Mumbles, and Captain Kangaroo, collected and analyzed data on the beer business and Coors competition. More importantly, we assessed the impact of Coors marketing programs on our rivals (i.e., whether Coors marketing weapons were working). As one might guess, some of The Crunchers were solitary figures, more comfortable with a table full of numbers than a table full of dinner guests. And, not surprisingly, these Crunchers were somewhat lacking in social graces.

One of the least-popular Crunchers, socially speaking, was Rip, who had a penchant for breaking wind in his office. When told to tone down the gas, Rip explained that his cubicle was the only place in the company "that's mine, where I can do as I please." Since *my* cubicle was next door, I was always braced for the next outburst, on a state of permanent alert.

Wee Willie's cubicle was across from Rip's. Wee Willie was a 265-pound behemoth who always seemed to be dieting, though never with much luck. An imposing physical presence afflicted with a laugh, or snort, like Mr. Ed's, Wee Willie had a zest for travel, and would gleefully call ahead to prospective hotels when he booked reservations, asking whether they provided a chocolate mint at night, and, most importantly, the *size* of the chocolate.

A bit more refined than Rip and Wee Willie, Dewey was the manager in charge of the Competitive Intelligence Department, and, as such, was the Coors historian on the beer industry. Besides maintaining close contacts with insiders at other companies, Dewey was closely connected with Coors own Cor-

porate Finance Department. He also had the unusual talent of
sounding inebriated when he was stone-cold sober. Dewey frequently bellowed lines like a drunk, changing the pitch and
resonance of his voice without any discernable pattern and
without warning. Even better, when he actually *did* start to
drink, he would begin to sound sober, projecting his voice in
even, measured tones.³

And, finally, one of The Marketeers' best and brightest think-
ers was Big Tim. A short, stocky, curly-haired former athlete
from Colorado State University, Tim worked closely with the
Sales Department, as a marketing information manager. Affable, reliable, and hard-working, Tim had an excellent rapport
with The Force, and was a major source of information on The
Force's activities and agenda. As testimony to their affection,
members of The Force would drawl, ''Hey, Beeeg Teeem,'' as
he passed them in the hallways.

It is not unusual for a business, or even the military, to be
comprised of diverse departments, each performing a distinct
task as part of an overall business or war effort. Nor is it unusual
for companies or bureaucracies to be afflicted with internal
strife, bickering, or turf battles. What *is* unusual is for members
of an organization to openly fight each other by design.

While successful generals have traditionally espoused teamwork and coordination, Herr Rechholtz believed in the survival
of the fittest, even within his own Marketing Department. Rechholtz spoke often of the brewing industry as being a ''war with
only one survivor.'' In order for Coors to win, all other competitors had to lose. According to this line of thinking, there
was no middle ground between winning and losing; only the
toughest and most fit companies would win The Beer Wars.

Thus, Rechholtz's core belief dictated his management philosophy. If departments within the brewery were in constant
competition with one another, they would be more likely to
perform at a high level on an ongoing basis. Always on guard,

---

3 Dewey was one of Coors taste testers.

these battle-tested departments would make Coors a more formidable opponent in The Beer Wars. This "kill or be killed"
management philosophy also helped Rechholtz to identify the
true warriors in his military; victorious warriors *within* Coors
were more likely to defeat Coors enemies without—that is, the
beer industry. Working at Coors became a game of survival,
with one warrior, or one worker, pitted against all the others.

Plus, reasoned Rechholtz, if his own High Command were
in constant turmoil, they would be more likely to remain loyal
to his plan, unable to turn mutinous while constantly covering
their own rear flanks. This was the same basic management
style used by Hitler in World War II to harness and channel
the ambitions of German High Command officers including
Goering, Jodl, Himmler, and Hess.

On one hand, the Coors High Command was balanced by
design, in that on any given issue, Rechholtz would hear per-
spectives or viewpoints from the Sales Department, the Marketing Department, and the Brand Development (New
Products) Department. But it was also designed for considerable
overlap, or conflict, in responsibilities. Would the sales strategy
for a new product, like Colorado Chiller, come out of the Sales
or Brand Development Department? When an existing product,
like Coors Light, was introduced into a new sales territory,
would the Sales Department manage the introduction, or would
the Brand Management Department? There was no shortage
of conflicts within the High Command. All three executives had
a natural beef with Rechholtz and with each other.

Big Wig was constantly irritated that sales activities in the
new expansion markets were coordinated by Gary Truitt's
group, the Development Department, instead of his Sales Department. Not part of the Schlitz Mafia (he had joined Coors
from Pearl Brewing in Texas), Big Wig felt that Rechholtz naturally favored his old Schlitz sidekick, Truitt. Worse, he had
little respect for Truitt's sales-management abilities, and often
blamed Gary for the "fuckups" on Masters III and Colorado
Chiller. Big Wig wanted *all* sales efforts consolidated in his

domain, for, as he was fond of reminding his staff, "Truitt doesn't know shit (pronounced 'sheeeet') about sales."

Gary Truitt, meanwhile, blamed the Sales Department's "good old boy" organization for sabotaging his new products, Colorado Chiller and Masters III. Truitt argued that the Coors Sales Department continued to focus almost solely on Coors Banquet and Coors Light, the two major established brands. "Coors [the company] will never grow successfully without the Development Department," Gary argued. "The Sales Department has got to support us. Coors Banquet is yesterday's news," Gary continually reminded Rechholtz, pointing to its rapidly diminishing sales. "If you give me the time, the money, and the authority," Truitt argued to Rechholtz, "I can do for Coors what I did for 'The Bull' [Schlitz Malt Liquor]."

And Rain Man, too, had a beef. He argued that Truitt's "dalliances" with new products were using up precious resources (time and money) needed to turn around the declining sales outlook for the Coors Banquet brand. Cognizant of the spectacular sales decline for Coors Banquet, which his group managed, Rain Man was very insecure about being "blamed" or held accountable for the Coors Banquet sales decline. "Give me more money, Bob, or I can't turn Coors Banquet brand around," he arued to Rechholtz. Worse, Rain Man was envious of what he perceived to be Rechholtz's "closeness" to both Truitt and Big Wig. "Big Wig's always taking the bows for any gains we make on Coors [Banquet], and Truitt is Rechholtz's caddie, another one of the Schlitz guys," he'd say.

This friction wasn't restricted to the High Command.

As part of his plan to gain indepenence from the dabbling of the Coors family, Rechholtz insisted on moving his marketing staff out of the company's corporate headquarters, into their own office building. In October 1985, Rechholtz's dream became a reality, and Coors entire marketing staff—including me—moved to a five-story building across the parking lot from the brewery. The building, set atop a hill, was officially named the North Office Building (no doubt to distinguish it from the

South Office Building), but was nicknamed "Snob Hill," by brewery employees, who resented the special treatment accorded the marketing staff. Pete Coors, who had approved the building's completion at Rechholtz's insistence, considered the gleaming new building a divisive luxury, and called it "The Taj Mahal."

What looked like "The Taj" on the outside was really a white-collar tenement. A month after the building opened, The Taj's tile floor collapsed in places, while the foundation settled. After the first rain, water poured through the atrium's glass roof. Visiting executives were no doubt impressed by the rows of buckets set out to collect water on the fifth floor whenever it rained. (This practice continued right up to the day I left Snob Hill.) When the wind blew, as frequently happens in the foothills of the Rockies, it whistled through the outside glass, which was a tad too small to cover the atrium frame.

Beyond these aesthetic problems, which forced the Central Command to rough it from time to time, the design of the building contributed to internal strife. In theory, a five-story atrium and waterfall were supposed to create a natural sound barrier that would drown out the excessive noise from the tightly packed, five-foot-high cubicles. In reality, the din from cubicles on Snob Hill sounded like Times Square during Dick Clark's "New Years Rockin' Eve." The waterfall was only noticeable on the second floor, where it was located. The cramped, noisy offices turned the staff at Central Command into cranky human sardines, and eavesdropping became the favorite office pastime.

The "kill or be killed" management philosophy also spurred open warfare between departments at Central Command. In theory, we all worked for the same company. In reality, we were often fighting each other for survival. Brand managers for Coors Light and Coors Banquet competed for funding, choice sales-promotion events (such as the Fourth of July or Memorial Day), and staff support. Coors Sales Department sabotaged sales programs of Masters III (by questioning the quality of the product and deliberately lowering the prices of Coors products) even though Coors owned part of Masters Brewing; sales success for the fledgling company would have cast the Coors Sales Department in a relatively unfavorable light. Even in the Market Research Department, managers sparred over staffing and budgeting for each of the company's brands.

Each of these internal skirmishes was really a prelude to the ultimate battle, a battle over the company's marketing philosophy and future direction. Rechholtz had promised the Coors family that he would increase the company's sales and profits by the end of his four-year contract (the end of 1986). His staff proposed two diametrically opposite philosophies, or plans, for achieving the promised turnaround.

The Force, motivated by hefty annual bonuses for increased sales volume, clearly favored using price discounting to increase Coors market share immediately. By aggressively discounting the price of Coors and Coors Light, Big Wig and The Force argued that Coors could become a more formidable competitor "almost overnight." He and The Force also proposed to Rechholtz that Coors should abandon its investment in new products, which was diverting the focus of the sales force away from the core beer brands. Big Wig and The Force buttressed their argument by noting that:

1. The Force had a demonstrated record of success at Coors. Coors overall sales volume increased 7 percent from 1983 through 1985. Measured against the sluggish growth of 1 percent to 2 percent for the industry as a whole, Coors growth seemed spectacular. Without the Sales Department, The Force argued, Rechholtz's overall program would have shown little success.

    Of course, The Force failed to point out that the amount of territory in which Coors was distributed had increased by far *more* than 7 percent during this period (on a population basis, it had almost doubled). So, in effect, Coors performance as measured by per capita consumption (or the amount consumed by the average person) had actually declined during the Schlitz Mafia's tenure. Many of the newest markets were unprofitable, with Coors eking out no more than a 3 percent to 5 percent market share in cities like Minneapolis and Chicago. And The Force's argument also failed to take into account the increased marketing and distribution costs in Coors expanded territory. *Net profits for the company actually declined by 50 percent in 1984,* with the emphasis on sales and expansion of Coors and Coors Light, and would never return to their 1983 high of $89 million. By 1985, profits had declined to just $53 million annually.[4]

2.   The Force also claimed that the millions of dollars lost on Colorado Chiller and Masters III diverted resources from the marketing of Coors and Coors Light, which accounted for 98.4 percent of the company's sales volume in 1986.

This argument, too, was flawed. There was no reason to believe that increased advertising spending on Coors and Coors Light would have boosted sales. As early as 1983, Coors spent more money advertising its Banquet brand, on a per-barrel-sold basis, than Anheuser–Busch spent on its Budweiser ($3.17, versus $2.01).[5] Despite Coors extra spending, sales of Coors Banquet continued to decline steadily—they were down 7 percent in 1986, even with the market expansion—while sales of Budweiser continued to increase.

The Marketeers countered that discounting was ruinous to the company's future. Rod Sterling noted that increasing sales through discounting was "a mirage. Yeah, Rechholtz can tell the Board that sales are up, but only because we're selling beer

4 According to Coors *1990 Annual Report.*
5 *The IMPACT American Beer Market Review and Forecast,* M. Shanken Communications, 1984, p. 55.

on the cheap. We can't keep that up forever, at least if we want to stay in business."

So The Marketeers, spearheaded by the ultimate deep thinker, Rain Man, formulated their own plan. According to The Marketeers, Coors needed to scale back drastically on price promotions, which were cheapening the company's image and conditioning consumers to wait for sales before buying Coors. More importantly, Coors needed to increase drastically its investment in viable new products, since the sales gains for Coors and Coors Light were due only to discounting and market expansion. In fact, if Coors hadn't expanded, The Marketeers argued, the company would be facing a serious *decline* in sales.[6] To support their philosophy, The Marketeers reported to Rechholtz that:

1. Coors Light, a new product in 1978, accounted for 47 percent of the company's annual sales by 1986. The company would never attain such success again without taking the risk of introducing more new products.
2. The company's new-product failures needed to be put in perspective:

- Statistics by major consulting firms indicated that, on average, eight out of every ten new products failed within a year.[7]
- While Miller had succeeded with Meister Brau and Lite, they were considerably less successful with Milwaukee's Best and Special Reserve. (Even top-notch marketers were fallible.)
- Anheuser–Busch, the industry leader, had experienced only marginal success with new products until Bud Light

6 Sales of Coors Banquet beer were declining at a rate of 20 percent per year in Coors traditional (non-expansion) markets.

7 Philip Kotler, *The Principles Of Marketing* (Englewood Cliffs, N.J.: Prentice-Hall, Inc., 1980), p. 332.

began to take off in the 1980s. And what about their spectacular failure with Chelsea (a controversial low-alcohol soft drink) in the late 1970s?

In essence, the clash of philosophies was a "tortoise or hare" dilemma faced nearly every day by business managers in free market economies. Should Coors invest for long-term competitiveness and profitability, as The Marketeers recommended, and risk suffering temporary setbacks? Or should Coors, like many other American companies, give in to the temptation to boost sales cosmetically in the short-term through price discounting, and risk the long-term consequences to the company's quality image and overall competitiveness, as well as to the bottom line?

Gradually, over the summer and fall of 1986, Rechholtz and his High Command sided with The Force. There was never a formal announcement; no puff of white smoke emerged to signal the company's shift. But, from 1986 on, Coors devotion to The Force's Doctrine of Discounting was unmistakable, as were the power of greed and the allure of hefty bonus checks.

Rechholtz and the High Command, as well as The Force, were paid bonuses based on the company's annual sales *volume*, as well as its profits.[8] The fastest way to cash in on this bonus

---

8 This was common knowledge around the brewery, although the company's annual report and 10-K filings did not specify the bonus formulas for any of the company's marketing executives. Confirmation that bonuses were largely driven by volume came in 1986, when Rechholtz's total compensation at least doubled, from less than four hundred thousand dollars per year to more than seven hundred thousand dollars. In the year in which this bonus was paid (1986), the company's net income increased by a scant 11 percent, far less than the compensation increase. And during the first four years that Rechholtz headed the Coors Marketing Department, total net annual income *declined* by exactly $30 million (from $89 million in 1983 to $59 million in 1986). Therefore, the most reasonable assumption was that the hefty compensation was a combination of short-term and long-term compensation for sales volume increases, totalling

"pot of gold" was to sell beer, the faster the better. In effect, reliance on discounting was a temptation the High Command at Coors couldn't resist. Wee Willie compared the temptation to discount with his beloved hotel-room chocolate mints. "How can you not eat it [the mint], when it's right there, in front of your face?" he asked, rhetorically. "The only way to avoid eating the chocolate is not to have the mint on your pillow each night. The same goes for them [the High Command]. If they didn't get bonus money, they wouldn't be discounting."

But discount they did. In 1986, the average price Coors charged for a barrel of beer declined, from $63.43 to $61.28 (a 3.1 percent decline), despite the introduction of high-priced Masters Beer and inflation of approximately 5 percent. This per-barrel price cut was a result of hefty discounts, price promotions, and special sales to distributors.[9] Not coincidentally, Coors sales volume surged to a record 15.2 million barrels, a hefty 28 percent increase since Rechholtz had joined the Coors Board of Directors. Despite the fact that annual net income at Coors during this same period *declined* by $30 million, Rechholtz was rewarded for the record sales volume with more than $700,000 in salary and bonuses in 1986, more than any other Board member, more than any Coors family member, and more than double his 1985 salary.[10]

At least for the High Command, greed wasn't solely a func-

3.3 percent in 1985, and 28 percent between 1982 and 1986, as well as a bonus for the modest net income increase (in 1986).

9 Calculated from the 1985 and 1986 Coors *Annual Report.*

10 Rechholtz's official compensation was never listed in Coors annual reports. However, an examination of Coors 10-K filing with the Securities and Exchange Commission from the years 1983 through 1988 indicates that: (1) 1986 was the only year in which Rechholtz was the company's highest-paid officer or director. (2) His pay in 1986 consisted of $487,018 in cash, $202,500 in stock, and $42,405 in deferred compensation. (3) Rechholtz's bonus in 1986 was listed as $103,000; but he was also awarded stock options for 4,600 shares of Coors Class B voting stock and $111,000 to meet tax obligations. (4) The next-highest-paid Coors officer was Pete Coors, who earned less than $500,000 in 1986.

tion of cash bonuses. Rod Sterling overheard two members of
the High Command talking in the fifth floor men's room in the
spring of 1987. "Have you dumped all your stock?" one general
asked as he washed his hands, unaware that Sterling was using
one of the stalls.

The conversation concerned the sale of their stock in advance
of a downbeat presentation on Coors earnings to Wall Street
financial analysts.

Rechholtz and the High Command also knew that they
couldn't continue to cash in on bonuses unless they maintained
the faith and trust of the Coors family. Losing millions on Colorado Chiller and Masters III had not exactly endeared the
Schlitz Mafia to Bill Coors, still the chairman of the Board.
According to Dewey's contacts in the Corporate Finance Department (who talked to him despite the fact that he sounded
inebriated), Bill Coors referred to the new-products effort as "a
bottomless pit." Investing in price discounting was far safer for
High Command, like a savings account. True, it wouldn't increase the profitability of the company in the long run, but it
did allow High Command to tout increased sales in each year
as a sign of "progress."

All the political infighting finally took its toll on The Marketeers, and tilted the balance of power in favor of The Force
and the Schlitz Mafia. Both Rain Man and Gary Truitt, the chief
advocates for The Marketeers, came under increasing pressure
to modify their views.

For Rain Man, pressure was spelled B-A-N-Q-U-E-T, as in
Coors Banquet beer. Rain Man was the company's most prominent Marketeer, believing that Coors would win The Beer Wars
not by discounting, but through slick advertising. Unfortunately, Rechholtz and the Coors family blamed Rain Man for
his inability to turn Coors Banquet around, despite increased
advertising outlays. Banquet had sentimental value to the Coors
family, and they didn't cotton to the Ivy Leaguer who, they
thought, was mishandling Adolph's legacy. Left to twist in the
wind, Rain Man gradually came to espouse The Force's view

of the company's future. This, he knew, was the only way he could retain Rechholtz's confidence and support—and, possibly, his own job.

For Gary Truitt, the shift from Marketeer to member of The Force came much more easily. He had once been a beer salesman for Schlitz, and felt a natural empathy for The Force, and for the Schlitz Mafia's mode of business. Plus, as the one man most directly responsible for both geographic expansion (which The Force claimed was working) and new-product development (which the Coors family bank accounts proved had not worked), Truitt had to fish or cut bait on the issue of the company's future direction. He chose to cut bait, relegating new products to the back burner, and taking an increasingly visible role in the geographic expansion efforts (which were primarily sales functions). In 1987, he would officially rejoin The Force as vice president of sales.

The first official shift in the company's marketing direction came in August 1986. Rechholtz announced that "regional sales and marketing" (a pseudonym for the old-fashioned relationship marketing from the pre-Philip Morris era), under the direction of the Sales Department, would become the company's primary marketing emphasis. Rechholtz wanted to maintain the "flexibility" of the "new-products option," he explained at the annual picnic in late summer of 1986.[11]

In effect, a few of us would continue to work on new products, but with a few "minor" constraints:

- Research budgets for development would be limited.
- Even if Coors did stumble upon a big idea, there was no guarantee that Rechholtz and the Board of Directors would support the commercialization/introduction of the product.
- Ideas would have to pay for themselves in a year or two.

11 These remarks were made in the Coors Industrial Parks/Softball complex, less than a mile from the so-called Taj Mahal.

There simply wasn't enough money to invest for the long-term.

By the fall of 1986, word from the front seemed to indicate that The Beer Wars were not going well for Coors, not well at all. Worse, the future seemed bleak, as the Coors image was plagued by not only the public-relations follies of the late 1970s and early 1980s, but by a gradual cheapening of its image through price discounting, and the de-emphasis of the company's new-product development effort.

"They sure took the easy way out," Rod Sterling noted after the annual picnic. "It's that goddamned Force running the company. They're good at sales, but we need more than just selling strategies right now. Yep, they [the High Command] sold out. They took the money and ran." True, sales volume was up because of the frequent price discounting. But this was a Pyrrhic victory. Coors Banquet was declining precipitously, and as The Force tightened its grip on the company and Rechholtz's High Command, the development of new products to replace Banquet, which appeared to be the company's only hope for winning The Beer Wars, would likely become even more difficult.

As Rod Sterling, who had been hired solely to develop new products at Coors, once said, "Working on new products at Coors is going to be as difficult as a one-legged man entering an ass-kicking contest." For the next year, whenever Sterling left on a business trip, he would bid me adieu by wishing, "May The Force *not* be with you."

6

Banished to the Cooler

What is courage? Courage means to be afraid to
do something and still going ahead and doing
it. If a man has character, the right kind of
energy, mental ability, he will learn that fear is
something to overcome and not
to run away from.

—*Knute Rockne*

Courage is doing what you are afraid to do.
There can be no courage unless you are scared.

—*Eddie Rickenbacker*

To appreciate fully the predica-
ment of the one-legged man, you must first understand how
he lost his leg, and the rules of the dérriere-kicking contest.

At Coors, new products were the "forbidden fruit." For more
than a century Coors had brewed one, and only one beer, Coors
Banquet. This was the family's pride and joy, billed as "America's Fine Light Beer." When Miller began brewing Miller Lite,
a beer that really *was* light, Coors Banquet lost its luster, for
the Coors family and millions of beer drinkers alike. Reluctantly,
Bill Coors and the Coors Board of Directors approved funding

for the development of a second beer product in the mid-1970s.

Coors Light, dubbed the "Silver Bullet" because of its silver can, was introduced in 1978, too late to be at the forefront of the light beer revolution in the United States. By this time, Miller Lite, Schlitz Light, Natural Light (from Anheuser–Busch) and a host of other lighter-style beers could be found on store shelves across the United States. Still, Coors had specialized in brewing a lighter-style beer for more than one hundred years, and the company "rolled the dice" on a late entry into the light-beer segment.

Drinkers joked that they couldn't really tell much difference between Coors Light and Coors Banquet. They were probably right; there wasn't much difference. Coors Light had fewer calories than Coors Banquet, and a little less alcohol, as well. (As a consequence, it was cheaper to make, and more profitable for the company.) Still, both beers were smooth-tasting and easy to drink. Some Miller Lite drinkers eventually switched to Coors Light because it was smoother tasting. But many hardcore beer drinker eschewed Coors Light, claiming it was just watered down beer (which, in fact, is true of any light beer).

Coors battles on the light-beer front were one of the company's few success stories in the late 1970s and early 1980s. Throughout the 1980s, sales of Coors Light increased by approximately 20 percent per year, and, by 1987, Coors Light actually outsold Coors Banquet. The success of this campaign left an indelible impression on the High Command, a phantom presence that would lurk in the shadows of other new-products efforts. Unfortunately, while Coors Light became the company's top-selling product, the High Command and the Coors family ignored several bitter lessons that should have been learned in the process of making Coors Light a success.

First, innovators and risk-takers were more likely to win The Beer Wars than followers. Despite the company's heritage in brewing lighter beers, Coors Light would never overtake (as late as 1992) a firmly entrenched Miller Lite as the top-selling light beer. Because Coors Light was so late in entering the fray,

Coors would have to be content battling Bud Light for second place. To many beer drinkers, there was only one light beer, and it wasn't Coors Light, much less Coors Banquet.

The second lesson that Coors should have observed was that success for "late bloomers" was expensive. By the time Coors Light was rolled out nationally, Miller had already spent hundreds of millions of dollars promoting its Lite. Coors would have to spend even more to convince beer drinkers to switch. In 1983, for example, Coors spent $4.68 per barrel of beer sold to advertise Coors Light, compared to just $2.96 per barrel spent by Mililer on Miller Lite.[1]

Finally, the High Command failed to note that many of the drinkers of Coors Light were formerly Coors Banquet drinkers. In marketing parlance, Coors Light was "cannibalizing" the sales of Coors Banquet. If Coors Banquet was America's Fine Light Beer, was Coors Light a *finer* light beer? Many drinkers thought so. Cannibalizing Coors Banquet amounted to the company's waging war against itself. The real trick to the new-products game was marketing a product that significantly *expanded* your customer base and generated incremental (additional) sales gains and profits, as Lite had done for Miller Brewing Company.

Unfortunately, the major, but patently false, lesson that the Coors High Command gleaned from the Coors Light battle campaign was that there was virtue in caution. "Let other companies do the pioneering work," Pete Coors said in assessing the Brand Development Department. "Then, we'll take what they've done, and do it better." This became the Coors battle strategy in the new-products war: track the enemy; absorb their initial attack; then counterattack.

After Coors Light, the company's next foray into the new-products arena was another "me too" counterattack product. The ignominious Herman Joseph's was a "super premium" or

---

1 *The IMPACT American Beer Market Review and Forecast,* M. Shanken Communications, 1984, p. 55.

higher-priced beer that was supposed to compete with the established and popular Michelob and Lowenbrau.

The lure of the super premium beers to brewers is that consumers are willing to pay more for "special" or "top-of-the-line" brands; hence, they are more profitable. Over a ten-year period of marketing trial, but mostly error, Herman Joseph's never came close to challenging Michelob or Lowenbrau, and never did turn a profit.

Contributing to the product's malaise was the odd brand name, which had been chosen to pay homage to a deceased Coors family member. In truth, "Herman Joseph's" sounded more like a brand of men's designer clothing than a beer that would compete with "Weekends Were Made For" Michelob or "Tonight, Let It Be" Lowenbrau.

The product's drab bottle, which lacked the distinctiveness and class of Michelob's (a patented tear-drop shape) and Lowenbrau's (which featured gold-and-silver foil wraps), didn't help, either. Herman Joseph's was bottled in a Coors standard brown bottle, the only type of bottle handled by Coors automated bottling machinery. As a result, beer drinkers decided that Herman Joseph's didn't *look* like a high-quality beer.

And finally, there was Herman Joseph's perpetual test marketing. Test marketing is the marketing profession's version of "war games," or limited battlefield engagement. In test marketing, a product is marketed and sold in only a few areas, for testing purposes. Then, when companies like Coors have perfected their marketing battle plan (and worked out all of the "bugs"), the product is rolled out nationally. (Imagine how much money Colorado Chiller would have lost if it had been marketed nationally instead of just in six test market cities.) For most companies, test marketing takes a few months, at most a year, to complete to perfect the marketing battle plan. But for Herman Joseph's, test marketing seemed to last forever.

Early sales results for Herman Joseph's, in 1981 and 1982, were disappointing. Beer drinkers didn't think Herman Joseph's tasted like it was worth an extra quarter or two per six-pack over the price of regular beers. At most companies, the marketing strategy for a struggling product—including the beer itself, its packaging, advertising, or even pricing—would have been changed in the face of such results; or else the product would have been canceled altogether. But not at Coors.

The Coors family, led by Bill Coors, stubbornly decided to continue brewing Herman Joseph's despite the flat sales in test markets. And rather than change the product marketing strategy, Herr Rechholtz and the High Command surprisingly recommended that Coors continue marketing Herman Joseph's in limited distribution, or test markets, to be rolled out in "phases." At a time when Gary Truitt acknowledged that it was time for "us [Coors] to either shit or get off the pot," Coors chose to do neither. Herman Joseph's wasn't going to be reformulated, but Coors also refused to pull the product from the marketing battlefield. All Herman Joseph's needed, according to the High Command, was time to "catch on" with beer drinkers. It never did.

One final effort was made in 1987 to resuscitate the brand. Attempting to cash in simultaneously on all of the crazes in beer marketing, the company renamed the product "Herman Joseph's Original Draft Light," and expanded distribution to twenty states. However, the cosmetic change to the brand name didn't fool consumers. As "Diamond" Dave from the Sales Department noted, "A dog with fleas is always ugly, even after grooming." Mercifully, after almost a decade of testing, the company finally stopped brewing Herman Joseph's in 1989.[2]

However, difficulties with Herman Joseph's didn't prevent Coors from introducing George Killian's Irish Red Ale, another super premium, counterattack product, in 1982. In order to battle imported beers (as discussed in Chapter 4), Coors contracted with the Irish brewer of Killian's to make the potent, full-bodied ale in Golden, under a licensing agreement. In re-

---

[2] Sales of Herman Joseph's never exceeded one hundred thousand barrels.

turn for the rights to brew Killian's, Coors paid a licensing fee to the Killian's company, and assumed all marketing costs for the product in the United States.

Like Herman Joseph's sales, those of Killian's Red Ale were slow, and an expensive nationwide rollout of the product at cash-strapped Coors wasn't feasible. (The High Command made several important decisions about the Killian's Ale product in 1987 and 1988, which are covered in later chapters.) Killian's, like Herman Joseph's, languished in limited distribution or "test" marketing, with minimal advertising support from Coors, its bottles collecting dust on store shelves.

Thus, the proverbial one-legged ass-kicking contest, or the attempt to develop new products at Coors, began anew in the fall of 1986. The past failures of new products (Herman Joseph's, Killian's Ale, Colorado Chiller, and Masters III) in combination with the High Command's tilt toward a sales-driven marketing strategy for the company, made working on new products at Coors about as popular as serving as a juror at the Charles Manson trial. But, as it was my job, I was determined to work on at least one success before moving on to greener marketing pastures.

My specialty at the time, market research, is crucial to developing successful new products. Market research improves marketers' odds for success by ensuring that, at each stage in the development process, a product is continually tested with consumers. (If you're developing a cooler, this means that you have to continually test the product with cooler drinkers.) By testing a product with actual consumers, and taking the guesswork out of marketing, companies are much less likely to make the kind of mistakes that doomed Colorado Chiller.

In order to explain the somewhat complicated and intimidating process of using market research to develop new products, I used to explain to clients that it was a lot like selling shoes. Imagine that you're the salesperson. You can sell shoes with one of two techniques.

Using the first sales method, called "instinct marketing," you simply size up the customer when she enters the store, and based upon your experience and prowess as a shoe salesperson, select the one pair of shoes that you think that customer will want. Of course, you're not quite sure if the shoes you've selected are the right size or right style for the customer; but, if you, an experienced salesperson, don't know what a customer wants, who does? And if the customer doesn't like your selection, she'll just take her business elsewhere. (This is the way Colorado Chiller was brought to market.)

The second sales technique, "consumer-driven marketing," is more involved and more effective. First, you ask the customer what type of shoe she's looking to buy. Then, you measure her foot, in order to make sure that the shoes she buys are the right size. Next, you bring out the types and styles of shoes that the customer says she's interested in buying. When she sees a style she likes, she tries on the shoes to make sure that they fit right. If they do fit and are the right style, you ring up the sale, and a satisfied customer walks out of your store. This is the way that market research should be used to develop new products— providing marketplace feedback at each stage of the product development process.

Shockingly, The General, a proponent of the "size 'em up and take your best guess" sales approach, was assigned the task of developing the Coors battle plan for reentering the wine cooler wars. Despite his troubles with Colorado Chiller, The General was saved by The Lazarus Syndrome.

Among Pepe, Big Wig, Herr Rechholtz and the rest of Central Command, as well as the other nine thousand employees of the company, The General was not exactly popular. But this was also his greatest virtue. The General's soul was considered so lost that Gary Truitt relished the opportunity to turn around his dying career. If The General, a boorish loser in the marketing game, could be turned into a more genial success, Truitt figured that *he* would be credited with a major accomplishment.

This is The Lazarus Syndrome of marketing management: Save a dead or dying career, and you, yourself, will be considered a miracle worker.

Of course, this line of reasoning assumed that The General would develop a new, more successful (than Colorado Chiller) Coors cooler product, and bid adieu to his tyrannical leadership style. But these were huge, if not improbable, assumptions.

At the request of Truitt and Rechholtz, the Coors Board of Directors approved funding for ''limited'' (meaning inexpensive) exploration of the cooler business in August 1986. From the start, though, the biggest limit to this exploration wasn't funding, but The General's pessimism, a pessimism founded in an inaccurate and distorted analysis of the cooler battlefield.

By 1986 sales of wine coolers were increasing by 75 percent per year. To most marketers, this would signify opportunity. To The General, this fact inspired fear. And fear was spelled G-A-L-L-O, as in Ernest and Julio Gallo's winery. Gallo introduced Bartles & Jaymes Wine Cooler in 1985, and within a year, *IMPACT,* an industry trade journal, estimated that Bartles & Jaymes had already become the top-selling cooler brand in the country, selling 4 million more cases than former industry leader California Cooler. Gallo's secret for success, beyond a quality product, was clever advertising.

Rather than sell America on the idea that Gallo, the McDonald's of wineries, was bringing out a quality cooler product, Gallo introduced the characters Ed Bartles and Frank Jaymes, two ingenious entrepreneurs who used dry, deadpan humor, and the ''Thank you for your support'' line to win a cult following. Bartles & Jaymes spent a small fortune beaming Ed and Frank into living rooms: $30 million, or about $1.76 per case of cooler sold.[3] (Remember that Coors spent $3.11 per barrel on Coors Banquet in 1983, and there are almost 30 cases in a barrel.) And Gallo wasn't alone. Seagram's spent $7.50

3 *The IMPACT American Cooler Market Review and Forecast,* M. Shanken Communications, 1986, p. 31.

per case advertising Seagram's Golden Wine Cooler. Stroh, one of Coors main competitors in the beer business, spent more than $13 per case advertising White Mountain Cooler. According to The General, it was simply too expensive for Coors to fight the cooler wars.

In 1986, *IMPACT* warned that because of the prodigious amounts spent on cooler advertising, the cooler business was "no place for the timid or underfinanced."[4] The General argued that Coors was both timid and underfinanced. He may have been right, but only in the beer business; Coors could have dominated the cooler business.

"Ahm not going to bring a slingshot to battle Goliath," The General drawled during one planning meeting.

"Who's Goliath?" I asked innocently.

"You know, Ernest and Julio [Gallo]. Heeh, heeh, heeh," he cackled.

"But we're [Coors] a lot bigger than Gallo," I reminded The General, wiping the smile off of his face. "Aren't *we* Goliath?" Coors was, in fact, about two times larger than Gallo, based on annual sales revenue.

"Burgess, stick to research," The General hissed back at me.

Not only could Coors have been the Goliath of the cooler business, but The General's analysis of cooler economics was far off the mark. Cooler marketers *should* have been spending more per case on advertising than beer marketers. There were only four, ten-ounce bottles of cooler per package (forty total ounces), versus six, twelve-ounce bottles in a beer package (seventy-two total ounces). Moreover, the forty ounces of cooler retailed for an average of $3.75, versus about $2.50 for the seventy-two ounces of beer. That is, coolers reaped about nine cents per ounce in revenues, while regular beer was worth about four cents per ounce. In essence, on a per-ounce basis, there was a lot more money to be made in marketing coolers.

4 *The IMPACT American Cooler Market Review and Forecast*, M. Shanken Communications, 1986, p. 31.

In addition, most of the top-selling cooler brands were relatively new products in 1986. Marketers spend more to introduce new products, so it was unrealistic to expect the 1986 rate of advertising spending on coolers to continue in the future.

While The General saw his glass of cooler as being half empty, I saw the glass as being at least half full, based upon my analysis of the industry. In talks with Gary Truitt, I had lobbied long and hard for the cooler project to be approved for development, based upon the following analysis:

1. Coolers were consumed primarily by women.[5] Beer was a man's drink. If Coors wanted to expand its franchise, or customer base, beyond male beer drinkers to include more upscale women, the cooler category offered the perfect opportunity.

2. Coolers were growing so much faster than beer that I projected the cooler category to be bigger than the imported beer and super premium segments of the beer industry within a few years.[6] If these segments had been large enough to warrant Masters III, Herman Joseph's, and Killian's Red, I reasoned, then a new cooler should be a top priority for Coors.

3. When looking at the competition, I was less than awestruck. True, Gallo and Seagram's had solid reputations. But after this dynamic duo, Coors would be competing against Stroh, Franzia Brothers (who?), Canandaigua, and other less savvy companies. One look at a cooler advertising reel containing the ads for some of these competitors, (which Coors advertising agencies routinely collected for us), was enough to convince me that the cooler business was a little like Ed McMahon's "Star-

5 According to an annual study of food and beverage consumption conducted by the National Family Opinion Center.

6 The super premium and import segments of beer industry accounted for approximately 8 million barrels each.

Search." Only this time the search was for marketing talent. (Such talent appeared to be in short supply: The amateurs were out in force. My favorite advertisement featured a plastic grapevine which chased cooler drinkers around from the tennis court to lounge chairs in their backyard, imploring them to drink its cooler.)

In the short term, this analysis, as well as marching orders from High Command, persuaded The General to develop a battle plan for reentering the cooler wars. He was, at best, a reluctant warrior.

I knew as much when, walking by The General's cubicle one night in the fall of 1986, I heard him tell Igor, "There's absolutely no way we're ever getting back in the cooler business again. I learned my lesson with Chiller. I'm not going to be a scapegoat this time. Let someone else take it up the ass."

Despite this negativism, The General, Igor, myself, and several chemists from the Research and Development Department formed a product development team. The first step in the product development process was to identify what *type* of cooler product Coors would develop and manufacture. (In the shoe store, the salesperson would be asking the customer what type or style of shoe she was looking for.) The first piece of market research to shed some light on this issue was an "attitude and usage" survey conducted among three hundred cooler drinkers throughout the United States in the fall of 1986. This research indicated that:

- 50 percent more households reported trying coolers in 1986 than in 1985, indicating continued robust growth for the business.
- Among the top five brands in 1986, more than 70 percent of the buyers of a given product were *first-time* buyers. These buyers weren't yet entrenched with, or loyal to, one product.
- Nearly 90 percent of the reported cooler consumption occasions were fun, festive, and social ones.

- While cooler drinkers drank the products primarily for the combination of fruit taste and alcohol (which was refreshing), many drinkers found the products to be too sweet (35 percent of drinkers), or too sour/bitter (9 percent of drinkers). In other words, while the fruitiness was appealing to women, there was still widespread dissatisfaction with the taste of wine coolers.
- Most importantly, existing cooler products, such as California Cooler or White Mountain Cooler, were perceived to be far from the ideal, and failed to fulfill the average cooler drinker completely. While Bartles & Jaymes came closest, it was still perceived to be too sweet, and not refreshing enough.

Marketers often use this type of information to conduct what they call a "gap" analysis. As the name implies, the goal of the analysis is to identify gaps in the marketplace which a new product can fulfill. Here, the gap appeared to be cooler drinkers' need for a less sweet, more refreshing product.

"Someone's already filled our gap," The General chirped, almost gleefully, upon learning that Anheuser–Busch had introduced Dewey Stevens Premium Light Wine Cooler in late fall of 1986. But Dewey Stevens was to Anheuser–Busch what Colorado Chiller was to Coors.

For starters, Dewey Stevens tasted like a watered-down wine cooler, because it *was* a watered-down wine cooler. There was no secret formula. Dewey Stevens simply contained less alcohol in order to be "lighter."

Additionally, Dewey Stevens, having been rushed to market, was packaged in an unattractive clear bottle with a twist-off plastic cap. Dewey Stevens even looked like a cheap wine cooler.

But Dewey Stevens worst sin was discovered in research we conducted on low-calorie coolers. This research indicated that cooler drinkers didn't want to drink a diet, or low-calorie cooler, because they feared it would taste "funny" or "different."[7] More importantly, this research project spawned Crystal Springs Cooler, the key to the Coors cooler battle strategy.

After Dewey Stevens was introduced, Coors invested in focus group research on concepts, or potential marketing strategies, for diet coolers. Conducting market research with The General was always interesting, though not terribly edifying. Traveling around the country talking to cooler drinkers provided exposure to the true luster of The General's personality.

The General was fond of micro-managing (known in layman's terms as "penny pinching"). Most of The General's management zeal was reserved for evaluating the cost of conducting research on the cooler business. The General, like many of his contemporary American middle managers, was far more adept at *not spending* money than at making money.

On one occasion, The General refused to authorize funding so that a focus-group moderator (market research consultant) could spend a weekend in Boston at the expense of Coors, instead of flying back and forth to focus groups scheduled, for logistical reasons, on a Friday and a Monday. In fact, it was *less* expensive for the moderator to weekend in Boston than to fly back and forth to his home. Still, "I'm not spending money for him to sit by the pool," The General told me emphatically, implying that the moderator was more interested in lounging than in conducting the research.

"But it's March, and he probably won't be sitting by the pool in Boston," I pointed out. "It's still a little cold there." The General relented, but only after I reassured him that the moderator would have to wear a fur-lined parka and sip hot toddies in order to enjoy the comforts of an outdoor pool in Boston.

---

7 The same had been true for light beers. Until Miller Lite advertised that light beers were not only less filling, but tasted great, they held little appeal. As a consequence, Dewey Stevens Premium Light, which advertised its lower caloric content, was an abysmal failure, and was pulled from the marketplace in 1988.

No amount of money was too small to be questioned by The General. He even wondered about the cost of food provided in the observation room at focus groups. "Why should we be eating well?" he wondered. Why, indeed? (Of course, Chinese take-out food or lasagna "to go" didn't quite fit my definition of living well.) So, for the next set of focus groups, I arranged for the focus group facility to serve only peanuts and chips. Not surprisingly, The General stopped questioning food expenditures for these occasions, and we went back to eating "well."

In his most bizarre act of cost control, The General berated me for tipping a cab driver in San Francisco. "He's probably a fag," The General reasoned.

"Why does that matter?" I asked, feigning innocence, knowing full well that an Archie Bunkerish response was forthcoming.

"We don't allow those type of people in the Army," The General reasoned, "so why should we make them rich at company expense?" It was hard to argue with that logic.

On this same trip to San Francisco The General refilled a scotch bottle with water at the city's posh St. Francis Hotel, in order to avoid being charged for drinking from his in-room "honor" bar. To The General, this was undoubtedly an act of fiscal responsibility. In my mind, this sort of cost control fanaticism was better left to an accountant, a junior marketing manager, or abandoned altogether. The amount of money saved by The General's micro-management was miniscule compared to the time and money exhausted on the financial audits themselves. Plus, his fanatical cost-cutting often obscured our true goal of finding a way for Coors to reenter the cooler business.

In between budget reviews, the project team actually found time to research the "light" cooler concept. This research was conducted in Denver, Phoenix, and Los Angeles, with focus groups of female cooler drinkers reacting to concepts for diet coolers. (Using the shoe store analogy, we were now trying to measure the foot size of cooler drinkers; we know that they wanted a lighter cooler, we just didn't know what kind.)

The advertising agency that Coors hired for the cooler project, Tatham, Laird, and Kudner (TLK), had brainstormed potential diet cooler concepts, or ideas. Even the best advertising agencies occasionally misfire, and one of TLK's concepts was a new cooler called "Tsunami," because the taste "exploded" in your mouth, like a "tidal wave of flavor." Predictably, most cooler drinkers were unable to pronounce the name of this product idea, much less understand how a cooler would "explode." (A cooler "fizzie," perhaps?)

Another concept was dubbed "Platinum," and was supposed to be an upscale cooler, like a liquid version of the Platinum American Express Card. Predictably, naming a drink after a precious metal lacked appetite appeal. One "literal" drinker noted that if she wanted to taste metal, she'd simply drink tap water from the rusty pipes at her home.

And then there was "Shimmer." A cooler drinker in the focus groups said it sounded more like something she'd buy at Frederick's of Hollywood than at a liquor store.

However, in the process of exploring the diet or light cooler concepts from TLK, as well as studying Dewey Stevens Premium Light, we stumbled upon a truly innovative idea. Cooler drinkers wanted a lighter tasting, less sweet drink. But they emphatically pointed out during the focus groups that they detested low-calorie drinks, since they usually tasted funny, and stigmatized the drinkers. One cooler drinker pleaded, "I want to count my calories in private."

While listening to the focus groups, a marketing research manager known as Big Mama, no stranger herself to dieting and calorie-counting, asked, "What if a cooler manufacturer made a drink that mixed sparkling water with wine, like Bartles & Jaymes combined with Perrier?" Big Mama went on to explain that not only would this sparkling cooler provide a rationale for a lighter tasting, less sweet beverage, but it would likely be perceived as more refreshing (and would avoid the stigma of being a "low-calorie" drink).

Building on Big Mama's idea, an account executive from

Tatham, Laird, and Kudner noted that the sparkling cooler concept would also provide the perfect explanation for why a seemingly "macho" beer company like Coors was bringing out a cooler product for women. Who else but Coors had advertised their pure sparkling mountain water for decades? (In marketing, this type of strategy is called "leveraging your assets.")

Sure enough, the idea "clicked" with cooler drinkers in focus groups. In Los Angeles, where bottled sparkling waters were (and are) all the rage, female cooler drinkers loved the sparkling cooler concept, which would soon be dubbed "Crystal Springs Cooler." One remarked, "It sounds really tasty, but I wouldn't feel bloated." Another typical comment was, "That sounds like the best of both worlds; wine cooler flavor without the sickening sweet taste and all those calories."

In a memo to The General in early 1987, I summarized the benefits of a light cooler product strategy:

1.   Would communicate fresh/all natural ingredients (juice/water).
2.   Would communicate refreshment.
3.   Would position the product as lighter than standard coolers.[8]

Now that Coors had a viable cooler concept, it was time for the Research and Development staff to brew a product that would fit cooler drinkers' expectations for Crystal Springs. This was no easy task, since their last effort, Colorado Chiller, was a slimy, greenish drink that had spoiled easily in contact with light. But R&D rose to the challenge.

After months of work, they were able to brew a malt product that was clear in appearance, poured without a beer head (through the use of natural foam retardants), and was flavored with natural peach or citrus. Using special cold filtration tech-

8 This memo was dated January 22, 1987.

niques, this Crystal Springs prototype product was, according to market research tests, better tasting than wine-based coolers, yet cost less to manufacture.

Once R&D worked its magic, Coors had both a marketing concept and a product prototype. At this stage, The General became obsessed with reasons why Coors couldn't introduce Crystal Springs Cooler. "I just don't think we can compete with Gallo," was his favorite irrational declaration.

"Why?" I would always respond. "Coke has Pepsi. United Airlines has American. GM has Ford. Why shouldn't Bartles & Jaymes have a strong competitor? And why shouldn't it be us [Coors]? We have more money, a stronger distribution network, and a great product concept."

My argument would usually be followed with a sigh, and then silence, recognition that there was no reason why Coors shouldn't jump back in to the cooler business. What made The General's opposition to Crystal Springs Cooler strange is that, under normal circumstances, the marketing manager in charge of a new product is usually that product's strongest advocate, since the project represents the extent of his or her marketing prowess. In this case, though, The General was the product's strongest critic.

And if the project manager wasn't a strong advocate for the project, no one else outside of our project team was willing to give Crystal Springs a boost. Certainly not the macho Force, which treated "fruity" coolers with disdain. "We're a beer company," Scooter repeatedly told me. "There's no way The Force is going to push hard for a product like this." And Scooter's sentiment wasn't unique. The Force, intent only on selling Coors and Coors Light in order to collect their bonus money, called Crystal Springs everything from "piss water" to "pussy juice."

A new product spearheaded by The General was reason enough for most departments at the brewery to hope, openly, for Crystal Springs failure. Pepe called The General "dipshit" to his face, and that was one of his kinder nicknames.[9] The Force, Research and Development, Corporate Finance, Distributor Development, and other departments all had been the object of one or more of The General's verbal tirades during the Colorado Chiller debacle. Now, it was time for retribution. They *hoped* The General would fail again, miserably, even though he was fighting on the same side, for the same cause, as they were.

Dewey, the drunk-sounding but sober-thinking analyst from Competitive Analysis, told me that Stroh, the brewer of White Mountain Cooler, was pulling hard for Coors to introduce Crystal Springs. (They didn't know the details of the project; they had only heard rumors that Coors was working on another cooler product.)

Incredulously, I asked, "But don't they know that we're not going to make the same mistakes this time around? And just wait till they find out what a great product Crystal Springs is."

"Yeah, but my friend at Stroh told me that they know that the same guy who managed Chiller is in charge of this project," Dewey bellowed in his best, but unintended imitation of Mayberry's Otis Campbell. "He says that's enough to make them feel pretty confident that our next cooler has no chance, either."

Nevertheless, the project team relentlessly forged ahead. At one stage of testing, in December 1986, our travels took us to Tempe, Arizona, to develop an advertising strategy for Crystal Springs. (At this stage in the shoe store, we were bringing out shoe samples for the customer to try on.) A female focus-group moderator named Brooke was conducting our focus groups, with an all-male contingent from Coors and Tatham, Laird, and Kudner in the back room observing the proceedings. The General and Captain Kangaroo, back at Coors after the failure of Masters III, repeatedly commented about "Brooke's fat ass,"

---

9 Other nicknames for The General included "Pinhead," "The Penguin," and my personal favorite, "Fat Wally Cox."

and observed that she'd be "a great lay." What they didn't know was that the walls of the focus-group facility weren't very well soundproofed, and Brooke heard *all* of their comments. Embarrassed, I apologized to her after the focus groups, but she refused to work as a consultant to Coors ever again.

The same duo pulled off the same caper, again in Tempe, a few months later. This time, I was interviewing female cooler drinkers about their flavor preferences in wine coolers. We had chosen Tempe because it was the home of Arizona State University, where it would be easy to recruit college-age women to participate in the research study. Again, throughout the two days of interviewing, The General and Captain Kangaroo made lewd comments every time a semi-attractive female was being interviewed. And unless each young lady regularly wore Walkman headphones or had ruined her hearing in some manner, she heard the comments as clearly as I did. I always wondered if these snide remarks affected the women's responses, and whether they biased the research results. But no matter how many times I asked The General and Captain Kangaroo to shut up, they persisted. It was like listening to two teenagers discovering the opposite sex for the first time.

But off-color opinions weren't The General's only commentary during the interviewing process in Tempe. I had worn blue jeans and a golf shirt to the focus groups in order to dress like the women I was interviewing, who were college students. But this wasn't formal enough attire for The General, who told me, "You look like a hobo."

When I explained to him why I was dressed that way, The General exploded, and his complexion turned a dramatic shade of crimson as he howled, "I don't give a Gawd-damn. You're representing this company, and you look like a hobo."

If I did, I didn't care, because it was part of my job. On top of that, I never told the interview subjects *who* I was working for, so they had no idea if I was a "hobo" from Coors, Gallo, Anheuser–Busch, or any other cooler company. Again, I couldn't help but wonder why The General was preoccupied with minutia in the face of our formidable marketing challenge.

After the work in Tempe, the project team was ready to conduct a simulated test market. (If we were back in the shoe store, it was time to ask the customer if we could ring up her purchase.) The simulated test market would tell us whether we could sell enough Crystal Springs Cooler there to warrant producing and selling the product nationwide. As mentioned in Chapter 3, simulated test marketing involves testing the advertising, pricing, and product prototype through shopping-mall interviews, in order to see how drinkers will react. Based on complicated forecasting formulas, the test results are used to predict sales volume, with a fair degree of accuracy.

Before this test was actually conducted, the project team flew to Chicago for a round of planning meetings with TLK and Foote, Cone, and Belding, the Coors advertising agencies. It was mid-December, and we were all stopping over after the company's annual distributor convention in Las Vegas (which is covered in Chapter 7). At this convention, most distributors and Coors marketing personnel made a habit of drinking heavily, each and every night. When we got to Chicago, The General, already in the habit of imbibing cheap scotch, forgot that he wasn't in Vegas any more.

By the end of dinner, at an Italian restaurant across from the Park Hyatt Hotel, The General was plastered. Then the fun really began.

While the rest of us enjoyed Rush Street, The General made a pest of himself. He got angry when I beat him in an electronic trivia game at Elliot's Nest, so he dunked my tie, which I'd removed, into a pitcher of beer.

As we hopped bars, The General stumbled into a cab waiting at an intersection on Erie Street and joined a young couple in a passionate embrace on the back seat. After we rescued The General from this cab, and apologized to the stunned couple, The General proceeded to get kicked out of nearly every bar we entered. At one watering hole, The General was thrown out after cutting in on several couples on the disco dance floor and singing, or more nearly shouting, a verse of "The Eyes of Texas."

But The General saved his best for last. In The Ambassador East's famous Pump Room, he was escorted out of the bar area by an alert maitre d', but not before he made an awkward pass at Big Mama, the market research manager. The General's idea of a great "line" was to slur "Mannequin" repeatedly to the object of his desire while trying to grope her. Mercifully, a bellman finally put him to bed.

The next day, The General missed his flight home and spent an extra day at the Ambassador sleeping off his hangover. On the way to O'Hare Airport, I asked Captain Kangaroo if we should call the hotel and have security check on The General, who hadn't answered repeated phone calls to his room that morning. "He might have died, you know, choked to death, or something," I suggested.

"Who cares?" responded Captain Kangaroo nonchalantly. "If he did kick the bucket, there isn't anything we can do about it. This kind of thing happens all the time."

"Are you sure?" I inquired again, now a bit more worried.

"Oh, sure. Besides, if he did die, I'm not carrying his goddamned corpse home. Let someone else arrange that asshole's funeral," Captain Kangaroo finished, confirming that he was another one of The General's ardent admirers.

We never did call hotel security, and, as Captain Kangaroo promised, The General didn't perish, to the chagrin of some members of the Crystal Springs project team. As the calendar slipped into 1987, the test results from our simulated test market rolled in, and they were encouraging:

- About 63 percent of cooler drinkers we surveyed were interested in purchasing Crystal Springs Cooler.
- After sampling the Crystal Springs prototype, 74 percent of the drinkers indicated that they would buy the product, confirming that the product actually fulfilled the drinkers' expectations of a smoother, lighter tasting, more refreshing product.

- The research company hired by Coors to conduct the simulated test marketing estimated that Coors would sell
  about 223,000 barrels of Crystal Springs. (After the citrus
  flavor was reformulated and improved, this estimate was
  later increased to 319,000 barrels.)[10]

Poised on the brink of success, the project team's request for
funding a full national marketing campaign to introduce Crystal
Springs Cooler was met with . . . silence. Despite the positive
test results, Crystal Springs Cooler was tabled in the summer
of 1987; a permanent tabling, I learned over time.[11]

In the end, Crystal Springs merely faded away, rather than
being killed outright. There was never an official announcement
of the project's demise. Nor did I ever stop working on, or
hoping for, Crystal Spring's approval. To this day no one, from
The General on up to Herr Rechholtz, has ever been able to
explain why Coors didn't pursue the Crystal Springs opportunity. At the projected three hundred thousand barrels of sales
in 1988, Crystal Springs would have been Coors third-largest
product, and the second or third best-selling cooler in the country. Financial forecasts showed that, after paying back the company's initial investment in new bottling equipment (within
two years), Crystal Springs would have generated millions in
pretax profit for Coors each year. As a business decision, Crystal
Springs should have been hard, if not impossible, to delay or
kill.

In retrospect, there are several reasons why Crystal Springs
was never produced. Greed, fear, shortsightedness, and excessive caution were likely contributing factors to the demise of
Crystal Springs.

---

10 The last volume estimate was provided by Bases Market Research
on March 4, 1987.

11 On July 31, 1987, I presented ''The Strategic Rationale for Crystal
Springs'' to Rain Man (then in charge of new products), Rechholtz, The
General, and Captain Kangaroo, among others. Despite this presentation,
the project remained shelved.

First, the idea of a spring water cooler was too revolutionary, and too risky, for cautious, risk-averse Coors. The company's most innovative products, Masters III, Killian's Ale, and Colorado Chiller, had all failed miserably. Coors Light, a copycat product, had thrived. "Let's see how the market develops," The General told me in announcing the postponement of Crystal Springs. Unfortunately, while Coors waited and observed, other companies were ringing up billions in annual sales.

Beyond this innate corporate caution, The General and the High Command simply lost their nerve. After the failure of Colorado Chiller, The General had confided to Igor that he wasn't about to "take it up the ass" again, a clear reference to his apparent fear of failure. Herr Rechholtz had warned Gary Truitt that he wouldn't support Crystal Springs Cooler "unless we've got absolutely everything nailed this time." For a marketer, fear of failure is debilitating, akin to a fighter pilot who is afraid to fly after a crash, or a jockey afraid to mount a horse after a fall. In the world of marketing, past failures needed to be analyzed, for a time, but then laid to rest, with any memories of failure quickly erased by the next marketing challenge. In retrospect, the only thing worse than the Colorado Chiller fiasco was assuming that Crystal Springs would turn out the same way. Clearly, based upon the research tests, it would not have.

Finally, greed may have contributed to the demise of Crystal Springs. Investing in the marketing of Crystal Springs Cooler would have diverted efforts from the expansion of Coors Banquet and Coors Light, which might have endangered the hefty bonuses at Central Command. This was a shortsighted viewpoint, though, since Crystal Springs would have added three hundred thousand barrels, or 2 percent, to the company's annual sales volume thereafter. With the Coors Banquet brand declining by 20 percent annually, a reasonable argument was made, but ignored, that Coors Banquet advertising money should have been allocated to Crystal Springs Cooler.

And what was the price of the decision to abort the Crystal Springs mission? A campaign without battles, a war that was never waged, cost Coors more than a million dollars in research and development and thousands of man hours over the better part of two years.[12] In the end, a company badly in need of a marketing victory, and cash, turned down an opportunity to make millions.

By 1988, mention of the words "Crystal Springs" failed to elicit a stir at Central Command. Like the Flying Dutchman's ship, the project vanished, seemingly without a trace. But a dusty bottle or two of Crystal Springs in my closet at home provide an occasional reminder that, as John Greenleaf Whittier claimed, the saddest words of tongue or pen really are, "What might have been."

---

12 By my own estimates, Coors spent well over $500,000 on market research alone, despite The General's constant vigil over the costs of travel, food, liquor, etc.

7

Creating Myths and Tarnishing Legends

> Do you always live your life like a beer
> commercial?

—*Kirstie Alley to Mark Harmon in the ABC-TV movie,*
Prince of Bel-Air, *1987.*

> I know half the money I spend on advertising is
> wasted, but I can never find out which half.

—*Department store founder John Wanamaker*

Like Germany in World War II, the Coors troops fought battles on two fronts. At the same time that Gary Truitt, The General, and I were fighting and losing the cooler battles, another division of the Coors military, led by Rechholtz and The Force, was fighting on a second, much larger, and more dangerous front. The battle for premium beer supremacy was joined rather inauspiciously in 1986, with a gulp, rather than a bang.

"And, so, in conclusion—" Gulp. "—I think next year will be a very big year—" Gulp. "—indeed for us." Gulp. "Thanks for all your hard work."

It was an annual Yuletide tradition for Pete Coors and members of the High Command to give a motivational talk to corporate headquarters marketing employees. Pete Coors was a dull, monotonous speaker, who regularly interrupted his own speeches to take large, audible gulps of water. (Maybe big gulps of beer would have smoothed out his rough edges.) Beer Wars veterans could recite Pete Coors's speech almost word for word, as it rarely varied from year to year.

"And now—" Gulp. "—I'd like to turn things over to our final speaker this afternoon," Pete Coors finished, to a smattering of polite applause.

In 1986, Pepe was assigned the dubious honor of speaking for the High Command, after Pete Coors. This was a test of sorts, to see if Pepe had the mettle to occupy a seat on the High Command. He chose an anecdotal theme for his talk.

"Last year, I was visiting one of our sales offices," Pepe began. "I asked our district sales manager why he hadn't sold in the Fourth of July promotion, and why his sales were down during the Fourth of July weekend." Slowly, the audience began to stir with interest, especially members of The Force.

"He told me that it had rained for one week straight," Pepe continued, his voice rising, "and no one went out and bought beer." The Force chuckled at this comment, no doubt having heard it or said it themselves in the past.

"Plus, the district manager told me that his sales reps hadn't had much time to sell in the promotion, because of the rain," Pepe continued, on a roll of sorts.

"And you know what I asked him?" Pepe recounted. "I says, how come sales were *up* for Budweiser over that same weekend?" Chuckles in the audience now turned to uproarious laughter.

"And do you know what this guy said?" Pepe inquired. "He says, 'Maybe it didn't rain on Budweiser.' " Now, the audience was a bit confused as to where this story was leading.

"And do you know what I say about next year?" Pepe roared. "I say, next year, let it rain on *Budweiser.*"

At first, the auditorium was silent, as we wondered whether we'd just heard the punch line, and, if so, what it meant. Reel-ing, Pepe roared even louder, "That's right, let it rain on *Budweiser.*"

Finally, polite applause arose throughout the auditorium, in acknowledgment of the abrupt, yet confusing end to the story.

Pepe knew he had misfired, and he quickly dismissed everybody with a wish for a "Merry Christmas and a strong sales New Year!" (What a sentimental send off.) Even though most of the Central Command warriors didn't understand the story, one point trickled through the confusion: Budweiser, competing against the declining Coors Banquet brand, was Coors major enemy.

Anheuser–Busch (or "A–B" to the High Command), the brewer of Budweiser, was indeed a very formidable enemy. St. Louis-based Anheuser–Busch was the titan of the beer industry in the mid-1980s, not only brewers of the "king" of beers (Budweiser, which accounted for two-thirds of the company's sales), but also a handful of other well-known brands, including Michelob, Busch, Bud Light, Natural Light, and King Cobra Malt Liquor. Under the direction of August Busch III, the company had grown faster than any other major domestic brewer in the 1970s and 1980s, nearly doubling its sales during the 1980s alone.

Anheuser–Busch had started the "war" in beer marketing. August Busch, a descendent of the company's founders, was a workaholic, a Wharton MBA who relentlessly drove his "troops," as he liked to call them, to battle Miller, Coors, and all other challengers. August knew that marketing warfare arose from the nature of marketing. You cannot pitch your products in a vacuum, but instead in relation to, and in competition with, other similar products. For a drinker to pound down Budweisers, bottles of Coors and Miller must sit on the store shelf unsold, collecting dust. August and his own High Command directed their war from Number One Busch Place, the company's corporate headquarters, where the "War Room" was used to map the success and failures of specific marketing battles on a huge map. "When they [Anheuser–Busch] decide where they're going," one friend of August Busch noted, "they're like an army on the march."[1]

In *Under the Influence,* a biography of the Busch family, Peter Hernon and Terry Ganey describe the marketing philosophy that drove Anheuser–Busch to new heights. "Using sophisticated demographics, August's team divided beer drinkers by race, income, sex, age, even ethnic origin. It was called target marketing, and there were targets everywhere. . . . The country was carved into some 210 markets, with the focus on big cities like New York and Los Angeles, where most of the beer was consumed. The result was an incredible number of different sales-promotion programs—as many as 10,000."[2]

Like Patton admiring his noble enemy Rommel, Rechholtz and the High Command wondered why this success couldn't be duplicated. If Anheuser–Busch could market Budweiser with as many as ten thousand different sales-promotion programs, each uniquely tailored to distributors and drinkers in various local markets, then why couldn't Coors? The answer was spelled M-O-N-E-Y.

Budweiser, the world's top-selling beer, was supported by more than $100 million in advertising, with more than half of that money spent on high-profile television advertising. Anheuser–Busch spent more on advertising than Miller and Coors combined, virtually ensuring that drinkers in every nook and cranny of America had heard of Budweiser and its slogan, "This Bud's for You." Coors simply didn't have as much money to spend, given the company's preference for cash over debt.

It was also unclear whether the marketing acumen of Anheuser–Busch's army, the creativity of specific local marketing programs, or the sheer number of programs, propelled Budweiser to its lofty heights. Anheuser–Busch was twice as large

---

1 Peter Hernon and Terry Ganey, *Under the Influence: The Unauthorized Story of the Anheuser–Busch Dynasty* (New York: Simon & Schuster, 1991), p. 327.

2 Ibid., p. 328.

as its nearest competitor, Miller, and could afford to spend money on lavish, risky, unproven sales-promotion programs that might or might not be effective. As one advertising executive noted, "In the 1970s, they [Anheuser–Busch] were so intent on beating back Miller's challenge that it was said you could dream up a quarter-million-dollar bartop tiddlywinks campaign . . . and sell it to somebody [at Anheuser–Busch]."[3] As Hernon and Ganey point out in *Under the Influence,* A–B's lavish spending amounted to "saturation" bombing of the enemy. If A–B kept dropping bombs, a few were bound to damage the enemy, including Coors. Only the well armed and well equipped, with virtually unlimited resources, could afford to saturation bomb. Coors was none of these things, and, therefore, would have difficulty duplicating the success of the A–B army.

Fortunately, Pepe had no rousing stories to tell about Miller Brewing Company, the last of the major brewers to still call "Beer City," or Milwaukee, home. But Miller was no less dangerous an enemy than Anheuser–Busch.

Using equal parts advertising savvy and creativity, Miller had achieved a stunning record of success since its purchase by Philip Morris in the early 1970s, including stealing the "light beer" mantle away from Coors, introducing Meister Brau beer, and producing a hilariously funny and memorable advertising campaign for Miller Lite (that featured famous ex-athletes who argued whether Miller Lite was "less filling" or "tasted great").

Like Anheuser–Busch, Miller Brewing Company had deep pockets. More than 20 percent of all beer sold in the United States, or about 40 million barrels in 1986, rolled out of Miller's seven nationwide breweries. Two of the three biggest brands in the United States, Miller Lite and Miller High Life, were brewed by Miller, and Miller spent lavishly (more than $200 million) promoting its products.

In 1985 and 1986, Miller not only was riding the crest of

3 Ibid.

success from Miller Lite, but was also attempting to revamp the sagging Miller High Life brand, which competed with Bud and Coors Banquet. Miller introduced a new advertising campaign proclaiming that Miller High Life was "Made the American Way," through a rousing, patriotic theme song and an endorsement by ex-Red Sox slugger Carl Yastrzemski (presumably to curry favor with Middle America).

As if marketing might alone weren't enough, Coors helped Anheuser–Busch and Miller to become even more formidable with its refusal to expand outside of the West. While beer drinkers nationwide watched thousands of ads for Budweiser and Miller High Life in the 1960s and 1970s, Coors Banquet hadn't even been available in most of the country until the 1980s. Worse, in the absence of advertising to help formulate opinions, Coors Banquet's reputation among drinkers was as an "in between" beer; it wasn't a true light beer (low in calories) like Miller Lite; but it was too light (or watery) to compete with macho Budweiser and Miller High Life, the top selling "premium" beers (which are one notch below "super premium" beers like Michelob).

When football players are trailing a superior opponent late in a game, they talk about completing a "Hail Mary" pass, which means, literally, completing a miracle pass to win a game. If ever there was a beer in need of a "Hail Mary," or miracle advertising campaign, it was Coors Banquet in the mid-1980s. Sales for the product had declined a hefty 14 percent in 1984, and, despite Coors massive geographic expansion, had increased a mere 3 percent in 1985. Matched against Budweiser and the newly revamped Miller High Life, the Coors High Command must have felt like Hitler had when sandwiched between the Eastern Front, with Russia, and the Western Front, with America and Britain. The competitors spent more to advertise their products, weren't saddled with the extra (negative) baggage created by the Coors family's political exploits, and had sold their products throughout the United States for years.

To create and deliver the miracle it needed, Coors turned to

Foote, Cone, and Belding, its main advertising agency. During The Beer Wars, advertising agencies were the Hessians, the hired guns, or mercenaries. As the management scholar Peter Drucker once said, "the aim of marketing is to make selling superfluous." A brilliant advertising agency could tip the scales in favor of an underdog like Coors Banquet.

The professionals at Foote, Cone, and Belding were quite unlike the fictional Darrin Stevens in TV's "Bewitched," who had been my archetype of an advertising executive. For one thing, Darrin was a jack-of-all-trades, who did everything from dreaming up advertising slogans to entertaining clients (between battles with witches and warlocks, of course). In reality, there were several different types of advertising executives. One breed of executive more closely resembled Larry Tate, Darrin Stevens's spineless TV boss, who did or said *anything* to keep his clients happy.

The Tates, as we liked to call them, were the account executives/managers. Their job was to coordinate all of the activities involved in creating advertising within their own agencies, and to make sure that their clients, at companies like Coors, remained clients. The Tates must have felt like baseball umpires, if not pincushions, perpetually stuck in the middle of the battle between their own instincts and tastes as to what made "good" advertising, and the whims and wishes of their clients. Foote, Cone, and Belding's Tates spent considerable time soothing the feelings of clients like Herr Rechholtz.

If a Tate disagreed with Rechholtz in a meeting, he or she might say something like, "Bob, that's a great idea, *but* . . ."

An angry Rechholtz would respond with, "Goddamn you, you son of a bitch."

And the ever-diplomatic Tate would counter with, "You're right Bob, I am a son of a bitch. But you need sons of bitches working on your business. Now, as I was saying . . ."

A good Tate also had the ability to make a client feel as if every idea was his own, and every one of the client's thoughts brilliant, in some context. "Bob, I'll bet you were thinking . . ."

a Tate would suggest, trying to translate even stupid or impractical client notions into workable ideas.

Tates were easily recognized by their stylish Armani suits, Gucci loafers (in which you could always see your reflection), and close-cropped, clean-shaven appearance (even among female Tates). Tates spent a lot of time and money entertaining clients, because business from large clients like Coors was usually worth millions of dollars to an advertising agency. These were the advertising men and women who epitomized the "Madison Avenue" image of the 1980s—somewhat vacuous, aggressive individuals, more image than substance. In effect, Tates were like high school cheerleaders. They earned their keep by being popular.

The senior Tate at FCB could well have been a 1980s version of Larry. Impeccably dressed, with a white, flowing pompadour hairstyle and a penchant for hyperbole, Big Tate usually agreed with almost anything that Coors managers said in meetings. "We'll look into it," or "You're absolutely right," were his favorite overused phrases.

I never really understood the need for Tates, even Big Tate, until I ran across other species of advertising professionals, the Creatives. The Tates were necessary, if for no other reason than to shield Creatives from the agency's clients; Creatives were, to paraphrase Merrill Lynch, a breed apart. Creatives closely resembled the whiny, rebellious, free-spirited advertising professionals portrayed on TV's "thirtysomething." These individuals were charged with dreaming up advertising campaigns, and translating their campaign concepts into effective advertisements. In order to encourage or incubate their powers of imagination, Creatives relied on somewhat unconventional rules for doing business.

Creatives usually dressed in jeans, flannel shirts, or T-shirts, in order to avoid the feeling of "confinement" that suits created. One Creative at Foote, Cone, and Belding wore a leather motorcycle vest to a set of focus groups—with no shirt underneath. He stood out not because of the vest (outfits like this were standard for Creatives), but because he had a two-day growth of stubble in the area where he normally shaved his chest. (His face, however, was fully bearded.)

Many Creatives played games like Nerf basketball or darts in their offices, in order to "keep the creative juices flowing." Few kept regular office hours. Some Creatives even used drugs to unlock their creative powers, while other read magazines, listened to the radio, or tuned into their own Walkman selections, in a constant battle to generate fresh advertising concepts.

In effect, almost anything was okay for a Creative: Like temperamental rock stars' quirks, Creatives' eccentricities were tolerated, as long as the person continued to produce advertising "hits." And who could blame the agencies for nurturing Creatives? A great, enduring advertising idea, like Wendy's "Where's the Beef?" campaign, could be worth hundreds of millions of dollars to an agency.

More than anything else, good Creatives had huge egos. It went with the territory. If a Creative hatched one brilliant advertising campaign, he or she began to believe that every idea was potentially brilliant, that it was not possible to misfire. Rather, clients lacked the "vision" to recognize what was good. This attitude helped to insulate Creatives from criticism. "Can't you see the concept?" they'd plead to a bewildered client. Or they'd say, "Bob, I think you're missing the point of the idea."

Despite, or perhaps because of these oddities, Foote, Cone, and Belding's Tates and Creatives delivered a miracle to Coors. His name was Mark Harmon.

Traditionally, mainstream beer advertising usually contained one of two elements: "male bonding" or "work reward." The best examples of male-bonding ads were commercials for Old Milwaukee and Miller High Life. Men would take along their favorite beer to go fishing or to a ball game, for playing cards, ogling women in bikinis, or any other traditional "male" activity. Beer was portrayed as the drink that facilitated the bond between males, cemented friendships, and brought on the good times. As Old Milwaukee commercials reminded drinkers after the tab was popped, "It [life] doesn't get any better than this."

Budweiser ads featured a heavy dose of work reward. This type of advertising treated working-class males like Pavlovian dogs. After a long day operating jackhammers, or building houses, the workers in the ads treated themselves to Bud. Apparently, simple pleasures sufficed; each day, the workers were motivated by the thought of an ice-cold Bud sliding down their throats. (A paycheck was only "icing on the cake.")

But Foote, Cone, and Belding hatched an idea for an ad campaign that wouldn't resort to bikinis, male bonding or work reward. Instead, the ads would tout the fact tht Coors *was* made differently from other beers, resulting in a unique, one-of-a-kind, smooth taste. The new ads would describe how Coors Banquet Beer was cold-filtered, brewed with special barley and Rocky Mountain spring water. (Other beers were heat pasteurized and brewed with flatland stream and tap water, which, Coors maintained, damaged the taste of the beer.) Coors would once again celebrate its uniqueness, and wouldn't try to imitate Budweiser and Miller ads.

Big Tate described the campaign (before Huey Lewis used the phrase) by saying, "We're gonna make it hip to be square. It'll be cool to drink a Coors again. We're not apologizing for being different anymore."

As if to underscore the different look of the planned Coors ads, Foote, Cone, and Belding compiled a "short" list of potential male spokespersons for the advertising. They wanted a ruggedly handsome, though not-too-famous actor, someone who epitomized Coors drinkers. The list of potential spokespersons contained a wide variety of names, according to Wee Willie, my rotund colleague in the Market Research Department, who was assigned to the project. Ed Marinaro ("Hill Street Blues"), Daniel J. Travanti (also of "Hill Street"), Pierce Brosnan ("Remington Steele"), Lee Horseley ("Matt Houston"), and Michael Biehn (of *Terminator* fame) were among the names on the list. But the actor Coors chose was Mark Harmon.

Harmon, a former UCLA quarterback, was the son of Michigan football legend Tom Harmon. One of his sisters was a spokesmodel, and another was the ex-wife of 1950s teen idol Rick Nelson (making Mark the uncle of the smash heavy-metal duo of Gunnar and Matthew Nelson, as well as TV star Tracy Nelson). Show business was in the Harmons' blood.

After his college football career ended (he was too small to play pro football), Mark Harmon bounced around as a male model and journeyman actor. Ruggedly handsome with piercing blue eyes and a broad, toothy grin, Harmon eventually became a leading man in several obscure TV movies and series, including "The Dream Merchants" (a 1979 TV miniseries with Vincent Gardenia), and "Flamingo Road" (an early 1980s NBC prime-time soap in which he starred opposite Morgan Fairchild as the character Fielding Carlyle).

By 1985, Harmon had landed a recurring role in the ensemble cast of NBC's offbeat hospital drama, "St. Elsewhere." Harmon's character, a doctor, was a gregarious, promiscuous skirt-chaser who also found time to perform plastic surgery. The role kept Harmon in the public eye, and at the time Coors came calling, beer drinkers were more likely to recognize his face than his name. Harmon had the right profile: not famous enough to overpower the ads, but far from an unknown.

Plus, Harmon was politically conservative. He had grown up in California drinking Coors, and wasn't offended by the Coors family's right-wing leanings. Harmon assured Coors that he would be an enthusiastic booster of the company and its products, as he himself believed in the brewery's products and the company's conservative credo. As Big Tate noted, Harmon was "made to order" for the Coors ads.

This was enough to convince the manager of Coors Banquet at that time, who was known as Preacher, that Harmon was the right man for the job of Coors Banquet spokesperson. (Preacher earned his nickname because of his habit of rendering passionate, zealous, long-winded soliloquies during business meetings in the Southern twang of a Baptist preacher.) A member of the Schlitz Mafia, Preacher had risen through the management ranks at Schlitz before joining Coors as a marketing manager.

The initial ads featuring Mark Harmon were nothing short of brilliant. Harmon appeared in stark, natural mountain settings. There were no girls in bikinis; no loud, raucous music; no male buddies; no hype. Just a single, solitary spokesperson, dressed in a flannel shirt, his straight brown hair dancing in the breeze, explaining why "Coors is the one." According to Foote, Cone, and Belding's research, Harmon was such a powerful spokesperson that he communicated effectively even when he didn't speak, with his mesmerizing eyes, hand gestures, arched eyebrows, and other nonverbal cues.

Test results confirmed the effectiveness of the ads. Awareness of Coors beer products increased, beer drinkers' attitudes and opinions about the taste of the product improved, and sales of Coors Banquet increased marginally (3 percent) in 1985. More importantly, test results showed that the Mark Harmon ads also were boosting sales of Coors Light, as beer drinkers reasoned that what Mark Harmon said about Coors Banquet also applied to Coors Light. Coors Light sales shot up by 30 percent in 1985, and by another 18 percent in 1986, the first two years of the Harmon campaign.

The Mark Harmon campaign boosted Coors in several other ways. First, women, traditionally not avid beer drinkers, reacted positively to the sexy actor. It was not uncommon for groups of women to talk about those "Mark Harmon" commercials whenever the conversation turned toward beer.

Second, Harmon himself generated tremendous free publicity for Coors. *People* magazine named him the "Sexiest Man Alive" in 1986, and he supplemented his "St. Elsewhere" stint with TV and big-screen roles. Magazine articles mentioned his connections to Coors, and distributors were excited by his (paid) personal appearances on behalf of the company. In short, Mark Harmon and his ads reinvigorated Coors Banquet, and the company as a whole, for at least a short time. Harmon was helping to make it "cool"—or "hip," in the words of Big Tate—to drink Coors once again.

But the Schlitz Mafia showed an amazing propensity to yank defeat from the jaws of victory. Basking in the euphoric glow of the successful Harmon advertising campaign, Coors committed a grievous error of omission when it failed to edit a commercial script. This was the birth of The Cold War.

For years, Coors had spent a staggering amount of money to ensure that Coors beer was kept refrigerated from the time it was brewed to the time it was consumed. Coors insisted that constant refrigeration created a superior-tasting product. So beer was brewed using the cold-filtration process. Coors bottling lines were refrigerated. Every Coors delivery truck was refrigerated. Even distributors were required to buy large refrigeration units to store Coors. The company was so devoted to this system that they refused to sell beer in Indiana, where state law prohibited selling beer from refrigerators. Coors, its distributors, and even consumers believed that refrigerating Coors was worth the effort, as well as the expense.

There was one small flaw in Coors devotion to refrigeration. Liquor stores and grocery stores *didn't* always refrigerate Coors. Once a retailer purchased beer from a Coors distributor, the brewery had no control over whether the beer was sold from refrigerated or non-refrigerated (room temperature) displays. And when Mark Harmon inadvertently pitched the beer in a commercial from an unrefrigerated store shelf, The Cold War was exposed.

Harmon himself had nothing to do with the commercial controversy. He merely read the lines he was given. But the Tates at Foote, Cone, and Belding and the Coors Preacher had all forgotten to screen out this one "little" flaw in the commercial script. The Coors family was livid. As Dewey, who kept one ear to the ground of the family's inner sanctum, told me, "Pete Coors wants to know how the Schlitz Mafia could have been so fucking stupid."

Consumers and distributors from around the country called Coors to say they were confused. If refrigeration was so important to Coors Banquet beer, then why was Mark Harmon pitching it on television from an unrefrigerated display? Had Coors been wrong for all these years? How could Coors be so callous and careless in shooting the commercials?

The distributors had a larger concern. As one unhappy wholesaler told me when I was on a visit to Minneapolis, "It's like going without food while the king builds a new palace. While we [the distributors] and the company spent all of this money on the fucking refrigeration, we could have spent *more* money on marketing, to stay competitive with A–B. Those fuckers [the Schlitz Mafia] ought to have their heads examined."

I never did find out whether members of the Schlitz Mafia ever visited a neurosurgeon; but it was clear that the momentum of the dynamic Mark Harmon campaign had been lost, at least temporarily. Big Tate confided to me in 1987 that he had "shit his pants" when he heard about the controversial ad. Dewey reported, via his contact at Stroh, that the Stroh family was "breathing easier now that Coors has messed up again." Harmon had been gold, but the fortune had been carelessly squandered because of an oversight.

The fallout from The Cold War was interrupted, briefly, by the Coors 1986 Distributor Sales and Marketing Convention. Coors staged an annual gala marketing extravaganza to promote its marketing programs and generate enthusiasm among the company's distributors. In December 1986, the convention was designed to inspire an almost evangelical fervor for The Doctrine of Discounting, and the push for growth at Coors, both prophecies from the wise men of Project Ten.

Project Ten was a special committee, headed by Pepe, which had been formed at Rechholtz's request to map out Coors future battle plans, or long-term strategic vision.[4] After months of top-secret meetings, the committee concluded that:

---

4 Members of this "secret" committee included Dewey, Captain Kangaroo, Rain Man, a corporate economist, a financial analyst, and at least one or two members of the company's production department.

- Coors needed at least a 10 percent share of the total U.S. beer market (a 33 percent increase over the 1985 market share of 7.5 percent) by 1990 to avoid being steamrolled by the larger, better-financed Anheuser–Busch and Miller.
- Ultimately, there would be only three major brewers in the United States. If Coors didn't grow, and grow quickly, Stroh or Heileman would survive instead (in addition to A–B and Miller).
- A 10 percent market share would result in significant economies of scale (savings) for Coors, because:
  —advertising could be purchased more cheaply
  —distributors' trucks could be completely filled with Coors products, minimizing their dependence upon those of other brewers.

Some of the committee's findings were questionable. Coors *did* need to grow, or else it would continue to sputter, and eventually succumb to titans Anheuser–Busch and Miller. But saving Coors demanded *profitable* growth. If sales volume increased, but profits continued their downward spiral, how could the debt-averse company stay in business? How long could the company survive, if growth in sales volume was achieved only by succumbing to the temptation to discount the price of Coors beer? The committee's twisted logic formed the core of the Coors marketing battle plan, from 1986 onward: sales volume growth, at any cost.

The wise men of Project Ten also officially sanctioned the company's practice of paying hefty bonuses based upon sales-volume increases, regardless of the profits generated by the new business. (Refer to Chapter 4.) Since the committee singled out sales volume, which they called "critical mass," as a key business objective for Coors over the next ten years (if it were to survive The Beer Wars), it was reasonable for Rechholtz and other top Coors managers to manage the company to achieve this objective, and to be richly compensated for doing so.

The 1986 convention, mentioned earlier, was the High Command's first opportunity to tout the Project Ten growth plans, and drum up support for The Doctrine of Discounting. But despite the best efforts of the meeting planners to whip up the desired enthusiasm among Coors distributors, the 1986 convention more closely resembled college students' spring break at Fort Lauderdale than a business meeting.

The four-day convention was held at the massive Hilton Convention Center in Las Vegas, Nevada. Inviting the members of the party-hearty Force to Las Vegas was similar to parading a herd of elephants through a peanut farm. Between visits to the gaming tables (with their complimentary beer and drinks), the Palomino Club (for topless burlesque), golf courses, and "escort" services, most members of The Force were unable to fit the convention into their busy itineraries.

Some members of The Force were spotted heading up the elevators with escorts as early as noon each day. One young sales executive from Denver introduced his date, dressed only in a halter top and leather miniskirt (with no telltale signs of underwear), as his cousin. He and his "cousin" spent several nights together, apparently to promote family closeness. And rumors were rampant that members of The Force were organizing orgies with members of their own extended "families" for interested distributors.

Still, a few members of The Force found time to attend the scheduled distributor meetings in the Hilton Convention Center's exhibition hall. A senior sales executive from Golden was scheduled to give a four-minute inspirational speech on Monday, the second day of the convention. Since all of the speeches were designed as part of a professional, coordinated multimedia program, befitting a company supposedly on the rebound, each speech was tightly edited, and speakers were told to read directly from the TelePrompTers at the front of the stage. And this they did, until the senior sales manager from Golden staggered up to the podium.

Under the glare of the stage lights and the influence of the last night's entertainment, this goodwill ambassador launched into a half-hour, shoot-from-the-hip speech, starting with "How the hell are you?"

While the distributors guffawed, embarrassed for both Coors and this sales executive, they were treated to a diatribe about: (1) Tennessee football ("We're [Coors] gonna kick some ass, just like the Vols"); (2) The heart attack of a Coors distributor in Dallas ("I think we [Coors] helped dig his grave"); (3) Rechholtz's demeanor ("C'mon Bob, lighten up!"); and any number of other extemporaneous topics of interest to the inebriated presenter. Rechholtz's secretary later reported that he was "furious" during the speech, insisting that she could see steam rising from Rechholtz's head. "He's history," Rechholtz said of the wayward sales executive. (He was, too, resigning from Coors several months after the convention.)

Though this inspirational talk didn't exactly drive Coors distributors to achieve the coveted 10 percent market share, the next day of the convention was set to feature an address by famed aviator Chuck Yeager. Yeager had been hired at considerable expense, to kick off the "re-launch" of Herman Joseph's Premium Draft Light.

"Chuck Yeager?" wondered Big Tim upon reading the meeting agenda. "What the hell is *he* doing here?" Yeager had been hired because someone at Coors thought he could provide the inspiration to back Herman Joseph's new advertising theme: "Take off with Herman Joseph's Original Draft Light."

The legendary pilot had an unenviable task. To begin with, Yeager, as Big Tim correctly observed, "didn't know a fucking thing about beer." Additionally, aviation heroes, whose piloting of multi-billion-dollar planes required excellent hand-eye coordination and split-second decision-making, weren't exactly the most credible advocates for drinking beer (or any other alcohol product). Only the Nevada Highway Patrol or Mother Teresa were less likely candidates than Yeager to be pitching Herman Joseph's beer from the podium at the Las Vegas Hilton.

Yeager probably *was* uncomfortable pitching beer because,

like the sales executive on the day before, he deviated significantly from the script on his TelePrompTer. Most of his speech centered on the difficulty of flying jets, especially when "pilots urinated and defecated in their flight suits when they lost consciousness," or how early jet pilots "had to urinate in their flight suits because there was no way to tailor the flight suits to urinating in the cockpit." The distributors were mystified as to how this speech related to beer (except, perhaps, in drawing a possible link between beer consumption and urination).

Finally, after a rambling twenty-five minutes, Yeager brought his talk back to beer by concluding, "And I'm sure that you're all going to make Herman Joseph's soar next year."

I looked around the convention center, amidst the applause, and imagined light bulb after light bulb blinking "on" in heads around the room, as we finally understood what this speech was supposed to be about. (The new Herman Joseph's would soar just like Chuck Yeager had!) Rechholtz's secretary never did let me know if Rechholtz wanted to fire Yeager, too.

While the other convention speakers, including Rechholtz, Preacher, and The General, failed to ignite a spark under Coors distributors, the main exhibition hall, packed with circus-like attractions and celebrities (including former football stars Ken Anderson and Willie Davis, race car driver Bill Elliott, and drag racer and former NFL quarterback Dan Pastorini), provided hours of entertainment for Coors employees and distributors alike. The big-top atmosphere was enhanced by the freely flowing samples of beer, which loosened tongues and encouraged instant camaraderie among the conventioneers.

Nearly every marketing program at Coors had its own display in the exhibtion hall, to assure distributors that Coors had the expertise and resources needed to achieve the infamous 10 percent share of the beer business. In one corner stood Bill Elliott's fire-red Ford Thunderbird stock car, which Coors sponsored on the NASCAR circuit. Nearby was Dan Pastorini's Coors Light drag racer, the Coors jumping combine (no doubt to promote beer drinking among farmers) and the Silver Bullet miniature airplane.

In addition to the machinery, booths were set up to hype the sales gimmicks for each of the company's major brands. Between swigs of beer, Cue Ball was handing out pins commemorating Coors introduction into Canada and Japan. Down the aisle from Cue Ball, hundreds of curious conventioneers were having their pictures taken with the Extra Gold Bulldog, Coors copycat answer to Budweiser's Spuds MacKenzie. A full-scale model set of the Silver Bullet Bar, featured in ads for Coors Light, was open for touring on the other side of the hall. And Mark Harmon commericals for Coors Banquet were playing continuously on big-screen TVs.

Like many conventioneers who wanted to avoid the temptations of the gaming tables at the Hilton, I spent most of my free time roaming the exhibit center. My picture was taken with the Coors Extra Gold Bulldog, who napped continually until prodded by his handlers. (Presumably, he was as bored with the proceedings as the rest of us.) I won a Coors Silver Bullet basketball by outshooting the Coors Light "sharpshooter" at a portable basketball hoop. To my utter delight, I met Sally, a sexy redhead and former model featured in the Silver Bullet Bar TV ads.

But for me, the highlight of the convention was the chance to finally meet and shake hands with Mark Harmon. As a college football fan and movie buff, I had been a Harmon fan long before I joined Coors. Despite the controversy over The Cold War, the line for Harmon's autographs was the longest in the exhibit center, as distributors' wives and other women (including a few of the Force's "cousins" and "sisters") waited to meet the star *People* magazine billed as the "Sexiest Man Alive."

While I waited in line, I remembered that Wee Willie, the gargantuan researcher, had told me that Harmon was outgoing and personable on the sets of his TV commercials. To break the ice, I decided to ask him about his football career at UCLA.

After forty-five minutes of inching forward in the queue , grasping a beer-can holder for Harmon to autograph, my moment in the spotlight arrived.

Harmon was shorter than I imagined, about five feet, nine inches tall with sandy brown hair and a perpetually furrowed brow. "Hi, Mark," I began. "I really enjoyed watching you play quarterback at UCLA, and I've been a fan of yours since 'The Dream Merchants.' " I extended my hand for him to shake.

"Who do you want the autograph for?" he asked, failing to acknowledge either my compliments or extended hand, while he reached for the can holder.

As I handed him the can holder, I said, "Make it, 'To Doris.' She's my mother."

While Harmon started to scribble, I decided to make one more stab at conversation. "This is the highlight of the convention for me. It's quite an honor to meet you."

"Hmmm," he responded. Then he handed me my can holder.

That's it, I wondered? "Well, thanks," I stammered.

"Sure," he responded, as the next person in line made her autograph request. *Not even "you're welcome."*

As I headed over to grab a beer in the reception area, I wondered if maybe I shouldn't have mentioned UCLA or "The Dream Merchants." Maybe Harmon was embarrassed by his early acting gigs, I reasoned. Perhaps he was distressed at having been a "jock" at UCLA. Regardless, Harmon lost a fan that day.

On the last night of the convention, Coors held a formal banquet for its distributors. Following the banquet, the Coors military, like a conquering army toasting the liberation of occupied lands, plundered Vegas, celebrating future victories in The Beer Wars with reckless abandon. The Coors military hosted parties at the Hilton, the Palomino Club, and scores of lounges on the Vegas strip. Many members of The Force escorted their kissing "cousins," sometimes two or three at a time, to the parties. Senior executives and well-heeled distributors lined the gaming tables, risking small fortunes on a roll of the dice or the draw of a card, far too giddy to add up their losses or walk away before risking and losing newly won fortunes. Big Tim observed that "we better sell a lot of beer next quarter, just to cover the expense reports coming out of the convention."

The High Command also used this temporary respite from the pressures of The Beer Wars to kick up their heels and enjoy the Vegas night life. During a predawn party hosted by Pete Coors in a Hilton lounge, one company officer, emboldened by the numerous celebratory brews he'd quaffed, begged his secretary to make love to him in, as he termed it, his "high-powered executive suite." He was promptly turned down. Another officer complimented a staffer on the "great job" she'd done for him at the convention, and then asked if she'd like to go up to his suite and do it to him again. A member of the Coors family spent several hours locked in a closet with a young public-relations assistant. When an unsuspecting beer warrior tried to open the door, he was told to "beat it. We're in the middle of an important meeting."

After four days of speeches, parties, exhibits, beer, and more beer, I was relieved and exhausted when my flight to Chicago (where I would be meeting with Coors advertising agencies) finally left Las Vegas's McCarren Airport. After the liftoff, I dozed, full of odd, dreamy thoughts. *Growth . . . wouldn't it be great if beer companies could take growth hormones? Maybe that surly little Mark Harmon should have taken growth hormones. Could Coors grow too quickly? How in the hell was Coors going to grow at all, without Masters III, Crystal Springs Cooler, or any other new products? What if Chuck Yeager took over for Rechholtz? Would we all have to wear flight suits to work? Why was 10 percent market share so magical for Coors? Why not 9 percent, or 90 percent?*

I woke up as the flight attendant asked the person seated next to me what he wanted to drink for breakfast. "Milk," he said.

"Two percent okay?" she inquired.

"No, *ten* percent," he said. I was still dozing, still dreaming. I think.

8

Spin Control

> . . . because it was the right thing to do, Pete
> Coors personally kicked off the Coors Pure
> Water 2000 program, a national commitment to
> help clean up America's rivers, streams, and
> lakes.

> —*Excerpted from* **1990 Coors Annual Report**

> The Adolph Coors Company officially became a
> toxic criminal on October 12, 1990, when it
> pleaded guilty to violating state environmental
> law by illegally pumping industrial solvents into
> Clear Creek from 1976 to 1989.

> —*Environmental columnist Mark Obmascik
> in* **The Denver Post**, *June 8, 1991*

> Coors Brewing Company could face
> a . . . fine . . . for killing all the fish in a 5.2-mile
> stretch of Clear Creek this month with a
> massive beer spill, the Attorney General's office
> said yesterday.

> —**The Denver Post** *May 29, 1991*

How many Coors employees
does it take to make a statement to the press?" Rod Sterling,
my comrade in the new-products war, asked me one day.

"I'll bite. How many?" I responded.

"One hundred and one," Sterling responded. "One Coors family member to say something dumb, and one hundred public-relations staffers to tell the press what the family member *really* meant to say."

In Nazi Germany, such P.R. mavens held the official title of "information ministers," though the Allies derisively called them "propagandists." Political reporters Jack Germond and Jules Witcover have referred to them as the masters of "spin control" in American politics, for their ability always to put the best complexion on events. At Coors, they were known simply as the Corporate Communications Department. As in World War II, propaganda would prove to be a potent weapon in the Coors arsenal, and an effective camouflage to hide just how badly Coors was faring in The Beer Wars.

As outlined in Chapter 2, a series of public-relations blunders in the late 1970s and early 1980s reinforced the Coors family's ultra-conservative image. Though Coors was by this time selling more than $1 billion in beer per year, and employed more than nine thousand workers nationally, these public-relations mistakes left a dark cloud hanging over the entire company. And despite more than 8,900 employees at Coors who were unrelated to the Coors family—some very liberal and even socially responsible—it was the Coors name that was emblazoned on the beer cans. For many Americans, buying or drinking a Coors beer was equivalent to supporting the Coors family's right-wing agenda. And what an agenda:

- Despite the fact that many working-class Americans were avid beer drinkers, Bill Coors called striking workers at the Coors brewery "monkeys" in 1977.[1] Many beer drinkers were aware of, and supported, the AFL–CIO's boycott of Coors products, according to Coors research.

1 Jeffrey Lieb, "Straight Talk," *Contemporary*, January 5, 1992, Times Mirror Publishing, p. 12.

- Joe Coors, the vice chairman of the Board, had provided funds to Lieutenant Colonel Oliver North to purchase weapons for the Nicaraguan Contras, covertly supporting the Reagan Administration and the CIA's controversial Central American activities. (See Chapter 2).
- Joe Coors was also a member of Ronald Reagan's "Kitchen Cabinet" of conservative, influential, wealthy advisors.[2]
- In spite of reams of academic research and financial theory outlining the benefits of issuing corporate debt, Bill Coors, the company's Chairman of the Board, continued to rail against the concept of issuing debt to finance a company's growth, and openly criticized the management at companies that already did so. (Consequently, *Financial World* magazine named Coors one of America's worst-run companies.)[3]
- Members of the Coors family provided financial backing to such conservative organizations as the Heritage Foundation, the John Birch Society, the Moral Majority, the Council for National Policy, and the Mountain States Legal Foundation.[4]
- Coors had been sued by the Equal Employment Opportunity Commission in 1975 for work force discrimination against minorities and women, in a case that was eventually settled out of court. (Coors, while not admitting any past discrimination, agreed to continue a program begun in 1972 to increase minority and female employees in all job classifications.)
- The Coors family continued to weed out "undesirable"

---

2 Jack W. Germond and Jules Witcover, *Blue Smoke and Mirrors* (Viking, 1981), p. 100.

3 Noted in the "Denver Inc." column of The *Denver Post* on May 21, 1991.

4 These ties are documented in Russ Bellant's book *The Coors Connection*, which was published in 1991 by South End Press.

employees, even after polygraph tests were outlawed. One senior Coors executive was quoted in the *Denver Post* as claiming that, despite the elimination of polygraph tests, Coors new screening procedure would allow the company to "find Communists." A company spokesperson explained to the *Wall Street Journal* that "If we [Coors] had Communists on our staff, we couldn't get government contracts."

- Coors was a major environmental polluter (as documented later in this chapter).

No member of the Coors family ever apologized for these actions and beliefs, in public or private. But with the company's financial fortunes sagging, Pete Coors acknowledged that the negative publicity surrounding the family's conservative credo was bad for business. "If we alienate anyone else on this planet, we're going to have to expand elsewhere in the Milky Way Galaxy," Pete Coors had intimated in closed-door meetings with Coors public relations managers. Rather than change the family's somewhat radical beliefs, management decided to change the public image of the Coors family. Enter the Corporate Communications Department, whose mission was to promote style over substance.

To a public-relations professional, Coors was either the ultimate challenge, or the ultimate nightmare. Not only was the company's image tarnished, but the anti-Coors factions were sometimes organized and well funded:

- The AFL–CIO organized a boycott of Coors beer in response to the company's strike-breaking activities in 1977. This boycott, which was supported by other unions including the Teamsters, extended from coast to coast, and generated negative publicity whenever Coors entered into new markets that were organized labor strongholds, such as Detroit and New York City.
- MADD, or Mothers Against Drunk Driving, while gen-

erally opposed to the marketing tactics of *all* the major U.S. brewers, prominently featured Coors bottles and cans in several ads and pamphlets, in an attempt to use Coors' controversial image to bolster its anti-drinking sentiment.

- Facing the threat of a boycott by the NAACP, the Urban League, and other civil rights groups after the flap over Bill Coors's alleged "intellectual capacity" remarks, Coors signed "covenants" which pledged $650 million in business and financial support to black and hispanic vendors from 1984 to 1989.[5]
- Numerous environmental groups criticized the Coors environmental record, and the Sierra Club frequently took the company to court for its polluting activities.[6]
- The late Harvey Milk organized a boycott of Coors beer in the gay community in 1975.

Spurred on by this organized resistance to Coors, millions of beer drinkers religiously boycotted Coors beer in the 1980s.

Gay and lesbian drinkers believed that the Coors family actively supported anti-homosexual organizations. I had convened a series of focus groups to help Coors assess the company's image problem in the gay community (discussed in depth in the next chapter); during these focus groups, one drinker told us, "I'd travel across the city to buy Budweiser, if I had to, instead of buying Coors if it was available across the street. I wouldn't drink a Coors if it was the only drink at a desert oasis." Anti-Coors fervor among gays was so strong that we were encouraged, off the record, not to mention our employer during business trips to San Francisco—especially not to cab drivers (for fear of retribution).

5 "Coors Agrees on Plan to Increase Business with Hispanic Firms," *The Wall Street Journal*, October 30, 1984, p. 27.

6 Lieb, p. 12.

Gay opposition to Coors not only generated negative publicity, but was very bad for business. According to research
conducted by Coors, a large portion of gay social life revolved
around clubs and bars, prime beer drinking situations. And
Coors wasn't welcome in most gay clubs. One bartender told
us in focus groups that, "I've never heard of a [gay] club that
carries Coors. No one would drink it, and even if they did,
you'd have a brick through your windows about once a week
if you were caught carrying Coors." A gay beer drinker in the
same focus group added, "If someone was caught drinking a
Coors, they'd be thrown out [of the bar]."

And gays weren't the only disenfranchised consumers who
vehemently opposed Coors. Throughout the years, nearly every
focus group that I observed or conducted was marred by at least
one consumer who, regardless of the subject, would opine, "I
never drink Coors because . . ." One beer drinker would say
that she grew up in a union household. Another drinker would
cite opposition to the Nicaraguan Contras as his reason for
boycotting Coors. Still another drinker would cite the company's use of polygraph tests (prior to 1987). Most would simply
lump all of the right-wing causes together and say that they
didn't drink Coors "because of the politics."

Over lunch one day, I discussed the public-relations nightmare with a manager from Corporate Communications, who
called himself Holy Man.

"I'm going to ask my boss for a raise," Holy Man told me
near the end of lunch.

"Why is that?" I wondered.

"Well, at CSU (Colorado State University), they taught us
that, at most big companies, you'll have about ten percent of
the population with fairly negative feelings about a company,"
he started.

"Yeah, so how does that get you a raise?"

"Well, I've been doing some figuring," Holy Man continued.
"Gays are ten percent of the population. Right? Blacks are about

ten percent, union workers are at least fifteen percent of the population, and women are fifty-one percent. So, I figure right there that at least eighty-six percent of the population hates Coors. And that doesn't even include liberals, environmentalists, MADD, or a lot of other groups. So I figure my job is at least eight or nine times harder than it would be at another company. So I think I should get paid eight or nine times more," he concluded.

"Well, that's a real interesting argument," I fibbed. "Good luck on the raise, and, if you get it, remember us little guys," I said as I got up to return to work. Though he had exaggerated the point somewhat (and had no chance of getting his raise), Holy Man had captured the essence of the Coors P.R. problem. Though Coors was America's fifth-largest brewery (having surpassed Pabst in 1985), a good portion of the population already had a natural inclination *not* to drink Coors, which was reflected in the sagging sales for Coors Banquet. The marketing challenge (helping the company to reach the infamous 10 percent market-share level) in the face of this barrier was formidable, if not impossible. Research indicated as much.

It was not uncommon for women in focus groups to say that they "loved" the Mark Harmon advertising campaign, but still wouldn't drink Coors (because of the "politics"). When testing new products, we'd often hear how good an idea was, until the Coors name was attached, and the "good" idea instantly became, "I'd never drink that." Surveys regularly indicated that 10 percent to 30 percent of the beer drinkers had a very negative opinion of an ad or new product that bore the Coors name. In effect, until the Coors image was rehabilitated, the company would have a hard time building its customer base.

Facing perhaps the toughest public-relations problem in America, the Coors Corporate Communications Department grew extremely large, with more than one hundred full-time employees and a sizeable budget. Its strategies for improving the Coors image, according to the Holy Man, were:

1. Deflect attention away from the family's activities to the positive accomplishments of the company.
2. Portray Pete and Jeff Coors as broad-minded, modern industrialists, not right-wing conservatives (a "new breed" of Coors).

The problem with this strategy wasn't its goals, but the tactics used to achieve them. The 1980s was a largely lawless and reckless decade in the business world: "Anything goes" was the motto, from Wall Street to Main Street, in pursuit of profit. While Wall Street robber barons like Boesky, Levine, and Milken grabbed headlines, the "me" generation values, or lack thereof, also penetrated the world of Madison Avenue marketing, and companies like Coors.

Traditionally, marketing and public relations have been used to entice American consumers into purchasing products like Coors beer. But until the 1980s, the Federal Trade Commission rigidly regulated the advertising industry to ensure that American consumers weren't conned by false and deceptive advertising claims. Due to this stringent regulation, most advertising claims were plausible, grounded—at least partially—in fact or reality.[7] In the 1970s, two out of three dentists really *did* recommend Crest; no one quibbled with the notion that many choosy mothers bought Jif Peanut Butter; and Coke *was* "it" for a generation of American soft-drink consumers.

When the Reagan Revolution of the 1980s ushered in a new era of government deregulation, the rules of the marketing game changed drastically. Under its new chairman, James

---

7 Among the companies cited by the Federal Trade Commission for using false and deceptive advertising claims in the 1970s were Warner–Lambert (Listerine), Wonder Bread, Ocean Spray, and Firestone. FTC rulings forced each of these companies to modify or cancel its advertising, and/or take remedial action. In most cases, the FTC also levied fines, a deterrent to other potential deceptive advertisers.

Miller, a Reagan appointee, the Federal Trade Commission relaxed its regulation of children's advertising, tightened the definition of "deceptive" advertising, and dismantled the government's "Substantiation Program," which had forced advertisers to document the authenticity of their advertising claims. As a result, marketing and public-relations "spin doctors" focused not on casting products and companies in the *best* light, but in *artificial* light. Half-truths and deception crept into advertisements for such formerly trustworthy products as Volvo cars, Purina dog food, and Pennzoil.[8]

Reflecting this shift in marketing tactics, the Coors corporate communications managers in the 1980s often acted as illusionsts, in the tradition of David Copperfield and Harry Houdini. In reality, the Coors family, and the company that was the crown jewel of their industrial empire, really *hadn't* changed much, if at all, from previous eras. In case after case, the Corporate Communications Department tried to create or reshape an image for the company and the family; an image that, no matter how desirable or commendable, didn't always square with reality. But the "new" image did square with the company's goal of selling more beer.

---

8 According to the September 23, 1991 edition of *Advertising Age*, Volvo's advertising dramatized the strength of the cars by driving a "monster truck" over the roofs. To the surprise and chagrin of consumers who tried to duplicate the feat, Volvo later disclosed that the roofs of the cars in the ads had been reinforced. The same magazine carried accounts of damage judgments for deceptive advertising against Purina, for a 1985 dog-food campaign (December 2, 1991), and Pennzoil, for its claim that Pennzoil "outperforms any leading motor oil against viscosity breakdown" (June 1, 1992). Both lawsuits were brought by competitors, not by the passive FTC of the post-Reagan Revolution.

PUBLIC RELATIONS MYTH 1:

The "New" Coors Brewing Company Is Concerned about the Environment

The Coors Corporate Communications Department attempted to portray the company as socially responsible and environmentally sound, earning headlines like "Coors Brewing Up Greener Image."[9] This program culminated in the late 1980s with the creation of the "Pure Water 2000 Campaign," a drive to clean up America's lakes and streams by the year 2000. The campaign was funded by a donation from the Adolph Coors Company, and through automatic contributions from beer sales. The campaign kickoff featured Pete Coors standing streamside in television and print ads, extolling the virtues of clean water. As Holy Man, my earnest but naive contact in Corporate Communications, told me, "This is something the whole company can get behind. Now we really *are* good corporate citizens."

REALITY: COORS STILL POLLUTES

Despite a massive public-relations effort to change its environmental image, Coors, according to *The Rocky Mountain News*, Sierra Club, and Citizen Action Group, has long been a major polluter, prompting a Sierra Club lawyer to comment that the company is "schizophrenic." The "lowlights" of the Coors environmental record since the 1980s include:

9 This front-page headline, which appeared in *The Rocky Mountain News* on February 6, 1992, is but one example of positive headlines about the company's environmental achievements since the mid-1980s.

1. In February 1984, the Colorado Department of Health
    found low levels of mercury, lead, cadmium, and silver
    coming from the Coors/City of Golden water-treatment
    plant.

2. In May of 1988, Coors was named by the EPA as the
    largest polluter of 154 industrial polluters at the infa-
    mous Lowry Landfill, one of America's largest toxic
    dump sites.

3. In June 1990, Coors was cited by the state of Colorado
    for violations of hazardous-waste and water-quality laws
    for pumping contaminated water into Clear Creek from
    1976 to 1989.

4. After killing more than ten thousand fish in Clear Creek,
    Bill Coors told stockholders that the fish were only "trash
    fish," and a company spokesperson defended Coors by
    saying the stream "was not a prime fishing stream."[10]

PUBLIC RELATIONS MYTH 2:

Coors Employs a Diverse, Racially Mixed Work Force At All Levels of the Company

The company coordinated a series of articles in newspapers,
trade publications, and mass-media magazines, which pointed
out that:

1. A woman, Sandra K. Woods, had been appointed a vice
    president of the company, and was named an outstand-
    ing corporate officer by *Business Week, Fortune,* and *Work-
    ing Woman* magazines. Two other women, Betsy Ross-
    Krieg and June Smith, served as brand managers for
    Herman Joseph's and Coors Light, respectively.

10 Mark Obmascik, "Coors Pure Water Promises Muddied by Pollution Record," *The Denver Post,* June 8, 1991, p. B1.

2.　Former Denver Bronco wide receiver Haven Moses was a sales executive with the company.

3.　The company no longer required prospective employees to take polygraph tests.

REALITY: AT ITS TOP LEVELS, COORS IS STILL A WHITE MAN'S COMPANY

Despite the articles in respected business publications, the truth is:

1.　While Sandra Woods was (and still is) a vice president of the company, she was the company's *only* female officer (in the mid-1980s, and one of two as of the summer of 1991). Employed in the company's Real Estate Division, Woods has never played a major role in the beer business. The two female brand managers no longer work in the beer business, and men still far outnumber women in the Coors executive suites.[11]

2.　Haven Moses was the *only* black marketing executive employed by Coors in the mid- to late 1980s, and, as late as 1992, all of the company's vice presidents were white. Typifying the company's attitude toward minority advancement, one of the leaders of the High Command had told me that the company didn't need any more black executives "unless they're good softball players."

3.　The company dropped mandatory polygraph tests only when forced to do so, with the passage of the Employee

11 The other female corporate officer was M. Caroline Turner, the vice president and chief legal officer for the company. Again, her department was not intricately involved in the brewery's day-to-day operations.

Polygraph Protection Act of 1988. The company then
switched to administering personality tests.

PUBLIC RELATIONS MYTH 3:

Coors Is Not Opposed to Organized Labor

In the fall of 1988, Coors Brewing rank and file overwhelmingly
rejected the right to organize a (Teamsters) union. This formally
ended the AFL–CIO's decade-old boycott of Coors.

REALITY: COORS STILL OPPOSES ORGANIZED LABOR

While Pete Coors spearheaded negotiations to end the union
boycott of Coors beer, culminating in the vote not to organize,
this did not constitute approval, tacit or otherwise, of organized
labor by the Coors family or company. In the days leading up
to the labor election in 1988, Pete and Jeff Coors conducted
"question-and-answer" sessions with workers (one of which I
attended), and attempted to dissuade them from unionizing.
Pete gave an impassioned plea to "save the brewing family,"
and to "allow Coors to treat you [workers] in the same dignified
manner that we've always treated you."

PUBLIC RELATIONS MYTH 4:

Coors Is a Modern, Diversified Industrial Empire

Central to the efforts of the P.R. staff to erase Coors negative
image was convincing the public that Coors wasn't a family-

owned business, but a modern industrial empire, publicly held and managed by professional business managers. By divorcing the company from the Coors family, the P.R. staff hoped to eliminate consumer avoidance of Coors beer products because of the Coors family's political beliefs. Holy Man summed up the merits of this strategy when he told me, "We've got to convince people that this is just a regular company, with a few employees who happen to be named Coors. That when they buy the beer, the money isn't funnelled directly to Coors family bank accounts. After all, people haven't boycotted Ford just because [the late] Henry Ford [II, grandson of the company founder] is a womanizer."

Coors took several steps to buttress this strategy. The brewing division, Coors Brewing Company, was set up as a separate subsidiary of the Adolph Coors (holding) Company. Next, the Coors family appointed several non-family members to the holding company's Board of Directors. The Corporate Communications Department also took great pains to point out to the media that Coors was a publicly traded company, with shares traded on the NASDAQ, over-the-counter market.[12]

REALITY: COORS WAS, AND IS, A FAMILY-OWNED-AND-OPERATED BUSINESS

Despite the best efforts of the spin doctors, Coors operated throughout the 1980s as it had for most of its first one hundred years. The brewery continued to fund the Coors family's agenda, as: (1) The brewing division provided 100 percent of the company's income until the late 1980s; (2) Despite the sale

---

12 However, all publicly traded shares are Class B, nonvoting stock, meaning that the Coors family still retains control of the company's Board, and, hence, the company.

of public stock, the Coors family and their trusts retained all of the voting stock in the company, ensuring that Coors was controlled and managed by the Coors family. The Coors Trust, the majority shareholder (controlling interest), which was run by Bill Coors, approved the mid-1980s management team consisting of Bill Coors (chairman), Jeff Coors (president of the holding company) and Pete Coors (president of the Brewing Company). In the late 1980s, Joe Coors, Jr. was appointed president of Coors Ceramics Company, while W. Grover Coors was appointed president of Coors Advanced Electronics Group.

In 1990, the family's control over the company was further tightened when the sitting Board of Directors was dissolved, and replaced by a new Board which consisted of five Coors family members.[13]

Further confirmation that the Coors Brewing Company was far from independent from the conservative interests of the Coors family was the company's newsletter, the *Coors Courier*. Before the 1986 mid-year elections, the *Coors Courier* featured an article instructing employees how to vote. Surprise! The company urged employees to vote for pro-life Republicans, and a strictly conservative agenda. After this piece ran, we began calling the *Courier* "Pravda," in honor of the state-controlled Soviet newspaper.

At numerous other times, the Courier featured "opinion" articles that advocated a conservative agenda, from tax cuts to government deregulation.

---

13 By 1991, four more "outside" directors (not members of the Coors family) were added to the Board. However, five of the nine directors were still Coors family members, ensuring family control of the company.

PUBLIC RELATIONS MYTH 5:

Coors is Dedicated to Quality

Even the Marketing Department wasn't immune from the temptation to put a positive spin on facts and events, though the spin bore no resemblance to reality. Historically, Coors had promoted the high quality of its beer products to consumers. Using a special strain of barley, pure Rocky Mountain spring water, and the cold-filtration brewing process, Coors drafted a quality image that fostered the beer's "cachet" status in the early 1970s. The Mark Harmon advertising campaign, touting how Coors really was better tasting because of the company's devotion to quality, had re-staked the Coors claim to a quality image. "Quality in all we are, and all we do," was even part of the company's official mission statement during the 1980s.

REALITY: COORS REGULARLY COMPROMISED PRODUCT QUALITY

Unfortunately, the standard of quality which had driven Coors for more than one hundred years was routinely compromised during the 1980s Beer Wars.

Coors regularly tinkered with the formulas for its products, in order to cut costs. At times, Coors merely blended two beers together, rather than brewing a beer from scratch, in order to save money. Retailers in Colorado charged as much as $5.50 per six-pack for the inaugural season of Coors Winterfest, a special holiday brew. In reality that first year, the beer was a blend of Coors Extra Gold and Killian's Ale, beers which sold for far less (as much as 50 percent less) than $5.50 per six-pack. (Blending leftover beer is much cheaper than brewing from scratch, but it significantly alters the taste of most beers. This is discussed in greater detail in Chapter 10.)

The alcohol content of Killian's Irish Red Ale was lowered,

in 1988, at the direction of High Command, again in order to cut costs. This changed the product from an ale to a standard lager, and significantly altered the taste of the product. Consumers were never told that the product had been changed, or why.

Despite Coors claims about the importance of refrigeration in the shipping and storage of Coors beer (The Cold War), the Coors family ordered a series of stress tests, which I coordinated, to assess whether Coors products could be shipped, by sea, to the Caribbean. Coors later exported their products to several Caribbean countries, undeterred by the intense heat from shipping beer to tropical areas via cargo ships.

The most dangerous, reckless cost-cutting move was the decision to brew Coors beers (including Coors Banquet and Coors Light) in Virginia, in order to reduce transportation expenses for East Coast markets. Coors had spent hundreds of millions of dollars, and more than one hundred years, telling beer drinkers that Rocky Mountain spring water was the special ingredient that gave Coors products their unique flavor. Yet, after expansion to the East Coast, Coors decided to use Elkton, Virginia, spring water to brew Coors beer.[14] Tantamount to a Presidential candidate disavowing his party's platform on the day before an election, Coors senseless decision left beer drinkers to wonder how special the Rocky Mountain spring water really was, if Coors altered its brewing recipe for East Coast drinkers.

Not all of Coors attempts to reshape the company's image were directed at beer drinkers. When the cost of providing health

14 In 1991, the Bureau of Alcohol, Tobacco, and Firearms ordered Coors to remove the claim, "Made with pure Rocky Mountain spring water" from the company's beer cans and advertising. Technically speaking, Coors beer is brewed in Colorado. Then, the beer is dehydrated to concentrate its mass for shipping in rail cars. The beer is rehydrated with Virginia spring water at Elkton, which ultimately prompted the BATF's order.

insurance for employees soared in the 1980s, Coors decided to push employees to limit their health care problems through a corporate "wellness" program—despite the fact that beer flowed freely in lunch rooms, the corporate wellness center, and break rooms throughout the brewing complex (it was free to employees), and despite the fact that Coors was in the business of plying the American public with the beer.

The company announced that Bill and Joe Coors had overcome hypertension through rigorous aerobic exercise and a low-fat, low-sodium diet. Thus, they incorporated this self-discipline into their conservative management credo, figuring that what was good for their own health must be good for that of all of their employees. They converted a Safeway grocery store into a Wellness Center, providing a free health club to all Coors employees. Ignoring the seeming incongruity between wellness and encouraging employees to drink beer, signs on the walls of the Wellness Center instructed fitness buffs on how to enjoy beer after workouts.

Herr Rechholtz, himself an avid exerciser, took the wellness philosophy to heart. "Healthy workers do better work," he pronounced when introducing his "Wellness Plus" program, "and can battle the opposition more effectively." To whip his army into fighting trim, Rechholtz decided to hold a mandatory contest in the Marketing Department, with employees having to monitor their wellness over a four-month period. Wellness included standard measures like blood pressure and cholesterol levels, weight, and regular preventive health care including mammograms and annual physicals. Points were accumulated according to a scoring system designed by the Coors Wellness Center. The winning department was to receive a party in its honor, where, of course, Coors beer would be served. Individual winners would also receive a free Wellness Center sweatshirt.

Despite the rigorous daily demands of competing in the billion-dollar beer industry, the contest became serious business in the "kill or be killed" world of Coors management. Group leaders were appointed in each department, and they religiously hounded and threatened employees who refused to participate in the mandatory contest. I was one of the more reluctant participants, until my manager, Big Mama, told me that wellness would be factored into my annual performance appraisal.

"But I'm very well," I pleaded when she confronted me about my nonparticipation.

"At this company, if you want to succeed, you'll have to prove it," Big Mama warned.

This is the rebirth of the Aryan Nation; only the physically fit can work at Coors. But I wonder how many members of the Central Command are really undertaking the program? Most are heavy drinkers, with the requisite beer bellies to show for their efforts. And what about Big Mama? She didn't earn her nickname through devotion to the Stairmaster or treadmill.

In a fit of rebellion, I decided, during my four-month wellness review, to lodge a silent protest against the mandatory contest. In filling out my health checklist, I claimed to have had nine testicular examinations over the past four months, worth a solid twenty-seven points in improved wellness. I figured the people running the contest would get a chuckle out of my claim, and I would be disqualified. Not quite.

As in the Olympics, Rechholtz honored the winning department, and those individuals with the most improved health during the contest, with a public ceremony. Coworkers were almost as stunned as I when my name was called.

"How did you win?" Big Tim wanted to know. "I know you pretty well. You haven't improved your health."

"If anything, it's gotten a lot worse," Rod Sterling contended.

"Pardner, you've been spending too many hours around the camp fire to win this," Cowboy chided.

They were right, I thought, as I carefully folded my new Wellness Center sweatshirt. "When I enter a contest," I told them, "I go balls out." *More than anyone will ever know.* I still have my Wellness Plus sweatshirt, a reminder of how strange it was for a company to promote beer drinking and good health simultaneously.

Even the citizens of Denver were unable to escape the Corporate Communications Department's spin control efforts. As hypocritical as the Wellness Plus program was, Coors actions in helping Denver gain a Major League baseball franchise were even more so.

As far back as the late 1950s, Denver had been vying for a Major League baseball franchise. More than thirty years later, in 1990, Major League baseball finally announced a timetable and criteria for awarding expansion franchises. Denver's problem in securing a franchise was its lack of a stable, wealthy owner. None of Denver's prominent citizens, including the Coors family, had stepped forward to spearhead an ownership group once real estate mogul John Dikeou's financial empire fizzled.[15]

In spite of their vast fortune, the Coors family had little interest in owning a Major League baseball franchise, or any other sports franchise. The company had turned down an opportunity to purchase the Colorado Rockies NHL team, for a paltry $6 million, in 1982. (The team subsequently moved to New Jersey.) True, Anheuser–Busch owned the St. Louis Cardinals, and Labatt's owned the Toronto Blue Jays. But baseball was not one of the conservative causes that the Coors family was interested in funding. At least, not until the baseball franchise became a public-relations and advertising bonanza for the brewery.

Metro Denver voters overwhelmingly approved a sales tax to fund the construction of a new baseball stadium in August 1990. According to the pundits, Denver was right for Major League baseball, except that the ownership group formed by Colorado Governor Roy Romer was short of cash and "deep pockets." Finally, just several months shy of the expansion vote

---

15 Dikeou was the owner of the Denver Zephyrs American Association Minor League team, and had indicated, prior to his financial troubles during the real-estate bust of the late 1980s, that he wanted to own Denver's Major League expansion franchise.

by Major League baseball, the Coors "cavalry" rode to the rescue. Coors announced, in March 1991, that it would commit approximately $30 million to the expansion franchise in return for "an equity investment and multiyear signage and advertising package," as well as the rights to name the new baseball stadium (which will be named "Coors Field").

Ultimately, Denver did get its baseball team, the Colorado Rockies, granted by the National League on July 5, 1991. But Denver area residents were left to wonder why Coors, a major enterprise in the area since the 1870s, waited until just three months prior to the expansion announcement to become a part of the ownership group. Why, despite their wealth, did Coors purchase only a minority ownership? And why did Coors insist on an investment with strings attached? (That is, with promotional rights and the stadium-naming rights attached?)

The answer was that the "new" Coors, while still committed to conservatism, was also committed to any cause that would sell more beer. As purely a civic gesture, the baseball package was unattractive. But when promotional rights and stadium-naming rights were included in the Coors package, the Colorado Rockies became an attractive investment. And the Coors P.R. department played the story for all it was worth in the Denver media, as stories were featured in major newspapers, TV, and on the radio, describing how Coors had "made the difference" or "put Denver over the top" in an effort to secure Major League baseball for Denver.[16]

Baseball wasn't the only cause where Coors acted only in its best interests. A clean environment was a cause, as long as Coors could continue to pollute while promoting its clean water program. Minority hiring seemed like a good idea, as long as the executive offices of the brewery were still dominated by

16 One radio interview with Pete Coors, conducted by KYGB's Irv Brown, ended with Brown stating that without Coors, "we [Denver] wouldn't have a team." Brown was later hired by the Colorado Rockies to conduct baseball clinics for the team.

white males. Quality was a good advertising theme, even as soaring costs and strong competition "forced" Coors to compromise quality.

Ultimately, the question is whether Coors big public-relations push helped the company. Did the attempts to change the family's image boost employee morale? Did beer drinkers really change their perception of Coors? Did the press? Did the "new" Coors appeal to a new generation of beer drinkers?

Employees were usually unaware of, and unconcerned with most of the Coors family's conservative agenda. Like many of the beer drinkers we surveyed, Coors employees were vaguely aware that the Coors family was conservative and controversial. The vast majority of employees were business professionals more concerned with their own careers than in supporting the political agenda of the Coors family. "I've got a job to do, and as long as I don't have to do anything illegal or unethical, I don't care about them [the Coors family]," Rod Sterling told me shortly after he had been hired.

As white-collar professionals, the members of the Marketing Department tried to ignore the controversy; knowing the facts and the family's true conservative agenda served only to depress morale. While fighting for survival, most of the marketing professionals in the Coors army didn't want to know that many beer drinkers would *never* drink Coors, or the reasons for consumers' negative feelings. Digging deep into the family's true beliefs and agenda was, according to Holy Man, like opening Pandora's box. By the time I left Coors, my once boisterous P.R. contact dubbed his department "Tass," in homage to the Soviet news agency known better for revisionism than journalism. He wasn't alone in his skepticism.

The attempted whitewashing of the Coors image sometimes backfired, creating dangerous disinformation for the Marketing Department. Pete Coors was featured in ads for Pure Water 2000 just months before the company's environmental abuses were publicized, harming the credibility of *all* of the company's advertising. Tampering with product formulas (unbeknownst to most employees) at times when ads touted the taste of Coors beers served only to further alienate remaining Coors customers. Marketing a product at Coors, according to Sterling, was like buying a house at the infamous Love Canal. "You don't know what disaster awaits, what poison or toxin will do you in. But you know it'll happen sometime. They're [the Coors family] always hiding something we should know before we run an ad or a [marketing] program."

So if the P.R. push didn't help the company's employees, did it change the opinions of beer drinkers? Not really. Despite Coors attempts to whitewash, rather than apologize for, past transgressions, the consuming public was not easily swayed. As late as August 1991, three years removed from the Coors inner circle and firmly established as a marketing consultant, I still ran across consumers who opposed Coors products and the family's politics, undeterred by the public-relations machine. As one African-American consumer said while looking at an ad from Coors saluting Martin Luther King, "Right message. Wrong company. Just because they say these things doesn't mean they really believe this stuff."

And sales figures and surveys tended to echo his comments. Despite the company's public-relations push, the Coors Banquet brand continued its spectacular decline in the late 1980s. Internal company surveys continued to indicate that Coors had the worst image of any of the major brewers, and a solid, undiminishing minority of beer drinkers still believed that the company was run by right-wing conservatives, whose politics crystallized opposition to the company.

Despite the brazen attempts at spin control, Coors scored few public-relations victories with the media, either. While the low profile of Bill and Joe Coors minimized the company's negative press, there were few laudatory, "puff" pieces resulting from the public-relations push. (*Forbes* magazine, in its March 4, 1991 edition, was an exception to this pattern.) The business press focused more heavily on the company's business problems, and those weren't easily glossed over. COORS PURE-WATER

PROMISES MUDDLED BY POLLUTION RECORD, SERIES OF SNAFUS PLAGU-
ING COORS, and PROFITS TUMBLE AT COORS were headlines which
reflected the harsh reality of The Beer Wars, not public-relations
gloss.[17]

Further, the attitude of the business press seemed to be that
while Coors was avoiding the intense negative publicity of the
1970s and early 1980s, that, in itself, was hardly a major accomplishment. Anheuser–Busch, Stroh, and Miller for years
had avoided the scathing criticism that the Coors family's actions had earned. By using the Coors Corporate Communications Department to shape the image of the Coors family, the
company inadvertently caused the fate of the family and its
brewery to become even more intertwined, not distanced or
divorced.

The Coors family and the High Command may have under-
estimated the business acumen and sophistication of the media
and American beer drinkers. As a result, Coors massive effort
to reshape the company's image and improve its fortunes fell
on deaf ears. The fact that Coors was trying to change its image
may have been commendable, but the ugly realities that still
lurked behind the image continued to cast a shadow. For Coors,
it was still dark.

17 These headlines appeared in *The Denver Post* on May 13, 1991, July
13, 1991, and July 19, 1991, respectively.

9

Naked Ladies, Natural Sodas, and the Search for a Secret Weapon

Don't be afraid to fail. It's the way you learn to do things right.

—Marian Wright Edelman

July, 1988

Dear Mom:

After all of these months and years, I can finally tell you what I worked on during the war. You know, ''The Beer Wars.''

Remember when I wrote to you that I was working on secret new products for Coors, the brewing giant? Well, I really was. Tell Aunt Jean and all of your friends at the country club that I wasn't working for the CIA, as they suspected. These new products can be worth millions of dollars, so companies like Coors keep them ''top secret.'' That's why I could never talk about my work.

Just so that you can be proud of my contributions to the war effort, I thought I'd list the new products that I worked on while I was at Coors:

- *Fruit Juice Sparklers*
- *Coors Dark Beer*
- *A "High Alcohol" Beer*
- *Menthol-Flavored Malt Liquor*
- *Imported Beers Brewed at Coors*
- *Springfest Beer*
- *Imported Malt Liquor*
- *No-Alcohol Beers*
- *Liquors (Scotch, Vodka) Brewed from Malt*
- *A Natural Soda*
- *Bottled Sparkling Water*
- *Gay Beer*

I know what you're thinking, Mom. This list does look really strange for a conservative beer company located in the Rocky Mountains, especially the idea for a gay beer. But it really was my job to try and develop marketing strategies for these new product ideas. That's what I did for a living, for more than three years. I'd include all the details in this letter, but that would take a whole book, or at least one chapter in a book.

Oh, well, I guess this story does sound improbable, strange, or as your Aunt Jean might say, "weird as all heck." On second thought, tell Aunt Jean and the gang at the club that I really was a CIA agent for the past three years. That's more believable.

Your Loving Son,
Bob

After The Cold War and the loss of momentum in the Mark Harmon advertising campaign, Coors was running out of options. The war on the new-products front, including the battles over Colorado Chiller, Crystal Springs Cooler, and Masters III, had failed miserably. The company was also running out of money, as constant price discounting of Coors Banquet and Coors Light were draining valuable cash reserves. Despite record sales in 1986 of well over $1 billion, Coors had earned a paltry $59 million, providing a scant return on equity to shareholders of only 6.1 percent (a figure only slightly higher than if the company's shareholders had invested their money in a standard passbook savings account).

Faced with defeat on two fronts at the end of World War II, Adolf Hitler and the German High Command stepped up efforts to produce long-range missiles and an atomic bomb, weapons of mass destruction that could tilt the balance of power back to the Nazis. Similarly, Rechholtz and the Coors High Command, searching for a weapon of mass destruction to repel Anheuser–Busch and Miller, reemphasized the Coors weapons program in 1987.

Modern marketing warfare consists of two types of weapons. Advertisements are the conventional weapons, with limited destructive capacity and capabilities. While the Mark Harmon advertising campaign (before the flap over The Cold War) had given a slight boost (3 percent) to Coors sales, it had little tangible impact on the surging sales of Budweiser. The Cold War had also uncovered the frailty of advertising as a marketing weapon; one slipup or oversight can scuttle a campaign, and even good advertising can't counterbalance an unwanted, unnecessary, or outdated product (like Coors Banquet, which was no longer "America's Fine Light Beer").

New products are marketing warfare's weapons of mass destruction. A successful consumer product, like Oreo cookies, Crest toothpaste, or Minute Maid orange juice, can be worth hundreds of millions of dollars in profits per year to the manufacturer, which can be used to fund further corporate growth and development (a chain-reaction explosion). Like a nuclear arsenal, new products in marketing warfare are expensive and risky. In order to reap millions in profits, a company must *spend* and *invest* millions to develop a viable product, packaging, advertising, coupons, etc. Often, this investment fails to pay off, as Coors million-dollar losses on Colorado Chiller, Masters III, and other new products proved.

It was the risk of losing millions of dollars that changed the new-products game for American businesses in the 1980s. Traditionally, innovative ideas, like Apple's Macintosh computer, Boeing's 767 jet, and Nike's athletic shoes, have fueled growth in the American economy. But "me" generation managers, in search of bonuses, executive perks, and stock-price appreciation, couldn't afford to risk money on innovative, risky ideas, so the Age of Innovation (during the 1940s and 1950s) evolved into the Age of Imitation (the 1980s), an era of new products with limited profit potential *and* risk. This period in product marketing was marked by new versions of successful products (for example, a new, improved Tide), extending prominent brand names to new products (e.g., Dole frozen dessert treats), and imitations of other companies' products (what marketers call "me too" products).[1]

The Age of Imitation found its way to Coors, too. Poorer, but claiming to be wiser after the Colorado Chiller and Masters III fiascoes, the High Command ordered Truitt's Development Department and the Market Research Department to explore a full range of new product ideas. If a "sure thing" emerged, Coors would quickly enter the new market. However, until Coors uncovered a risk-free venture, the company would simply continue exploratory efforts. During the Age of Imitation, innovative products, like Crystal Springs Cooler, would be relegated to the back burner.

The foundation for Coors new weapons-development program was a set of idea-generating sessions that were held in March 1986. Idea-generating sessions are just that: meetings in which participants use their creativity to identify ideas for potential new products.

For this market researcher, being invited to an idea-generating session was akin to stumbling upon a oasis in a desert. Researchers are paid to critique other people's ideas, not to create marketing strategies on their own. "Don't step on other

---

1 According to *Gorman's New Products News,* almost 90 percent of the "new" products introduced into the United States in 1991 were variations of existing products, continuing a 1980s trend.

people's [i.e., The General's] toes," Big Mama had told me a few months after joining Coors. "We can analyze, but we have to make sure that the brand [marketing] managers always think the ideas are their own, for their egos." It wasn't surprising, then, that market researchers at Coors developed a reputation for being cooly analytical, but utterly lacking in creativity, something like a high school nerd who was smart, but not part of the "in" crowd.

Unfortunately, creativity *was* a requisite quality for any Cruncher (from the Market Research Department) hoping to one day advance up the career ladder at Coors. In a company dominated by machismo, instinct marketers, and "good old boy" members of The Force, Crunchers had to show the ability to abandon their logical, analytical approach to problem-solving, in order to join the inner circle of "beer men." Therefore, I decided to use the idea-generating sessions to which I'd been invited as a "coming out" party: I would suspend logic and reason, if not my better judgment, and operate with reckless abandon, on intuition alone.

Given their creative nature, idea-generating sessions are largely free-form, uninhibited discussions. The *only* rule for this type of session is to refrain from criticizing someone else's ideas, so as not to inhibit creativity. But if looks could kill, my first idea at these sessions was dead on arrival.

"Why don't we introduce a thick, hearty, sipping beer," I suggested to a group of eight managers and executives. Their deadpan expressions in response to my idea spoke volumes. "You know, it would be the sort of beer you'd drink out of a brandy snifter." Failing to elicit an arching of eyebrows, or even a nod of the head from anyone in my group, I took one last chance at this idea. "We could charge a lot for a sipping beer, something you could only drink a bottle at a time . . . it would have a lot of alcohol . . . it would be dark in color . . ." I finished, my voice trailing off as someone from the group moved on to another idea, the ultimate judgment on my first attempt at creativity.

Later during that first session, another of my "creative" ideas was so bad that it forced a member of The Force to break the golden rule of idea-generating sessions.

Having failed with the idea of a sipping beer, I decided to take another stab at displaying my creative prowess by suggesting that Coors develop a premixed, tomato juice/beer drink, dubbed a "Bloody Martha." *Come on, show you're one of the boys.* "Hey, beer drinkers like us already mix tomato juice with beer as a hangover cure. Why not legitimize the product?" *Good touch, especially the part about "beer drinkers like us." You're on a roll, kid. Now, show that you've been out in the field, pounding down beers with distributors.*

"Plus, this product would help us to compete against Bloody Marys. I was talking to a distributor in Minneapolis who said he'd love to have a share of the breakfast business. We'd be on store shelves right with the Bloody Mary mix." *Get ready for that promotion! Boy, this creative stuff is easy. Tomato beer doesn't taste very good, but it sure sounds creative.*

Unfortunately, as soon as I finished, a member of The Force from New York bellowed, "Man, that's a *stupid* idea."

"What?" I replied, in disbelief.

"I said that's a stupid fucking idea," he roared. "None of my distributors would buy that shit," he said, shaking his head.

"Hey, you're not supposed to criticize ideas," I retorted. "That's one of the ground rules." *Even though it* was *a really stupid idea. Wait a minute! Better repress that logical, analytical side of the brain. Don't think, just react, talk, say something macho.*

"You dumb ass," I continued. "Didn't you listen to the rules?"

"You candy-ass fucking number-crunchers," he responded. "All you do is bitch. Would you like to step outside to settle this?"

"Settle what? That you have no brains?" I responded. *Oh well, so much for being "one of the boys" on the inner circle. Didn't really want that promotion anyway. I just hope Coors doesn't spend any time researching the idea for "Bloody Martha"; consumers would skewer the idea.*

"Don't forget, if it wasn't for us sales guys, you marketing pussies wouldn't have jobs, and . . ." he droned on and on.

While the sales manager continued his diatribe, I couldn't help but notice that the professional facilitator we'd hire to run the meeting appeared to be taking notes on this argument. I chuckled, thinking of how this conversation would appear in the facilitator's final report.

I also suspended my blind ambition for a moment and remembered that it wasn't necessarily the source of the idea that was important in developing successful new products; it was the quality of the idea that mattered. (Or at least that's how I rationalized my lack of creativity at the idea-generating sessions.) This maxim became glaringly apparent over time.

Despite the early tension, the idea-generating session continued for two days. Ideas were systematically collected, and then handed over to Truitt, The General, and the Research Department for analysis. Our formal exploration of this new batch of product ideas began, according to Rod Sterling, "when The General got a burr up his ass." The burr was Coors Dark Beer.

During the Age of Imitation, many of the ideas for Coors weapons of mass destruction were generated by observing the competition. The General noted that Michelob Dark (A–B), Lowenbrau Dark (Miller), and a variety of imported dark beers were available throughout the United States. Though the idea of imitating the competition seemed relatively risk-free, closer examination of intelligence reports identified few opportunities for Coors in the dark-beer market.

Research collected by the Crunchers indicated that dark beers accounted for less than 3 percent of the beer sold in the United States, with sales having flattened out in 1984 and 1985. Plus, Coors was known for its lighter beers. A number of Crunchers and Marketeers at Coors were of the opinion that Coors would be deemed by beer drinkers the company *least likely* to produce a dark beer. With products like Guinness Stout, Michelob Dark, and Lowenbrau Dark already satisfying the demand for dark beer, why would Coors, brewers of "America's Fine Light Beer," want to enter the fray? After a few months, The General finally dropped this idea, apparently convinced by the overwhelming objections.

While scouting the front lines of the competition in The Beer Wars, The General also noticed that Coors was the only major brewer without a malt liquor product. While Colt 45, King Cobra, and Schlitz Malt Liquor dominated this market, The General decided to explore the opportunity for Coors to market a menthol-flavored malt liquor (an idea which had been raised during the idea-generating sessions).

Six million barrels of malt liquor were sold in the United States in 1985, a little more than 3 percent of the total beer industry. But it wasn't the size of the category that made malt liquor intriguing to Coors; it was the drinkers. Malt liquors were consumed primarily by young, urban, African-American males, who drank the high-alcohol products because, in the words of one drinker, it provided a "cheap buzz." After the flap about Bill Coors's alleged remarks in 1984 many African-Americans boycotted Coors products. A new malt liquor product could bring black beer drinkers back into the Coors fold. Or, as The General noted, "We [Coors] need the coons."

The concept of adding menthol, which smoothed out the bitter taste of malt liquors, was not new. Schlitz had experimented with a menthol beer in the late 1970s. Thus, this project became the perfect vehicle for The General to ingratiate himself with the Schlitz Mafia. He decided to proceed with Project Cool, commissioning focus groups to test consumer interest in the product idea. (The name of the project referred to the taste sensation caused by menthol flavoring.)

Focus groups were conducted with black malt-liquor drinkers in Chicago and Los Angeles. Focus group participants in Los Angeles were enthusiastic about a menthol-flavored product, and loved the taste of the "Cool Beer" sample served during the groups. As one drinker in Los Angeles noted, he would drink the Cool Beer because it would "keep his shit off the streets." (Presumably, this was a worthwhile civic benefit to the city of Los Angeles.) In Chicago, the reaction was much the same.

With several failures already under my belt, I was ecstatic that Coors had finally discovered a new-product idea that was (almost) unique (save for the dabbling by Schlitz in the 1970s), and popular with beer drinkers, too. The mood on our project team was so upbeat that we decided to celebrate after the focus groups with drinks at the famous Acorn on Oak Street bar, in Chicago.

There, The General entertained the bartender and our traveling party with his macho stance that the United States should attack Libya with nuclear bombs.[2]

"What about innocent children?" a Tate from Foote, Cone, and Belding wondered.

"Who cares?" The General slurred, emboldened by his first drink. "They'll all just little Khadafys, anyway. Let's just take care of this problem right now." This idiotic pronouncement was apparently provocative to at least one Chicagoan. Right after the words left The General's mouth, a lovely, long-in-the-tooth prostitute, all dressed up with no place to go, snuggled up to The General.

"I love you militaristic types," she cooed, desperately searching for business.

Shortly after we returned from Chicago, Project Cool, like Crystal Springs Cooler, was tabled. According to The General, engineers from the brewery had warned that menthol could contaminate Coors beer lines. Since Coors had only one brewery, this was deemed too risky by the High Command.

---

2 The week before the focus groups, the United States had conducted an air raid on Libya in which Colonel Muhammar Khadafy's adopted infant daughter was killed. Many Americans feared an immediate terrorist response in the United States.

"But if we can't brew it here, can't we brew it somewhere else?" Dewey wanted to know.

"We have higher priorities," The General countered. Plus, he informed the project team that "the Coors family would never approve us buying an existing brewery. It just wouldn't be up to the Coors standards."[3]

Other ideas, some as bad as Bloody Martha, surfaced, were briefly explored, and then quietly dismissed as quickly as they had arisen. No-alcohol beer? The company lacked the brewing capacity to produce it. An imported malt liquor? Low-income blacks couldn't afford it.[4] Want to brew a special beer in the spring of the year, named "Springfest"? Drinkers probably wouldn't buy an expensive beer at this time of year, concluded The General. Some of the ideas that we spent time and money exploring were downright strange, and probably deserved to die an early death.

In August 1987, Preacher and Captain Kangaroo asked me to conduct some research into the advisability of producing a "high-alcohol" beer, or "Hi-Test Coors Extra Gold." "I can see it now. We'll revolutionize the business . . ." Preacher had explained to me with evangelical fervor, at the start of one of his long sermons. What made this request strange was that it came at a time when alcoholic-beverage marketers were under increasing pressure to market their products more responsibly. To come out with a high-alcohol beer at a time when concerns over alcohol abuse were soaring was like waving a red flag in front of a charging bull.[5]

Fortunately, reaction from consumers in focus groups to this

3 Ironically, Coors purchased a brewery in Memphis from Stroh in 1990, disproving The General's theory about breweries meeting the Coors family's "standards."

4 Molson currently sells Brador, an imported malt liquor, in the United States.

5 G. Heileman Brewing Company was severely criticized by black activist groups and the Federal Trade Commission for marketing a high-alcohol malt liquor, Powermaster, in the spring of 1991.

idea was mixed at best. While some younger drinkers thought they could get a quick "buzz" from drinking a high-alcohol product, most beer drinkers felt that it would be bitter tasting. (In fact, they were right. A higher alcohol content *would* make the product more bitter tasting, according to the Coors taste experts that I talked to at that time.) Like many other brain-storms from the Schlitz Mafia, this concept quickly faded away.

And then there was "LeCoors." While dabbling at the pilot brewery, a few chemists discovered that Coors could concen-trate alcohol, a waste product in the brewing process, flavor it with natural or artificial flavors, and brew spirits, like vodka or scotch. But unlike distillers, who had to pay higher federal excise taxes on their product, "LeCoors," as we dubbed it, would be taxed at a much lower rate, as a malt (beer) product. In essence, Coors could make a synthetic scotch at a much lower cost than, say, Dewars.

The General convened a sample panel to taste an experi-mental batch of LeCoors, in every flavor from mint vodka to straight scotch. Since we weren't taste experts, there was no way to draw definitive conclusions from this test as to how good LeCoors actually tasted. In my opinion, the flavored liq-uors were passable, while the synthetic brown liquors were poor imitations of real scotch and bourbon. But the idea was intriguing.

Like other ideas, though, LeCoors died a quick death. Ac-cording to The General, the Coors family was dead-set against producing synthetic liquor products. Plus, "We don't have the distribution network for it," he reminded our new product-development team.

The strangest idea of all, though, had to be gay beer. In the fall of 1987, Captain Kangaroo passed along a request from someone in the Coors Community Relations Department to conduct exploratory research with gay beer drinkers. Gays, like most minority groups, refused to drink Coors because of the family's right-wing politics.

Alienating gay beer drinkers was, as noted in Chapter 8, bad business, as gays tended to drink more beer than the average beer drinker. Research also showed that, in stark contrast to prevailing gay stereotypes, most gays were avid drinkers of the very macho "king" of beers, Budweiser. (Perhaps gays were one of the 210 markets that August Busch's troops targeted, as noted in Chapter 7.)

My marching orders were to conduct focus groups with gay and lesbian beer drinkers, in order to search for marketing opportunities for Coors products. Captain Kangaroo told me that part of my assignment was to "see if we [Coors] could introduce a new beer for gays." How unique (and not at all patronizing).

We spent about thirty thousand dollars to conduct nine focus groups in San Francisco, New York, and Chicago, though we needn't have spent a dime. Most gays, according to the research, would never, *ever* drink Coors no matter what the company did to remedy past sins. One gay beer drinker told us matter-of-factly, "If they don't do anything in terms of marketing [to gays], I'll never drink Coors again, because of their politics. And if they did advertise the beer to gays, I'd feel it was some kind of insincere approach to take our money. Leopards don't change their spots."

In late fall of 1987, I presented my final report on Coors marketing opportunities in the gay community, and the report could be summed up in one word: "Not!" Gay Beer was the wrong beer, sponsored by the wrong company. In my mind, the project was over—that is, until newspapers began flooding into our offices, and it appeared that my career at Coors might be over, too.

"Coors Thinks Its Image Is Hopelessly Homophobic," screamed a headline in the *Windy City Times*, Chicago's leading gay newspaper. The article began.

An Adolph Coors Company marketing employee states that the company would be wasting time trying to convince the gay community in Chicago and two other major cities that it should drink Coors beer. A lengthy March 3 intracompany memorandum that was sent by a Coors marketing researcher, Bob Burgess, to John Meadows, Coors director of community relations, concluded that any attempt by Coors to change its negative image among gay people 'may exacerbate, rather than alleviate, gay opposition to the Coors company.' *The memo was released by a source that chose not to be identified.* (Emphasis added.)

Ginger, a Sales Training Department staffer whose cubicle bordered mine, told me, "I knew your big mouth would get you in trouble some day. You've really done it now."

Pepe, standing nearby, chimed in, "The day of reckoning is at hand. I always got the feeling you were different."

Cowboy, talking with Mumbles, reassured me that "the posse is sure going to be riding after you, pardner."

Mumbles agreed, I think, telling me, "You . . . know . . . they . . . fired . . . believe . . . what they said."

The Coors Marketing Department was aghast that I had (apparently) leaked my secret gay memo to the press. At the conservative Coors Brewing Company, leaking this memo was tantamount to a member of President Bush's Cabinet routing a top-secret memo to Baghdad. And the news wasn't just reported in Chicago, but in gay newspapers in San Francisco, Los Angeles, New York, and any other major city with a sizeable gay population. I was summoned to Captain Kangaroo's office for interrogation.

"Did you leak it?" he asked.

"No, of course not," I told him truthfully. "Why would I do that?"

"I don't know. Where else would they get it?"

"I'm telling the truth," I reemphasized to Kangaroo.

"Yeah, but maybe you developed some sympathy for them [gays] while doing research. Or maybe you just wanted to embarrass the company," he opined, searching to see if he was nearing the truth.

Knowing that I was being observed for any overt physical reaction, like squirming in my chair, I remained impassive. "You know that's not true. No one's worked harder for the company [than I]."

Just then, Pepe stuck his head into Captain Kangaroo's office, and asked, "Did he crack yet?"

As Captain Kangaroo shook his head and said "No," Pepe's face sunk, and he skulked out of the office, clearly disappointed.

"Okay, we'll investigate. Maybe we'll even take a look at your polygraph test, to see if you're one of them [that is gay]. And in the meantime, don't worry about your job. *At least not yet.*"

Not yet? Great. Not only do I have to worry about letter bombs, threatening phone calls, and vandalism at my house, once the Denver gay community gets wind of my report; now, on top of that, I have to worry about losing my job.

But I didn't. A few days after the papers were printed, a Coors sales representative admitted that he'd leaked the report. The leak had nothing to do with me. He thought he'd be creating good public relations in his area if he disclosed that Coors was working to smooth out its problems with the gay community. I applauded his *chutzpah,* especially since I kept my job. Gay beer, like most other new-product ideas Coors investigated, faded into the distance. (No word yet, on whether Captain Kangaroo has completed his investigation.)

One area where Coors *should* have been searching for opportunities was nonalcoholic beverages. In a memo that I sent to The General in March of 1987, I argued that Coors had to search for growth outside of the alcoholic beverage business because:

1. Nonalcoholic beverage sales were growing twice as fast as alcoholic beverage sales (1.3 percent annually versus 0.7 percent per year). Soft-drink sales alone had grown by over 4 percent per year in the 1980s, making soft drinks the single biggest beverage category in the world.

2. The number of eighteen-to-twenty-four-year-old males, traditionally the heaviest drinkers of beer, was shrinking. Nearly 18 percent of the U.S. population in 1970, this group of young adults was projected to make up just 13 percent of the U.S. population by 1990.

3. There was mounting evidence that alcoholic beverage consumption would decline for the foreseeable future:

- Drunk-driving laws were being toughened throughout the country.
- Aging Americans were concerned about the effect of alcohol consumption on their health.
- Groups like MADD (Mothers Against Drunk Driving) were continuing to exert pressure to make alcohol consumption uncouth and socially less acceptable.

My argument was buttressed by the marketing activities at Anheuser–Busch and Stroh, two of Coors major competitors. When they started looking outside of the beer business for growth, so did Coors (since this was the Age of Imitation).

When Anheuser–Busch purchased Saratoga Springs sparkling water and introduced Zeltzer Seltzer in 1987, Coors, according to the High Command, had no choice but to look more closely at the sparkling water business. Rain Man, in charge of new-products marketing after a management shake-up, agreed that, "Weeeee've . . . gooooooooottttttt . . . to start looking outside of the beer business. We want to see the forest through all the trees."

In the late 1970s, Perrier had turned water into a hot commodity, importing naturally sparkling water from underground springs in France into chic American cities like Palm Springs and Palm Beach. The bottled sparkling water was refreshing, and, served with lime, tasty. Perrier also became a status symbol for up-and-coming "Yuppies." After all, you needed some money, aspirations, and pedigree to *pay* for bottled water, when the rest of the country drew their water out of kitchen and bathroom faucets, for pennies a gallon.

The popularity of bottled sparkling water soared in the 1980s, as health-crazed, aging Baby Boomers consumed the refreshing, noncaloric beverage in record quantities. Domestic sparkling waters, including Calistoga and Crystal Geyser, which were less expensive than Perrier, entered the market, which helped spread the bottled sparkling water craze to middle-class Americans.

No company was better positioned to take advantage of this craze than Coors. For years, Coors had touted the purity and good taste of its Rocky Mountain spring water, claiming that the purity of its water contributed to the fresh, clean taste of Coors beer. Still, Coors was reluctant to "take the plunge" into the water business.

Rod Sterling, given the rank of brand development manager by the High Command, had been hired away from Gallo specifically to help Coors enter the sparkling-water business. The first time I met him, Sterling gushed that "this is going to be so easy. Can you imagine how lucky we [Coors] are to have this source of water in the Rockies? We're going to dominate this business. I mean *dominate.*" Months later, he wasn't quite so ebullient, having encountered significant resistance to Coors Sparkling Water within the company itself.

First, Bill Coors, the company's chairman and, according to Dewey, the "soul of the company," was fearful of running out of spring water. Bill wondered whether Coors would have enough money to brew beer *and* bottle sparkling water. Internal studies showed that the Coors spring water supply was plentiful, and that bottling a sparkling water product would pose no serious threat to it. Plus, Sterling pointed out that the company could always purchase additional sources of mountain spring water on Colorado's Western Slope (of the Rockies), if the existing water supply was ever seriously threatened.

A more serious obstacle was the lack of packaging capacity at the company's Golden plant. According to company engineers, Coors had the capacity to bottle approximately 17 million barrels of beer, and/or water, per year, in Golden. In 1986, the company sold 15.2 million barrels per year, and projected sales of 16.2 million for 1987. "There's no way we're going to run out of capacity," Rechholtz warned Sterling. "Water has to take a back seat to beer. Remember, beer is what made this company what it is today." Undaunted, the resourceful Sterling negotiated an agreement with Safeway's Denver bottling plant to bottle Coors spring water (that was trucked to the plant from Coors own springs).

A major dilemma for Coors was deciding which flavors of sparkling water to market. Most competitors, including Perrier, marketed lemon, lime, and orange-flavored water. The General's answer was to order Coors pilot brewery to mix up a batch of lemon-mint bottled water, for test marketing with sparkling-water drinkers.

"Can you believe that guy?" Sterling wondered. "What the hell is 'lemon-mint?' It sounds like a cough drop, or vapor rub."

"Ah want to offer something different," The General promised Rain Man in explaining this experiment with a new flavor.

The General commissioned a special research study, at a cost of eight thousand dollars, to test this inspiration. About one hundred bottled-water drinkers at several locations throughout the United States tested the lemon-mint concoction during a "sip" test (during which drinkers rate the beverage after one or two sips).

"It's different, all right," Sterling concluded when I shared the results of the sip test with him. "Different in the same way that shit-flavored water would be different." The sip study showed that lemon-mint sparkling water was the lowest-rated beverage Coors had ever tested.

After Rain Man saw the results of the study, he was succinct with The General. "Lemon-mint . . . lemon-mint . . . lemon-mint . . . Thaaat . . . woulddddd . . . sssseeeem . . . Presumably, the only way we're going to get people to drink this new flavor is shove it up their asses. You know, lemon-mint enemas." Lemon-mint, mercifully, was history.

Sterling commissioned state-of-the-art market research to resolve the flavor question, once and for all. This research (which I managed) showed that the same drinkers preferred lemon and lime, and used them interchangeably. If Coors wanted to maximize the appeal of its water line, it should sell only one citrus flavor, and a berry flavor, along with plain sparkling water. This would attract more drinkers overall than if Coors sold two citrus flavors.[6]

Unwittingly, *I* raised the issue that became the biggest obstacle to Coors finally entering the bottled-water business. It came to be known as the "Naked Lady Theory."

Our research had shown that American beverage drinkers believed that Coors source of water was unparalleled. A drinker in Boston had summed up this belief by saying, "The Rockies are the highest peaks on the continent. So water that comes from that high *has* to be the purest." Purity translated into a belief, or expectation, that the water was more refreshing than any other type of water, including Perrier.

This expectation didn't square with the research results from taste tests. About 80 percent of bottled water drinkers expressed some interest in trying Coors Sparkling Water, but, once they tasted the drink, they were less than awed. In nontechnical terms, the water was only "so-so," a major cause for concern. This reaction indicated that despite the expectation that water from fourteen thousand feet up in the Rockies would taste the best, it *wasn't* very different from other waters in terms of actual taste.

When I tried to sound the warning siren over this finding in a meeting with Sterling, The General, and Captain Kangaroo,

---

6 Pepsi introduced a new water in 1988, called H2OH!!, using this same flavoring mix. I often wondered if Pepsi had somehow obtained the results of the Coors research study, or merely conducted the same kind of study.

I was met with immediate resistance. "What the hell are you talking about?" The General said anxiously.

My mind raced. *This is an important research finding. If consumers ever find out that Coors water, by itself, isn't much better tasting than any other source of water, the entire Coors empire, including the beer business, could be in trouble. This is a secret weapon of mass destruction, all right, of mass self-destruction. But how can I explain this to The General?* Then, a light bulb clicked "on" in my head. *Explain the problem with an analogy, in a context The General can understand: either sex or bathroom humor.* I chose the former.

"Have you ever been to a strip club?" I asked The General.

"Of course I have, when I was in the army," he responded.

Yeah, probably last week. "Well, drinking Coors water plain is a little like looking at a naked woman."

"What the *fuck* are you talking about?" The General screamed.

"Well, sometimes a woman looks sexier when she has some clothes on than when she's totally naked," I continued. A faint smile creased The General's round, Wally Coxish face. Maybe this analogy *would* work. "Coors water is the same way. The mountain mystique works best when the water is mixed with hops and grain. When the lady is naked, or the water is plain, some of the sex appeal, or mystique, is taken away." I felt like a cross between Dr. Ruth and Louis Rukeyser.

"So if we cover the lady up with lingerie, to make her sexier, it's like adding flavoring to water. What I'm really saying is that if we ever sell the water by itself, we could be risking the credibility of the mountain mystique," I concluded. (Female readers should take note that the analogy works equally well using a naked man.)

"What do you call your theory, the 'Naked Lady Theory?'" Captain Kangaroo asked. He had clearly understood my analogy, and had christened it with a memorable name. For weeks in 1987, the Brand Development and Research Departments talked about little other than the Naked Lady Theory. A Tate from Foote, Cone, and Belding even titled a memo, "Agency Position on Naked Lady Theory." (I'm sure this pun was accidental!) As late as 1991, Rod Sterling told me that a Coors distributor in Illinois was *still* talking about the theory.

The theory took on a life of its own. The sexual nature of the name was somewhat regrettable (though hardly offensive at the macho Coors offices), but if it helped communicate the danger of this project to High Command, it was worth the shock value.

The theory didn't say that Coors should avoid the bottled sparkling water business. In fact, it proposed just the opposite. Given the mythical qualities that drinkers ascribed to Coors mountain water (maybe it even healed paralysis), Rod Sterling and I proposed that Coors should bring out a full line of beverage products containing Coors unique water, *as long as the water was always combined with flavoring, or other ingredients.* Coors Natural Soda. Coors Fruit Juice Sparkler. Coors Seltzer. We even tried to resuscitate Crystal Springs Cooler. "We could set up a whole separate subsidiary to handle these spring-water beverages," Sterling contended. To make our argument more compelling to High Command, we pointed out that Hershey's marketed their chocolate in much the same way. Chocolate bars. Chocolate milk. Chocolate syrup. All contained Hershey's special chocolate.

Sterling and I pointed out to High Command that mountain spring water could be Coors ultimate weapon of mass destruction. Anheuser–Busch's water wasn't special, since they brewed beer everywhere from Boston to Los Angeles, and points in between. The water used by Miller, Stroh, or even Heileman wasn't special either, according to consumers. Only Coors, nestled in the foothills of the Rockies, could lay claim to the purest, most refreshing source of water in the United States. Outside of the beer business, Sterling and I argued to High Command, Coors could attain some dominance over Anheuser–Busch and Miller. (How could Miller, with their standard, nothing-special water, introduce a natural soda? Or

Anheuser–Busch?) Besides, nonalcoholic beverage businesses were growing faster than the alcoholic beverage field. Maybe Coors was the *only* company that could survive the coming apocalypse in the beer business—and all because naked people are sometimes less sexy than partially clothed people.

High Command agreed, and granted the Brand Development and Market Research Departments the funding to explore the idea of a Coors line of spring-water beverages. Unfortunately, we never did have the opportunity to use this money, and Coors never did develop its secret weapons of mass destruction.[7] Though we didn't know it at the time, Coors was about to be blitzed.

7 Bucking the wisdom of the Naked Lady Theory, Coors eventually introduced Coors Sparkling Water, both with and without flavoring, into limited test markets in 1989. This product apparently failed, as predicted by the taste tests we had conducted in 1987, and was pulled from the marketplace in 1992.

10

"Nipples on the Long Necks"

Real difficulties can be overcome; it is the
imaginable ones that are unconquerable.

—*Theodore Vail*

Do you like what you see?"

Startled by a shrill, piercing voice, I quickly opened my eyes.
Then, as if to remind me that my dream was over, the voice
shrieked again.

"I'm asking, do you like what you see?' For a brief moment,
I mistook the voice for that of Jackie Gleason's oddball bartender, Crazy Gugenheim. But as I blinked, and looked around
the auditorium, with its brightly lit stage, ornate chandeliers,
plush theatre seats, and hundreds of cheering members of The
Force, my bearings returned. This was late fall of 1987, and I
was attending the Coors Annual Distributor Convention at the
Denver Center for the Performing Arts.

The man on stage was The Silver Fox, one of the Coors
marketing managers, an astute field-sales general who was
"generally" given credit for Coors Light's surging sales. After
each new commercial for Coors Extra Gold Draft, his newest

management project, he'd screech, "Do you like what you see?"

In response to his rhetorical question, Rod Sterling whispered in my ear, "Wouldn't you just love to scream out, 'No!'?"

"You bet. Coors Extra Gold *Draft?*" I answered. "Original Coors Draft? Young-adult advertising? What's happening to this company? How in hell did things get so messed up?" Before Sterling could answer, I closed my eyes again, hoping that I'd wake up to discover this strange convention was part of a dream, a fantasy sequence like the ones I'd watched on scores of TV shows over the years. . . . *This'll be like Bobby Ewing's "death" on "Dallas" . . . Dick Loudon's "Vermont Inn" on "Newhart" . . . Gilligan's stint as "Agent 014" on "Gilligan's Island". . . .*

But the TV dream sequences cascading through my mind were rudely interrupted by another cry of "Do you like what you see?" No, this wasn't a dream, but Coors plan for the decisive battle of The Beer Wars. Before this day was over, Coors distributors would learn that a new High Command was mapping Coors fighting strategies, and that Mark Harmon had been eliminated from the Coors marketing arsenal.

After World War II and the end of the Great Depression, stability in management became an integral part of the American business scene, and contributed to the biggest economic boom in history. Workers often joined management-training programs right out of college, and it wasn't uncommon for American managers to spend their long, lucrative management careers with a single firm.

Like many "golden rules" of American management, the concept of lifetime employment was itself retired in the 1980s. Top executives in search of their own personal "pot of gold" demanded slim payrolls, minimal investment in employee training, and immediate, bottom-line results from their managers. Employees were no longer regarded as human capital, but as an expense or commodity, to be added to or deleted from the ledgers at the whims of top management.

Herr Rechholtz, too, was a firm believer in the concept of job instability. His "kill or be killed" management philosophy demanded constant reshuffling within Coors management ranks in order to retain the loyalty of his generals and keep the troops in a constant state of battle readiness. As Rechholtz himself noted with a rather mixed metaphor, "A caged animal is the most dangerous fighter, and I want to lead an army of caged animals."

By 1987, wholesale changes in middle-management ranks at Coors were routine. One "Friday Night Massacre" in 1986 included the firing and demotion of eight marketing managers, including most of the Coors Sports Marketing Department. In 1987, many of the company's top sales managers were fired, demoted, or transferred. Most of the interoffice memos announcing these changes used the fateful line, "[Blank] has left his position as Marketing Manager, and will be pursuing other opportunities within the company." (Translated: The person is no longer wanted, but will be hanging around until he can find another job, or uses up his severance pay.)

The defections, demotions, and firings hit close to home, too. In the span of three years, I reported to four different managers, and the Market Research Department was headed by no less than four different directors. The Sales and Marketing softball team, which won the Coors Industrial League championship in 1986, had but four returning players in 1987. The others no longer worked in Golden.

The revolving door in the Marketing Department did have a bright side, though. During the summer and fall of 1987, there seemed to be a going-away luncheon nearly ever week, almost always at company expense. Most of the luncheons were held at the Morrison Inn, a quaint mountain restaurant famous for its menu of "101 Shot Drinks," ranging from the provocative "Sex on the Beach" to the intellectually stimulating "Vulcan

Mind Probe." As the pace of the farewell lunches picked up in 1987, Big Tim predicted, "At the rate we're having these lunches, we'll have sampled all hundred and one shots by the end of this year. That's the best fringe benefit of all."

Even the High Command, the most powerful officers in the Coors marketing military, weren't immune from management purges. Following the flap over The Cold War, Coors Banquet sales plunged nearly 8 percent in 1986. Sales of Herman Joseph's dropped by 25 percent in 1986, and sales of Killian's Ale were flat. With but one major growing brand, Coors Light (up 18 percent in 1986), Rechholtz took drastic action to shake up his staff and the troops.

The shakeup started when Big Wig resigned as vice president of sales in order to purchase a lucrative Coors beer distributorship in Utah. He bid the company adieu by bragging, "Sheet, I'm gonna make more greenbacks than you assholes [on The Force] have ever dreamed of before."

Rechholtz filled this breach with Gary Truitt, the tough-talking man of action who had risen to fame as manager of Schlitz Malt Liquor, but had achieved little as the Coors vice president of new products. Displeased with the decline of Coors Banquet and the flap over The Cold War, Rechholtz transferred Rain Man from Coors established brands to fill Truitt's shoes. Rechholtz then promoted Preacher, formerly the manager of Coors Banquet and a member of his inner circle, to vice president of marketing for the established beer brands, Coors Banquet and Coors Light. To complete his revamping of the High Command, Rechholtz also appointed Pepe, the director of Coors Pricing Department, to a newly created seat on the High Command.

At this same time, one more significant officer appointment was announced. The Silver Fox, a former member of The Force and the manager of the company's lone marketing success, Coors Light, was assigned the unenviable task of turning around Coors Extra Gold and Coors Banquet.

In theory, Rechholtz had built a command structure which would drive Coors toward Project Ten's infamous 10 percent market-share goal. A member of the Schlitz Mafia and trusted confidant (Truitt) ran the Sales Department. Another member of The Force and Schlitz alumnus, Preacher, held the reins on the company's established brands. With Pepe representing the Pricing Department on the High Command, the price-discounting strategy could be fully coordinated and enforced at the highest levels of the company. And if The Silver Fox worked the same magic on Coors Banquet as he had on Coors Light, the company's biggest marketing weakness would be eliminated.

In reality, the newly reorganized High Command was routed in its first major battle of The Beer Wars, in the fall of 1987. While plotting changes in Coors battle strategies, and keeping an ever-watchful eye on industry behemoth Budweiser, the new High Command allowed larcenous Miller Brewing to launch a sneak attack against Coors and steal the company's marketing crown jewels, a near repeat of 1975's ceding of the light-beer crown to Miller Lite.

While the radical management purge had been prompted, in part, by the dying Coors Banquet brand, Miller Brewing Company, too, had struggled with a dying premium brand, Miller High Life. High Life's "made the American Way" advertising campaign (which is detailed in Chapter 7) failed to halt the brand's declining annual sales (it was down 14 percent in both 1985 and 1986). Coors research showed that High Life was a staid, conservative beer, consumed primarily by aging, blue-collar drinkers. Unfortunately for Miller, these aging blue-collar drinkers, while loyal, consumed approximately one-third less beer than the average younger beer drinker (age twenty-one to twenty-four).[1] Deciding that it was foolish to try to capture the lucrative young-adult market with the hopelessly old-fashioned High Life, Miller tested a new product, Miller Genuine Draft, in 1985.

---

1 Alix M. Freedman, "Upstart Miller Brews Up Beer Market," *The Wall Street Journal*, October 5, 1988, p. B1.

Coors seemed unconcerned with the potential threat posed by Miller Genuine Draft, right up until the 1987 Distributor Convention. One night after work, I was summoned to Captain Kangaroo's office. Expecting another inquisition, like the flap over gay beer, I was surprised when I was assigned the task of flying to Los Angeles for top-secret focus groups.

"What are the focus groups about?" I asked Kangaroo.

"Draft beer," he responded.

"Isn't Cowboy handling the monitoring of Genuine Draft?" I asked, although I was somewhat interested in conducting research on the threat posed by that brew.

"Yeah. Well, this isn't about Genuine Draft. Budweiser has circulated a pamphlet in Los Angeles that rips draft beers. We want to find out if this could hurt us."

"But we're not a draft beer," I stammered, a little confused.

"Yeah, but we're brewed the same way that Genuine Draft is, and if Bud blasts draft beers, or cold filtration, we need to know how dangerous this pamphlet is. It could turn into an ad," he reasoned. "Besides, we just can't afford to give up any more ground to Budweiser."

While the Budweiser threat was omnipresent, Miller Genuine Draft ads had targeted not only younger beer drinkers, but Coors Banquet drinkers, as well. Miller spent millions to convince consumers that Genuine Draft was a cold-filtered, smooth-tasting draft beer that was packaged in bottles (what Miller referred to as "bottled draft beer," which has always seemed an oxymoron to me). Miller also claimed that its cold-filtration brewing process produced a beer superior in taste to heat-pasteurized beers. (Heat pasteurization is the method used to brew Budweiser, Stroh, and Miller's own High Life).

Not surprisingly, the ads for Miller Genuine Draft failed to point out that one other premium beer was cold-filtered: *Coors Banquet*. Though Coors had used the cold-filtration brewing process for more than twenty-five years (remember The Cold War), Miller Genuine Draft was spending millions to become known as "the" cold-filtered draft beer, as Lite has become America's premier light beer.

Though Coors touted its cold-filtration brewing process in the Mark Harmon ads, the company had never called Banquet a "draft" beer. Thus, when millions of American beer drinkers tasted cold-filtered draft beer for the first time (at least in their own minds), sales of Genuine Draft skyrocketed, from just 70,000 barrels in 1985 to 1.5 million in 1986, and to almost 3 million barrels in 1987. Flush with success, Miller introduced another draft product, Miller Genuine Draft Light. Analysts at Stroh, quoted in *The Wall Street Journal,* attributed Miller's success with draft beer to its appeal with younger males, under the age of twenty-five.[2]

Incredibly, Coors didn't respond to Genuine Draft's threat with a new batch of Mark Harmon ads, or ads touting *Coors* as "the" preeminent draft beer. Instead, Coors responded to the new challenge on the premium beer front with: silence.

Though Harmon had brought prestige, credibility, and, for a short time, increased sales to Coors, Preacher announced that "We want to take Coors Banquet in a new creative direction." Foote, Cone, and Belding, the brand's advertising agency, was replaced by GSD & M, a relatively small and unknown agency, based in Austin, Texas. During most of the last half of 1987, while Miller Genuine Draft cemented its hold on the young-adult market, Preacher, The Silver Fox, and the new Coors ad agency worked to develop another advertising theme for moribund Coors Banquet.

Thet termination of Harmon as the Coors spokesperson crushed morale among Coors marketing troops. "Why would they get rid of Harmon," Big Tim wondered, "when he's the only good thing we had going for us?" Cowboy noted, ruefully, "We lost ourselves a gunslinger, all right."

Sterling guessed that assigned new tasks, many of the Coors

2 Ibid.

officers felt pressured to "make their mark" by initiating a radical change to the company's marketing programs. "I didn't get appointed to stand still," Preacher reminded his staff, in announcing the switch from the Harmon campaign. Even anointed saviors, like The Silver Fox, felt compelled to justify Rechholtz's confidence in their marketing abilities.

After ignoring Miller Genuine Draft for the better part of two years, and then watching with dismay as Genuine Draft trounced Coors Banquet in the young-adult market, one of The Marketeers conceded that "Genuine Draft is admittedly a success story in a few selected markets."[3]

Indeed, the new commanders on the premium beer front finally decided that instead of ignoring Miller Genuine Draft, Coors Banquet would copy it. In December of 1987, Coors introduced its new advertising campaign, "The American Original," which touted Coors Banquet as a cold-filtered draft beer. Coors Brewing Company President Pete Coors announced that Coors was capitalizing on consumers' new awareness of draft beer, and "It's helpful to be able to ride on Miller's media exposure."[4]

"Do you like what you see?"

The thousands of Coors employees and distributors in attendance at the 1987 Distributor Convention were the first audience to preview the "American Original" advertising campaign. The new Coors Banquet advertising was a radical departure from the conservative, product-oriented Harmon ads; instead, the new campaign featured what Marketeers liked to call, for obvious reasons, "T & A" advertising. The "American Original" campaign featured young, active beer drinkers, partying to loud, raucous, rock 'n' roll music. Coors Banquet was

3 Ibid.

4 Marj Charlier, "Coors Beer Gets New Look as It Tries to Ride Coattails of Other Draft Beers," *The Wall Street Journal,* August 2, 1988, p. 27.

now targeted at the same young-adult market which Miller Genuine Draft seemed to own.

"Loud music, quick scene cuts, partying, work reward . . . this looks just like any other beer commercial," Sterling commented, as we sat in our plush theatre seats in the raucous auditorium at the 1987 convention.

"So much for Coors being 'the one,' or whatever Harmon used to say," I added. "These ads could be for any other major premium beer. Cross out 'Coors' and write in 'Bud' and no-body'd know the difference. Who's going to remember this?"

"That's not even Coors audience," Sterling continued. "We're the white-collar, upscale, Yuppie-type beer. Not a teen-agers' beer."

Big Tim added, "If we go any younger with our target [audience for the ads] we'll have to put nipples on the long-neck [beer] bottles."

If the young-adult segment had been a park bench, it was terribly overcrowded by January 1988, when the "American Original" ads debuted. In addition to the chic, clear-bottled Miller Genuine Draft, Budweiser was using the now-world-famous Spuds MacKenzie, the ultimate party animal, in humorous, young-adult ads for the "King of Beers." *The Wall Street Journal* had noted in August 1987 that Schlitz and Pabst had developed ads specifically to appeal to young adults.[5] By the time Coors "American Original" Banquet arrived, young-adult beer drinkers were already dazed, confused, and spoken for (in terms of beer preferences, that is).

The decision to target Coors Banquet at young adults was also curious given population projections. Dewey, a beer-industry historian, had warned as early as 1985 that the number of young adults in the United States, ages eighteen to twenty-

5 Ronald Alsop, "Two Once Popular Brews Woo a New Generation of Beer Drinkers," *The Wall Street Journal,* July 23, 1987, p. 33.

four, was shrinking drastically. According to Dewey, there were 30 million eighteen to twenty-four-year-olds in 1984, comprising 17.2 percent of the U.S. population. The Census Bureau predicted that this market segment would shrink substantially by 1989, and dwindle even further by 1994. (See Chart 10-1.)

More significantly, the twenty-five to forty-four-year-old segment, traditionally the heaviest Coors drinkers, was projected to *grow* substantially, by 12 million Americans, over the same ten-year period. The middle-aged segment, even without the projected growth, was already more than twice as large as the young-adult segment.

I first caught wind of Coors Banquet's young-adult strategy

CHART 10-1

Population Projections

YOUNG-ADULT SEGMENT (18–24-YEAR-OLDS)	U.S. POPULATION (IN MILLIONS)	% OF U.S. TOTAL POPULATION
1984	29.7	17.2
1989	27.1	14.6
1994	25.1	12.9
STANDARD ADULT SEGMENT (25–44-YEAR-OLDS)		
1984	71.0	41.0
1989	80.5	43.4
1994	84.0	43.2

Source: U.S. Census Bureau

from Valley Girl, a novice market researcher hired by Coors in 1986, and assigned to the company's flagship brand less than one year later. Valley Girl, though energetic and enthusiastic, was known for her somewhat careless presentation of statistics. In her first major presentation, she responded to repeated questions about columns of percentages not adding up to one hundred with the phrase, "Oh, okay, let's move on."

"Look at these numbers," I said to Valley Girl a few months later, relating my concerns about a young-adult marketing program based on the Census Bureau projections.

"Oh, that's, like, pretty interesting. But did you know that, like, young adults consume about fifty percent more beer, on average, than the twenty-five to forty-four-year-olds?" she countered.

"Yeah, that's true, but there are more than twice as many twenty-five to forty-four-year-olds as young adults. Even though they drink less, on a per person basis, than young adults, they drink more overall as a segment, because there are so many more twenty-five to forty-four-year-olds. If you do the math, you'll see that twenty-five to forty-four-year-olds consume about fifty percent more beer overall than your vaunted young adults," I asserted.

"You're so hung up on numbers, ya know. Young adults are, like, trend-setters. If we can get them to drink Coors, it'll start a trend, like, everyone will want to drink Coors."

This assertion probably wasn't true, either. Baby Boomers were, and are, famous for starting their *own* trends. It wasn't, like, Baby Boomers would start, like, talking like Valley Girls, just because, like, young adults spoke that way. Or that forty-year-olds would suddenly wake up with a yearning for Coors Banquet, just because college students were slamming it down.

Which is not to say that Coors should have neglected the young-adult segment. In a 1992 magazine article, Bill Coors acknowledged that, "I think we [Coors] lost a generation [of consumers]. We're still in the process of trying to repair that damage."[6] Marketing to young adults was necessary for growth, but not to the exclusion of the traditional, more mature Coors audience.

The young-adult focus was compounded by the High Command's decision to change the can design and brand name of Coors Banquet, eight months *after* the start of the "American Original" campaign. Until 1987, Coors Banquet was the company's best-selling product, peaking as the fourth-best-selling beer in America in early 1983. But Coors continued to tamper with tradition by changing the company's traditional can color from golden to almond, and the product's name from "Coors Banquet" to "Coors Original Draft."

But at least the can didn't feature an upside-down waterfall. In the process of testing new can designs, Valley Girl showed the Market Research Department prototypes (simulated can designs) created by the Coors Creative Services Department for the new Coors Original Draft's beer can.

"Missy," Cowboy interrupted after seeing the first prototype, "you've got a problem."

"Like, how? They're just prototypes for testing," Valley Girl responded, with nary a hint of concern.

"Well, one of your waterfalls is flowing *uphill*. I've never seen that happen out on the range."

Four months after the new can and brand name debuted, they were judged a flop in Southern California, the company's largest beer market. Coors oldest and most loyal customers rejected the new product targeted at young adults, fearing that the taste of the beer had changed, too. The sales manager in Southern California noted, "We tried hard to convince them [consumers] it was the same product, and they'd say, 'Oh no it isn't.' "[7] The traditional golden can, and "Coors Banquet"

---

6 Jeffrey Leib, "Straight Talk," *Contemporary*, January 5, 1992, p. 13.

7 Marj Charlier, "Beer Drinkers in Texas, California Don't Swallow Changes in Coors Label," *The Wall Street Journal*, December 29, 1988, p. B4.

brand name, were reintroduced into both Southern California and El Paso, Texas, in late December 1988.

Far from solving Coors Banquet's problems, the new campaign, brand name, and focus on young adults predictably accelerated Coors Banquet's decline. From a marketing perspective, trying to cash in on—rather than quash—Miller Genuine Draft's success was disastrous. Instead of responding to Genuine Draft with hard-hitting ads claiming that Coors Banquet was the *real* (or genuine) draft beer, and had been for more than twenty-five years, Coors tepid claim of being an "original" was shrouded in ads featuring loud music and young-adult beer parties, a new beer can, and a new brand name. To many beer drinkers, Coors, which had made radical changes in response to Genuine Draft, seemed like the imitator trying to cash in on a craze; in reality, Miller Genuine Draft had been the imitator.

The radical switch from Mark Harmon's product-oriented ads to more traditional "beer and bikini" ads also alienated many of Coors Banquet's remaining drinkers. Female beer drinkers, estimated at 10 to 20 percent of the Coors market, complained loudly about Harmon's removal from the airwaves.[8] The new, stereotypical beer ads said very little about why Coors beers were different from other beers, and, in fact, made Coors look much the same as any other beer, especially Miller Genuine Draft. In effect, Coors no longer stood out from the crowd of beer marketers pitching beer and good times.

Coors Original Draft's targeting of young adults was disastrous, too. By the late 1980s, most of the fifty states, reflecting societal concern over alcohol abuse, had raised the legal drinking age back to twenty-one. This further reduced the size of Coors Original Draft's new target market, to much less than

---

8 According to "A Demographic Profile of the Beer Market," a research study conducted by Coors researchers Paul Petersky and Sally Rivera, released on May 15, 1986.

half as large as the twenty-five to forty-four-year-old segment which Coors Banquet had once owned.

"Do you like what you see?"

As the large screen brightened the auditorium with new television advertisements for Coors Light, Rod Sterling mused, "Coors Light is what Coors Banquet used to be."

Big Tim agreed, shouting over the loud commercials, "Yeah, a smoother, lighter beer, just like Banquet used to be."

"So why do we have both beers?" Sterling asked rhetorically.

"Yeah, the world doesn't need two lighter-tasting beers," I added.

"Why don't we change the taste of Coors Banquet, then? We're not getting outsold by Bud just because of advertising," noted Big Tim. "We always change Banquet's advertising, but we never change the product," he finished in a soft whisper, as if talking to himself.

Americans decried their country's lack of industrial competitiveness in the late 1980s and early 1990s. Leveraged buyouts, merger mania, management perks, declining worker productivity, and soaring health-care costs during the Gilded Age of the 1980s forced debt-plagued American companies, which had once invested resources to produce the world's highest-quality goods, to churn out overpriced, shoddy products. Madison Avenue marketing contributed to this malaise with a battery of gimmicks, including provocative advertising, coupons, promotions, and rebates, which were used to seduce (or bribe) consumers into buying the low-quality goods (at least for a time).

Following this national trend, Coors Original Draft in 1991 was rechristened "Original Coors" (no longer a draft beer), and touted in another new series of ads which called it a "Rocky

Mountain Legend." Despite these revisions, Coors sold just 3.5 million barrels of Original Coors in 1991, 67 percent less than Coors Banquet's 1983 peak level of sales. Once the country's fourth-best-selling beer, Coors accounted for less than 2 percent of the American beer industry in 1991.[9] Ironically, Coors didn't significantly improve the quality of its Banquet/Original Draft/Original Coors beer during the course of The Beer Wars.

Even in Banquet's best sales years, Budweiser sold four times more beer. By 1987, when High Command decided to revamp Banquet's marketing program, the margin was six to one. Yet, the company clung to the belief that Coors Banquet was a superior product to Budweiser.

"Why should we change the taste," Valley Girl told me, when "taste tests show Original Draft [Banquet] is at least as good, if not better than Budweiser? We already make a great beer. All we need is the right marketing program to get young adults to try it, and see how good it really is." I wondered, were consumers really drinking inferior-tasting Budweiser, year after year, simply because of its marketing program, or the design of its cans?

While Valley Girl's viewpoint reflected the company line, she and the rest of Central Command ignored the ongoing success story of Coors Light. From 1983 through 1987, sales of Coors Light nearly doubled, because of its taste. According to Coors own taste tests, Coors light was the best-tasting light beer on a "blind" basis—smoother, more refreshing, and easier to drink than Bud Light or Miller Lite. Plus, Coors Light wasn't watered-down beer; it had more alcohol than Bud Light.

Yet, research also showed that many consumers couldn't recall, or didn't like, Coors Light's "Silver Bullet Bar" TV advertising. Others were confused, and thought Mark Harmon was Coors Light's spokesperson. The quality of the beer, not

9 These sales estimates first appeared in *Advertising Age* magazine, which cited *IMPACT* magazine as its source, on February 17, 1992.

its marketing campaign, fueled Coors Light's spectacular growth at the expense of Miller Lite.[10]

"Do you like what you see?"

"Can you believe this?" Sterling asked in amazement as the 1987 Distributor Convention was winding down. "Herman Joseph's is now 'Herman Joseph's Original Draft Light'? Is that a world record for longest brand name in history?"

"Well, at least Chuck Yeager isn't up there talking about relieving himself in his flight suit this year," I noted, searching for a bright spot.

"What I don't understand is, how can both Herman Joseph's and Coors Banquet be the 'original' drafts?" interjected Big Tim, quickly muting my bright spot. "How can they both be original?"

Big Tim then answered his own question, claiming that the High Command's new strategy appeared to be "harmonic convergence marketing."

"What the hell does that mean?" I asked.

"All of our marketing campaigns seem to converge at the same point. Every one of them is a 'draft' beer," Tim noted.

"No, every one of them is targeted at young adults," Sterling countered.

They were both right.

The "harmonic convergence" at young-adult draft beers was attributable, in part, to the fact that Coors new commanders,

---

10 Sales of light beer in the United States grew 37 percent between 1983 and 1987, about triple the growth rate of Miller Lite during this same period (11 percent). In contrast, sales of Coors Light during this five-year period grew 108 percent, triple the total industry growth. The logical conclusion, given that Miller Lite far underperformed the industry, while Coors Light outperformed the industry in the 1980s, is that Coors Light grew at the expense of Miller Lite.

mostly veterans of The Force (Coors Marines), weren't marketing strategists, but salesmen. Most of the new commanders, front-line veterans of The Beer Wars, were trench fighters, not officers versed in planning grand battle strategies. It wasn't surprising, then, that the focus of the Coors marketing army after the management purges wasn't advertising, or product development, but sales—especially when the beer was sold at a discount.

Everyone on the High Command, except Rain Man, was a former member of The Force. One rung below the High Command in the corporate hierarchy, half of the company's brand managers (with day-to-day responsibilty for marketing management) were former members of The Force. Departments such as Sales Forecasting, Distributor Economics, Pricing, Training, Sales Promotion, and even Sports Marketing were also havens for The Force after the 1987 management upheaval.

These new officers measured success in The Beer Wars by current sales, as Marines measure success by territory won or lost in battle. Advertising campaigns, which could boost sales down the road, were almost extraneous to the marketing war conducted by these new officers. The real marketing battles, which boosted sales this week, or this quarter, were over pricing.

The Force's Doctrine of Discounting thrived with the new High Command. The average price of a barrel of Coors beer sold in 1987 was $62.61, up marginally from 1986, but still almost one dollar below the 1985 level. These discounts helped prop up Coors sales by providing beer drinkers with an incentive to keep drinking Coors, regardless of whether the new brand names and advertising proved popular. Unfortunately, gaining or keeping territory (market share) in The Beer Wars through discounting came at a steep price. If Coors prices had been held at their 1985 levels, the company would have reaped from $5 million to $15 million more in profits in 1987 alone.

To these new officers, countering Miller Genuine Draft with Coors own draft beers may have seemed like an obvious (even the only) battle plan. Coors Original Draft and Herman Joseph's Original Draft Light, in theory, would slow the growth of Miller Genuine Draft with young adults, and earn Coors a share of the burgeoning draft beer business. Or, as The Silver Fox told Sterling during a softball game, "How else could we respond to Miller? Besides, what the hell do we have to lose?"

"Do you like what you see?"

"I don't think it's 'harmonic convergence marketing.' I think it's 'me too' marketing," Sterling commented.

"Coors Extra Gold is a draft beer, too?" I asked rhetorically after seeing new ads introduced by The Silver Fox. Unwittingly, I had just backed up Sterling's contention.

"Yeah, I think The Silver Fox wanted to enter the most-confusing-brand-name contest against Herman Joseph's Original Draft Light," Sterling replied.

"He might win," Big Tim added. "Extra Gold used to be a heartier version of Coors. What's Extra Gold Draft? Extra heavy draft beer? A darker draft beer? A gold draft beer? By the way, what's 'me too' marketing?" Tim asked.

"You know, copycat marketing," Sterling responded. "If imitation is the sincerest form of flattery, then Miller's going to be real flattered after today."

"Me too" marketing, whereby Coors simply mimicked competitors' successful marketing strategies, thrived after the management purges of 1986 and 1987. For the macho Force, "me too" strategies sparked a feeling that Coors was fighting back. "We're giving as good as we're getting," Bash, a sales manager, told me when I questioned the wisdom of Coors Original Draft.

Lacking the training and perspective for mapping battle strategies, Coors sales-oriented officers often had no other choice but to study the enemy for inspiration (as noted in Chapter 9).

America's Age of Imitation also fueled "me too" marketing at Coors.[11] Imitating enemy successes rarely generated big profits for the imitator (as in the case of Coors Original Draft), since the "if we can't beat 'em, let's join 'em" strategies were defensive in nature, initiated in response to competitors' forays. However, to the manager chasing sales gains, adopting a "me too" strategy was tantamount to purchasing an insurance policy. "Me too" strategies were *proven* strategies, as imitators figured that if a marketing strategy worked for a competitor, it was bound to work for their product, too (though usually not as well as it had for the competitor, who had initiated the strategy).

"Me too" strategies also helped to mute, counter, and limit competitors' successes. Sales at Anheuser–Busch, already five times larger than Coors, were growing 5 percent per year, and Miller had posted sales gains in both 1986 and 1987. Thus, when Budweiser introduced a popular Dracula character for their Halloween promotion, Coors created a character that Preacher proudly dubbed the "Beerwolf."[12] And when Miller introduced Genuine Draft, Coors responded not with one draft beer, but three.

Coors Extra Gold, introduced in 1985, was originally marketed as the Coors answer to Budweiser. Acknowledging that Banquet was smoother and lighter-tasting than Budweiser (perhaps too smooth to suit Bud drinkers), Coors Extra Gold was a darker, heartier-tasting Coors beer.

In military terms, the introduction of Coors Extra Gold was a flanking maneuver. Instead of attacking Budweiser head-on with Banquet, which many Bud drinkers said was weak and

11 The Age of Imitation, as noted in Chapter 9, refers to a stretch in the 1980s and 1990s when many American companies chose to imitate other companies' successes, rather than innovate with new products and new marketing strategies.

12 Oddly, the Beerwolf was also used during Coors Light's St. Patrick's Days promotions, despite the fact that he was a frightening Halloween character, and presumably, was Transylvanian, not Irish.

watery-tasting, Coors attempted to steal share from Bud using the new, heartier Extra Gold. Befitting its status as a macho, full-bodied beer, the product was promoted with humorous ads depicting feats of brute strength by Extra Gold's drinkers.

Though sales of Coors Extra Gold increased by 150 percent in 1986, The Silver Fox decided to stop attacking Budweiser, and turn the Extra Gold artillery on the pesky new threat, Miller Genuine Draft. Like Coors Banquet, Coors Extra Gold was re-christened "Coors Extra Gold Draft," and ads targeted at young adults celebrated the beer's smooth draft taste, not its heartier, full-bodied taste. Unfortunately, this change in battle plans once again left the "King," Budweiser, unopposed in its quest for premium beer supremacy.

Predictably, the image change also confused beer drinkers. Was Coors Extra Gold a macho, full-bodied beer like Budweiser, or a smooth-tasting draft beer? Were Extra Gold drinkers macho, middle-aged males, or frolicking young adults? And what *did* the brand name mean? Despite expanded distribution (nationally) by the end of the 1980s, sales of Extra Gold peaked at just 1 million barrels per year, far below the 4 million barrels of Miller Genuine Draft sold annually, and a mere drop in the ocean compared to Budweiser's 50 million barrels in sales.[13]

In 1991, at about the same time that Original Draft became Original Coors, Coors scrapped Extra Gold's draft beer campaign. Extra Gold went back to the future, with new ads touting Extra Gold's superior taste compared to Budweiser's (in consumer taste tests). The Coors artillery had been shifted back to shelling Budweiser, perhaps too late, and judging by Extra Gold's dismal sales, certainly with too little firepower.

When Coors finally retreated from the draft beer battlefield (Herman Joseph's was finally pulled from the marketplace in 1990), a three-time loser, Miller Genuine Draft was officially declared the victor in the Draft Beer Wars.

13 According to Coors *1990 Annual Report*.

* * *

"Do you like what you see?"

"At least they haven't done anything to ruin Killian's yet," Big Tim noted with a slight sigh, as the parade of draft beer commercials targeted at young adults continued.

"Yet," I noted, as a reminder, if not a warning.

While most of the High Command's new battle strategies centered around product names and advertising campaigns, changes to the battle plan for Killian's Irish Red Ale focused on the beer itself. Unfortunately, these changes were driven by the company's dismal financial fortunes, not customer tastes and preferences.

Killian's Irish Red Ale was a relatively small product in the Coors marketing arsenal, accounting for less than 1 percent of the company's total sales. As a full-bodied, reddish-brown ale, Killian's was considered a "specialty" beer, too expensive for everyday use, but unusual enough to offer an occasional change of pace to American beer drinkers.

Brewed in Golden under a licensing agreement, the Irish product was advertised using the slogan, "Killian's Red Instead," a reference to its specialty status and supposedly unique taste. (Inside the company, this slogan was referred to as "Better Red Than Dead," a satirical send-up of the Coors family's notorious hatred of Communists.) Sales of Killian's peaked in 1985, and then leveled off at approximately one hundred thousand barrels annually, though it remained popular with Coors distributors and avid beer drinkers.

But because Killian's sold only one hundred thousand barrels of beer per year, Coors cleared little, if any profit, on the product. In 1988, the product's new management team—Igor, of Colorado Chiller fame, and Cue Ball—attempted to fatten Killian's profit margins. "If we just change it from an ale to a lager, and lower the alcohol content, we could make a lot more money,"

Igor told Sybil, an intern in the Market Research Department. "Drinkers won't know the difference. It will still be called Killian's, and it will still be red. It just won't have as much alcohol," he added. Accordingly, the name of the product was officially shortened to "Killian's Red."

To prove Igor's point, the Market Research Department conducted a taste test between Heineken, Corona, and the new Killian's Red lager. Based on test results, Cue Ball and Igor spent their entire 1988 advertising budget purchasing ads in *Time, Sports Illustrated,* and *People* magazines touting that American beer drinkers really *did* prefer Killian's Red (lager) instead of imported beers.

Unfortunately, after the ads started running, the Research Department intern received a phone call from the testing company which had conducted the research. A principal in the research company informed Sybil, the intern, that he had some "bad news. The test results are off slightly."

"Oh, that's okay, as long as it's not significant."

"Uh, Sybil, it is significant. The test is wrong."

"What do you mean 'wrong'?" Sybil screamed.

"Well, drinkers really don't prefer the taste of Killian's, on a statistical basis," he calmly noted. "We made a mistake in our calculations."

"Oh, is that all," Sybil mocked, almost frantically. "Do you know that we just started running ads this week based on that test?"

"I know," the research company president replied meekly. "But look at the bright side. Killian's is such an insignificant product, that no one will challenge the claim."

He was right. Killian's was so small and insignificant that the Federal Trade Commission, and Heineken and Corona, were uninterested in challenging the deceptive advertisement. With such a modest advertising budget, the ads quickly disappeared, and the claim that had no basis in fact disappeared, too. Unfortunately, the change to a lower-alcohol lager beer stayed, an acknowledgment of the sovereignty of the bottom line and the fading importance of Coors customers.

"Do you like what you see?"

"Hey, wake up, someone might see you," Sterling whispered as he jostled me from my TV sitcom dreams.

As I watched ebullient members of The Force march out of the auditorium after the Distributor Convention, I asked, already knowing the answer, "You mean this isn't a dream?"

"No, it's just the beginning of a long nightmare, for all of us," Sterling responded, without smiling.

11

Keystone Cop-Out

If you can keep your head, when all about you
are losing theirs . . . then yours is the earth and
everything that's in it.

— *From Rudyard Kipling's* **If**

The air in the conference room
on this early spring day in 1988 was thick, almost stale, with
equal parts anticipation and perspiration.

I looked up from my briefing papers, across the conference
table, at a row of seemingly interchangeable Tates from Foote,
Cone, and Belding. Well-dressed, neatly groomed, with affable,
if not vacant smiles, the Tates differed only in the hues of their
complexions and blow-dried hair. At the end of the Tate side
of the conference table, the billowy white thatch of Big Tate
bore silent, though stunning, testimony to his senior status at
the advertising agency.

To my immediate left, marketing commanders from Coors
had assumed their standard adversarial position, across the table
from and staring eye to eye at the Tates. Slouched over his
briefcase, with his droopy moustache, unstarched shirt, and
sloppy khaki pants, The General sat in vivid contrast to the

neat, buttoned-down, almost regal presence of Herr Rechholtz. Next to Rechholtz, Rain Man stared at the ceiling, apparently in one of his autistic trances. Next to me, Captain Kangaroo, with his thick gray bangs, but absent a "Treasure House" suit jacket (red, with white outline stitching on the pockets and wide lapels), hurriedly studied the management summary of a recent research report.

"Let's take a look," boomed Herr Rechholtz in his deep, TV announcer's baritone, instantly calling the meeting to order and snapping Rain Man out of his trance.

As if on cue, one of the young Tates from Foote, Cone, and Belding stood and began lining large, square boards featuring mock advertisements along the conference room wall, just as Big Tate, with a used-car salesman's grin, promised, "Bob, I think you're really going to love what you see."

Without acknowledging Big Tate's pitch line, Herr Rechholtz, Rain Man, and The General began perusing these concepts, or mock ads, for a new Coors beer product. Big Tate, in turn, kept an eye on the Coors commanders, analyzing their reaction to the advertising agency's work. And I, at the other end of the conference table, watched the drama between Coors and its agency unfold.

As the Coors commanders silently sized up the advertisements, Big Tate attempted to diffuse the tension by claiming awkwardly, and with a nervous laugh, "Boy, you can cut the tension in this room with a knife."

The tension in the stark conference room, on the fifth floor of Snob Hill, the Coors Command Center in Golden, was understandable. For Foote, Cone, and Belding, winning the account for this new beer product would be worth millions of dollars in advertising commissions, and help salve wounds opened by Coors sudden firing of both Mark Harmon and the agency when Coors turned Banquet into Original Draft. (As noted in Chapter 10, GSD & M of Austin, Texas, was awarded the Coors Banquet/Original Draft account.)

For the High Command, the tension was no less palpable.

As Rod Sterling had predicted at the end of the 1987 Distributor Convention, the nightmare was really just beginning at Coors in 1988, as it was for many American companies.

Since the beginning of the Gilded Age, scores of American businesses had been managed to increase profits and bonuses in the short term, with little regard for the long-term consequences of the "glory through greed" style of management. A leveraged buyout which made Macy's managers and shareholders rich in the 1980s had bankrupted the company by 1991. Years of labor strife, price discounting, and shoddy service due to cost cutting bankrupted Continental Airlines in 1991, for the second time in a decade. And the looting by Don Dixon of Vernon Savings as well as the failure of hundreds of other S & Ls across the country cost the federal government billions in bailout money.[1] These companies were but the tip of the mismanagement iceberg of organizations plundered by executives seeking instant gratification.

Coors, like many other companies in the 1980s, had been managed as if there would be no tomorrow. Mired in a quest for the pursuit of growth at any cost (which also plagued the S & L industry), Coors hadn't invested in new products, had discounted the price of beer in order to increase sales, compromised quality to fatten the bottom line, and had made a dramatic jump onto the draft beer bandwagon, despite fears that draft beer was nothing more than a passing fad. Then, in 1988, tomorrow finally arrived at Coors.

By 1988, Coors financial health was failing. Years of discounting Coors beer products, combined with the cost of marketing Coors on a nationwide basis, had gradually eroded profits. In 1983, Herr Rechholtz's first year on the Coors Board of Directors, Coors had netted over $89 million in profits on sales of $1.1 billion, a respectable 11 percent return on share-

---

1 The story of Vernon Savings & Loan is covered in the book *Daisy Chain: The Tale of Big, Bad Don Dixon and the Looting of a Texas S & L,* by Don O'Shea, which was published by Pocket Books in 1991.

holder equity, and 8 percent return on sales. In the ensuing five years, marketing and administrative expenses, including the cost of sales discounts and promotions, exploded from $221 million to $408 million. As a consequence, though net sales had grown by more than $400 million in Rechholtz's first six years, to over $1.5 billion annually, profits were sliced in half, to just $47 million annually.

To put this diminished prosperity in perspective, Coors was now returning only 4.5 percent on its shareholders' investment in the company in 1988, far less than they would earn from the average passbook savings account. In the span of six years, Coors sales had grown by 37 percent, while profits had *dipped* by nearly 50 percent; the growth in sales was achieved only at the expense of profitability. With Coors barely able to turn a profit, the 37 percent increase in sales was nothing more than a mirage. It was visible on the sales reports, but vanished on the profit ledgers.

Not clearing a sizeable profit when the Coors Board of Directors refused to borrow money was like fighting a war without weapons and supplies. "How can we compete," Rechholtz asked his staff rhetorically in the winter of 1988, "when we're

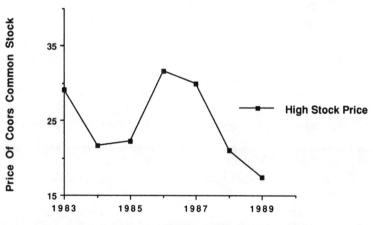

being outspent three or four to one by A–B and Miller? The Confederacy lost the Civil War because of supplies, not battle-field superiority." The High Command knew that even the most brilliant commanders and the most valiant warriors couldn't win a war without supplies; and the Coors commanders had shown at the 1987 Distributor Convention that they were far from the most brilliant in The Beer Wars.

I first became aware of the cash squeeze at Coors when working on income projections for Crystal Springs Cooler during the summer of 1987. In the course of preparing a presentation to the High Command, I asked Dewey why the company's Board of Directors were reluctant to fund the project, despite positive financial forecasts.

"We're a lot worse off [financially] than anybody, and I mean anybody, is saying," Dewey told me.

"What do you mean, a lot worse off? How bad can you be when you don't have any debt?" I asked. "I mean, I know profits are way down since the early nineteen-eighties. But that's not what I'd call a major financial problem."

"Think about it," Dewey countered. "If you won't borrow money, you have to operate on a cash basis. And if you have no cash, what do you do?"

"What do you mean, 'no cash'?"

"Well, according to a friend in Corporate Finance, some days we could have less than ten million dollars cash on hand, maybe as little as one million dollars. For a company this size, that's like you or me having a dollar ninety-eight in our checking accounts. We're not broke at that amount, but we're close to it," Dewey finished.

"So what happens when we run out of cash?" I asked.

"They just sell the place to Australians, or some other for-eigners, I guess" Dewey slurred, with a shrug. (An Australian financier had purchased Heileman in 1987, providing Dewey with his inspiration.)

I dismissed Dewey's wild speculation about selling the company, until the evidence began piling up that Coors *was* strapped for cash. First, Coors had completed plans to build a $400 million packaging plant in Elkton, Virginia, in 1987, the first step toward constructing an East Coast brewery. Since the Board of Directors refused, as a matter of policy, to issue debt, this major capital investment would have to be paid for with current earnings, or cash on hand. As a consequence, the company's working capital (roughly equivalent to cash on hand) plunged from $270 million in 1985 and 1986 to only $197 million in 1988.

There were other financial clouds on the horizon. According to the company's 10-K annual report filed with the SEC in 1988, the Environmental Protection Agency had warned Coors that it would be fined and assessed clean-up fees in the millions of dollars for polluting the toxic Lowry Landfill. Coors, the public would subsequently learn, was the largest industrial polluter at the landfill site just outside of Denver.[2]

Coors also lost a $14.3 million law suit in Texas state court, filed by Joe Rodriguez, a former Coors distributor. The judgment held that Coors had improperly terminated Rodriguez's distributorship agreement; therefore, the company was liable for damages.[3]

Throughout 1987 and 1988, rumors spread that Coors was for sale. One day, Big Tim walked into my cubicle grinning, and said, "Did you hear that the brewery is going to be sold?"

Reassured by his wide grin that this *had* to be a joke, I replied casually, "Oh, really?"

"Yeah, well, you've been to Tivoli and the Jackson Brewery in New Orleans, haven't you? Well, you're standing in the future home of Denver's largest shopping mall." (Both the Tivoli brewery in downtown Denver and the Jackson Brewery in New Orleans were converted, in the 1980s, into urban shopping malls.)

---

2 According to the Environmental Protection Agency.

3 After the verdict in March 1988, Coors immediately appealed the judgment.

While the Coors Brewing Complex in Golden would no doubt have made a splendid mall site, the rumors of an imminent sale were apparently unfounded. But not because the company was thriving.

At the same time that the Coors marketing military was running short of supplies, it was also running out of territory to defend. By 1988, Coors had expanded to every state (except Indiana)—the U.S. is the world's largest market for beer—and to Canada and Japan, as well. Expansion to these new markets, along with the robust growth of Coors Light had, for a time, countered the spectacular decline of the Coors Banquet brand. Reflecting financial analysts' bullish outlook on the profit potential from Coors expansion, the price of Coors stock climbed to as high as thirty-two dollars per share in 1986.

By 1988, the financial community's outlook for Coors had changed dramatically. Market expansion had generated scant profits. (In fact, profits had plunged after the marketing expansion, due to price discounting and the costs associated with marketing products nationally.) Worse, analysts concluded that with no new products, and few remaining new markets to conquer, Coors would be unable to increase either sales or profits in the future. The price of Coors stock plunged as low as sixteen dollars in 1988, and never reached higher than twenty-one dollars per share that year.

Squeezed by a cash crunch, disastrous draft-beer marketing campaigns, and a lack of new weapons with which to combat Anheuser–Busch and Miller, the Coors High Command, like the German High Command stashed in a bunker beneath crumbling Berlin, developed in late 1987 what Rod Sterling termed their "bunker mentality."

"Bunker mentality. How do you figure that?" I asked Sterling when he first broached the concept.

"Well," Sterling began, "remember when Hitler got desperate in his last days in the bunker?"

"Sure, he organized the Hitler youth, and . . ."

"Made plans for the Thousand Year Reich," Sterling inter-

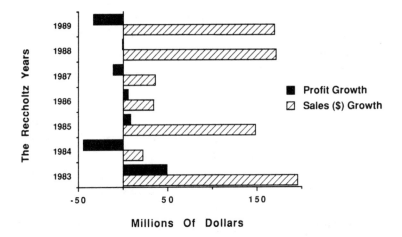

Note: In 1986, the year when Coors stock price reached its peak, Rechholtz cashed in lucrative bonuses and stock incentives to become Coors highest paid executive. By 1988, the stock had lost about one third of its value.

rupted. "He ordered his generals to counterattack to defend Berlin, even had a few shot. He was absolutely desperate, because he knew the war was about to end."

"Well, how does that compare to what we're doing?" I asked, still failing to grasp his analogy.

"You don't think we're desperate? First, we change not just one, but *all* of our beers to draft beer, even though we're not sure that draft beer is anything more than a fad," Sterling reasoned. "Then, you're out looking for opportunities for Coors with gay beer drinkers? Gays? Get real. Gays are the last market on earth that would ever drink Coors. We're getting so desperate, we're looking for new markets for Coors products that'll never pan out. Who's next? Unions? Environmentalists? Liberals? Man, you better believe this is the bunker mentality. Nothing but utter desperation," he finished.

"So what do we do?" I asked. "We're stuck in the bunker [with the High Command], too."

"That's what worries me," Sterling responded. "I don't want to command one of the suicide missions on the horizon. Remember what happened to Hitler's generals at the end? They either shot themselves, were shot by Hitler, or were killed leading one of the suicide counterattacks."

Unfortunately, as one of the beer warriors left in the Coors bunker, I was given the commander's mantle on several projects designed to seek new markets for Coors products, what Sterling termed "suicide counterattacks."

In 1987, I was assigned the dubious honor of conducting research into Coors long-term battle strategies. At the time, this seemed akin to being placed in charge of the presidential transition team for perennial Republican also-ran candidate Harold Stassen. By late 1987, I was fairly certain that there wouldn't *be* a long term at Coors. However, like most of the warriors at the Coors front line, I thought little about the impossibility of my assignment. Instead, I decided humbly to call this project "Cosmos," because, as I explained to Rod Sterling, "We'll search to the ends of the universe for marketing opportunities and the plan we'll develop will be so big, it'll be bigger than the cosmos itself."

Initially, though, our search through the beer-drinking "cosmos" took us no further than Milwaukee, Dallas, Boston, and Fort Lauderdale, during a series of focus groups with beer drinkers. Specifically, the Cosmos project was designed, at the request of the High Command, to identify marketing opportunities for Coors with one of the strongest anti-Coors factions: black beer drinkers.

Coors popularity in the African-American community, though never very strong, plummeted after reports of Bill Coors's alleged racist remarks before a gathering of minority businessmen in March 1984. *The Rocky Mountain News* reported that the Coors chairman of the Board not only claimed that blacks in Zimbabwe lacked the intellectual capacity to govern, but that "one of the best things they [slave traders] did for you is to drag your ancestors over here in chains." Though Coors later sued the *News* for libel, in a case which was settled out of court with an apology from the paper, *The Wall Street Journal* reported the news account to its national readership on March 8, 1984, setting off a storm of controversy in the black community.

A Coors spokesperson attempted to mitigate the damaging publicity by noting that some people were "one hundred percent behind William Coors because they know his record in the minority community." Still, the spokesperson conceded that some retailers were ordering Coors distributors to remove the allegedly "racist beer from [store] shelves."[4]

In response to threats of a boycott of Coors beer by the NAACP, Coors signed an agreement in the fall of 1984 pledging $325 million in business over a five-year period to black vendors. Fred Rasheed of the NAACP noted that the $325 million would "help foster understanding of Coors and its products in the black community." Ultimately, Coors hoped that this "understanding" would consist of more consumption of Coors beer by black drinkers.[5]

Five years later, it was evident that the $325 million hadn't quite fostered any appreciation for, much less an understanding of, Coors products in the black community. Blacks comprised just 5 percent of Coors total market, according to research, compared to a sizeable 16 percent of Miller's total market. In summarizing the results of the Cosmos research, I noted that black consumers' desire to drink Coors was being outweighed by Coors questionable reputation. In sum, most blacks still wouldn't drink Coors beer because of a lingering negative per-

4 Reported in *The Wall Street Journal* on March 8, 1984.
5 Norm Udevitz, "Coors to Put Millions into Black Groups," *The Denver Post,* September 19, 1984, p. 1.

ception of the company, despite the $325 million investment in the black community.[6] This first suicide mission had failed.

Undaunted, my next mission for the bunkered High Command was code named *"Reinheitsgobot."* It had about as much promise as the black market-outreach program. For centuries, German beers had been christened with the *Reinheitsgobot* seal of approval, which stamped the beer as a natural Bavarian beer, according to recipes passed down through the generations by German brewmasters.

Several brewmasters from the Coors Research and Development Department suggested that Coors, brewed with all-natural ingredients, could claim to be the first American beer to earn the *Reinheitsgobot* designation. According to one brewer, "Miller can have Genuine Draft, but we [Coors] can have the only genuine *Reinheitsgobot*."

A junior marketing manager in Rain Man's New Products Marketing Department jumped on the *Reinheitsgobot* bandwagon, claiming that earning the official German beer designation would dispel the Coors image of being weak and watery. "*Reinheitsgobot* sounds like a macho man's beer," she said.

Unfortunately, the vast majority of beer drinkers had never heard of the *Reinheitsgobot* designation, and were rather unexcited about its use on Coors beer cans. Worse, most consumers in several focus groups were unable to pronounce "*Reinheitsgobot.*" One beer drinker in Boston summed up the miniscule marketing potential of *Reinheitsgobot* labeling by saying, "I doubt if I'd go around the neighborhood bragging about drinking the '*Reinheitsawhatever.*' People would think I'm nuts."

Other tangible evidence indicated that Sterling's judgment about the "bunker mentality" wasn't without foundation. In the fall of 1988, Coors attempted to make peace with labor unions by sanctioning a Teamsters organizing vote (see Chapter 8) at the Golden brewery. In 1989, the company attempted to

---

6 My memo, dated October 20, 1987, was originally sent to Preacher and The Silver Fox.

mend fences with environmentalists by launching the ill-fated and ill-timed Pure Water 2000 campaign (also discussed in Chapter 8). These desperate attempts to jump-start sales by burying the hatchet with anti-Coors factions ultimately failed.

However, the bunker mentality did foster one mission in which I not only participated, but helped to mastermind. In retrospect, this project, code-named VOX, seems to have been a rather obvious, though desperate course of action for the beleaguered High Command. VOX, which the High Command hoped would be the keystone of the company's survival, was, in the words of Rechholtz, "a natural." Faced with imminent defeat in The Beer Wars, the High Command decided that Coors should brew an economy beer.

Economy beers, no-frill brews like Schaefer, Red, White, & Blue, Pearl, and Olympia, were popular with older, blue-collar, "shot-and-a-beer" drinkers—what we called the Joe Six-Pack segment. The charm of economy beers wasn't their taste, or even their advertising, but their low price.

Given Coors devotion to The Doctrine of Discounting and growth without profit, an economy beer *was* a natural. "Hell, we're just giving all of our beer away, anyway," Big Tim conceded one day after a planning meeting. "Coors Banquet is an economy beer, right now. Coors Light will be soon. VOX will just legitimize what we've already been doing for years. We'll just save a lot of money on coupons and sales calls to push through our special [sales] deals."

During the Age of Imitation, VOX also became a natural when the High Command observed that Coors was the only major brewer *without* an economy beer. In the fall of 1987, Pepe noted in a staff meeting that "Miller's got Meister Brau, A–B has Busch, Stroh has Old Mil[waukee]. We've got a real gap to fill." He went on to note that an economy beer was essential "if we're going to achieve our Project Ten objectives." (This objective was the ten percent share of the 190-million-barrel beer industry.)

What looked like a gap to Pepe more nearly resembled a

bottomless pit to the Market Research Department. Economy beers, dubbed "popular" beers when discount prices made cheaper beers appealing to inflation-battered consumers in the 1970s, lost their luster in the booming, prosperous 1980s. While the beer industry was growing 1 to 2 percent per year in the 1980s, the economy segment was actually *shrinking*, from almost 25 million barrels in 1983, to just under 23 million in 1987. Once-viable economy brands like Schlitz, Hamm's, and Pabst Blue Ribbon withered during the 1980s. Already straining from slim profit margins (because of the economy price) many brewers of economy beer lost money on this increasingly competitive segment.

Undaunted by the sales decline in the economy beer market, the push at Coors for an economy beer also gained momentum from the brewery's commitment to boost the bottom line through cost cutting.

"We can't make any money off a popular [economy] beer," Sterling told The General in late 1987. "With prices so low and advertising budgets soaring, how could we clear a profit?"

"The price we charge isn't important. It's the cost that matters," The General responded.

"Do you think economy drinkers really care about quality?" retorted The General. "Hell, they're just happy to get anything even close to beer taste. This stuff won't taste that bad. If it's refiltered Herman Joseph's, it might taste pretty damn good."

Despite the potential for added sales volume, and the low cost to brew an economy beer, the plan to market an economy beer faced strong opposition from the Coors family. According to Dewey, Bill Coors was strongly opposed to VOX, fearing that an economy beer would further tarnish the company's image. "I was talking to Bill at the hospitality center," Dewey told me, "and he says we've always been known for brewing quality beers, and we aren't going to change now. We've resisted the temptation to brew a cheap beer before, and we will now, if Bill has his way."

However, Bill Coors's opposition to VOX melted away when

research indicated that Coors could market an economy beer without advertising the product as "cheap," or "discount." The revolutionary marketing strategy which legitimized VOX with the Coors family and beer drinkers alike didn't arise from so-called Creatives at Foote, Cone, and Belding, but from my own infamous Cosmos project.

In the spring of 1987, I had flown to Boston to watch focus groups conducted by Andy Greenfield, a prominent and talented focus-group moderator based in New York. On a cold, snowy afternoon in March, a day better suited for savoring a steaming bowl of clam chowder than listening to consumers ruminate about the wonders of beer, we discovered how to brew and market a good-tasting economy beer. While sitting in the observation room at the focus-group facility, before the "hatch" to the back room was closed, Greenfield asked me, "Okay. What do you mean when you say you want consumers to describe a beer that really tastes different? How could a beer be different? Don't they all have hops, grain, and foam?"

"I don't now," I responded, caught off guard by his question. "That's what we're here to learn," I added somewhat sarcastically.

"No, I really mean it," Greenfield persisted. "How could a beer be different?"

"I don't know. Maybe it has extra foam, or maybe it's clear colored, or maybe it smells different."

"I see," Greenfield responded, his flat tone betraying a noticeable lack of enthusiasm for my ideas.

Desperate not to appear dense, especially after the Bloody Martha fiasco, I blurted out, "Jeez, if Miller can have draft-beer taste in a bottle, then why couldn't we [Coors] have bottled-beer taste in a canned beer?"

"Yeah," he responded excitedly. "Yeah! Beer drinkers are always telling us that they don't like the 'tinny' or metal taste of canned beer. Why couldn't we give 'em the smooth, cool taste of bottled beer, but in a can?"

A broad grin creased my face, and with that, Greenfield

marched into the focus group room and sprung the new idea on this unsuspecting group of Boston beer drinkers. In September 1987, I published a final report on the focus groups, which noted that beer drinkers universally preferred the taste of bottled beer over canned beer.[7]

The report went on to make two more critical points. First, beer drinkers were skeptical that a canned beer could taste as fresh as bottled beer, and needed evidence that the aluminum can had been altered to make the beer taste like bottled beer. More importantly, the report noted that the preference for this idea was strongest with economy beer drinkers.

Unfortunately, the High Command was preoccupied in the fall of 1987 with staff shake-ups, the threat posed by Miller Genuine Draft, the firing of Mark Harmon, and the "drafting" of the Coors product line. Therefore, the Cosmos report, as well as the potentially exciting news about the "bottled beer taste in a canned beer" concept, collected dust in desk drawers. That changed, though, in December 1987.

"Tell me about this bottled beer thing," Captain Kangaroo asked me from behind the desk in his small office. Whenever I stared at his piercing eyes, bushy moustache, mutton-chop sideburns, and thick, gray bangs, I expected Bunny Rabbit, or even Mr. Green Jeans, to join our meeting at any time. Or a batch of Ping-Pong balls to drop on his head, courtesy of the mischievous Mr. Moose.

"The Cosmos research shows that bottled beer taste in a canned beer could be a very powerful marketing claim," I began, somewhat formally. I quickly switched to a more casual tone, and continued, "Beer drinkers just don't like the 'tinny' taste of beer cans."

"That's just a myth," he responded. "The cans don't really taste like tin. We use processed aluminum. Everybody does."

"Maybe so," I allowed. "But beer drinkers *think* that alu-

7 This report was issued in September 1987.

minum cans taste different. And in marketing, customer perceptions are as good as reality. You know that."

"I guess so. But how do we make the beer in our cans taste different?" Captain Kangaroo asked.

"Well, that's the part we're going to have to figure out. Maybe we could brew it differently, you know, with a new process or something. Or maybe . . . can we do anything different with the can?" I asked.

"What do you mean?"

"Well, someone in the [focus] groups suggested we line the beer can to make the beer taste like bottled beer."

"With what?" he asked. "Trash-can liners?"

"No, glass."

"Glass. Sure, each beer can will weigh five pounds. I don't know, you may have something here," the good Captain finished. "Bottled beer taste in a canned beer. What's next, tap-water taste in a bottled water?"

That's the last I heard of bottled beer taste in a canned beer, until that fateful spring day when the VOX project team met with Foote, Cone, and Belding to discuss potential marketing strategies for VOX. As the junior Tate from the agency unveiled the agency's concepts for Coors new economy beer, I was generally unimpressed: *Tommy D's, a beer that was brewed in a fictional character's basement . . . the first economy beer brewed Australian style . . . Bighorn, a Canadian-style economy beer . . . Nightlife, the beer for after dark . . . and then finally . . .* a canned beer that tastes like bottled beer.

"I like Australia. Australia's really a hot country," bellowed Rechholtz, breaking the uncomfortable silence in the conference room. "My daughter and her friends would love that one. It would have young-adult appeal."

"Uh, Bob," I interjected. "Most economy beer drinkers are somewhat downscale. This is the 'shot-and-a-beer' or blue-collar crowd. They've never been to California, much less Australia. Australian beer might not mean anything to them."

Rechholtz glared at me, his contempt for my comment obvious.

"That 'Tommy D' feller looks like a fruit," someone offered. "Popular [economy] drinkers are too macho to buy a fag beer from some faggot named 'Tommy D.' "

"Uhhhhh . . . Thaaaaat . . . What are you thinking of with Golden Lager?" Rain Man asked one of the junior Tates, totally ignoring the gay bashing.

"Well," interrupted Big Tate, "It sounds like a rich-tasting, full-bodied beer, something an economy drinker could really learn to love."

"Uhhhhh . . . youuuuu . . . know that we already tried a beer called Golden Lager in 1984, and it failed." ("Golden Lager" was the original name of Coors Extra Gold.)

"I say, let's go with Australia. We know it's hot," Rechholtz countered.

"What about the bottled beer can thing?" Captain Kangaroo asked rhetorically. "The Cosmos research says it would really fly with economy drinkers. It could be as big as Miller Genuine Draft."

"But . . . thaaaaat . . . how do we deliver on the advertising claim?" Rain Man queried.

"Burgess says we should line the beer can," came Captain Kangaroo's instantaneous response.

"I didn't say that," I noted. "*Beer drinkers* said it in the focus groups. They said they'd love to drink a canned beer that tasted as cold and clean as a bottled beer, as long as we could convince them that it wasn't just advertising hype."

"How are you going to do that?" Big Tate wondered. "Does Coors have the ability to make a special beer can, or put a lining in the beer can? Put glass or something inside?"

"Not right now. It's too costly," Rechholtz countered. "Plus, we already line all of our aluminum cans right now. Everyone sort of lines their beer cans. It's all processed aluminum. Haven't you ever seen the aluminum at the rolling mills?"

"But is that enough to back the advertising claim?" Big Tate wondered out loud.

"You're wasting your time," Rechholtz responded. "We're not going to need to line the beer cans. Australia is in. I say let's go with it."

"Bob, should we test these [concepts] with beer drinkers first, and then make a decision?" I asked.

"Heeeeee's . . . thaaaaat . . . He's right," Rain Man stammered. "We have nooooooo . . . idea what will work. Let's let beer drinkers decide."

"Inarticulate or articulate, we have to find out how they'd react to our marketing strategies," I added. "We have no choice."

"Heeeeee's . . . right," Rain Man responded. "Like it or not, the economy drinker's our market. The Creatives are just going to have to lump it."

"Okay, do it [the research] quickly. We need to roll, people. We've got to get VOX out of the doors as soon as we can. It's part of our [strategic marketing] plan. Move it," Rechholtz finished as he quickly got up to leave the room.

"In the meantime," Big Tate interjected hurriedly, "can you have R and D look into the can-lining issue?"

"Sure, sure, whatever," Rechholtz responded offhandedly. "Bob [Rain Man], why don't you look into it? But it's going to be Australia, I'm sure."

Despite the advertising agency's protestations over the next four months, the VOX project team researched the agency's marketing strategies for the new Coors beer product, in an odyssey that took us from Cleveland to Tampa, and from Salt Lake City to Syracuse.

In the course of conducting these focus groups, we learned that:

1. Australian beer, despite its popularity with Rechholtz's daughter, held no allure for Joe Six-Pack. Many drinkers had no idea that Australians even brewed beer. "I've heard of Australia," noted one beer drinker, "but I had no idea that they brewed beer. Of course, I don't know

anything else about 'em, either, except for the freakin' kangaroos."

2. The infamous Tommy D character was perceived to be too quirky, weird, and feminine to act as a role model for Joe Six-Pack. In a sentiment eerily similar to that expressed in the planning meeting, one focus-group respondent said, "Tommy D's looks like queer beer to me. I wouldn't touch the stuff."

3. Bottled beer taste in a canned beer struck a nerve with economy drinkers. Avid fishermen, bowlers, softball players, and outdoorsmen, they admitted a penchant for the taste of bottled beer, while admitting that they usually brought canned beer because of the convenience and portability. "I'd love if it really tasted like bottled beer," was the most common sentiment expressed in the focus groups.

In the spring of 1989, after I had left the company, I was startled out of my usual early morning fog by an article in *The Wall Street Journal*, which reported that Coors was launching a new economy beer, dubbed "Keystone Beer." The *WSJ* account stated that Keystone had a *specially lined beer can*, which allowed the product to retain the freshness and smoothness of bottled beer, with the convenience and low cost of canned beer.

I immediately placed a call to Big Tim at the brewery. "Keystone? Where in the hell did they get that name?" I asked.

"Well, The General liked it, and he said he wanted a mountain type of name, to compete against the mountains on the Busch beer cans."

"Keystone?" I repeated again.

"Well, at least it doesn't have the name 'Coors' emblazoned on the can," Big Tim responded. "This new shit can't make our company image any worse than it already is."

"Yeah, other than the mountains, the fact that Keystone is

the name of Colorado's biggest ski area, and the words, 'Brewed by the Adolph Coors Company, Golden, Colorado,' no one will have any idea it's a Coors product." There was silence on the other end of the phone, so I switched gears. "Did they ever develop a special lining for the beer can?" I asked.

"Uh, not that I know of," Big Tim responded. "But I do know that all of Coors aluminum cans are lined, sort of."

"Yeah, but according to the paper, the Keystone ads are going to say 'specially' lined beer cans are responsible for the bottled beer taste. What's special about the new can?"

"Oh, you're just playing with semantics," Tim chided.

"I guess you're right," I said, as I hung up.

A couple of years later, I was watching late-night TV when the screen flashed with a Keystone advertisement. "Wouldn't it be great if you could have the great taste of bottled beer in a can?" the announcer asked.

As I watched the ad, I recalled that in December 1990, a Coors spokesperson claimed in Denver's *Rocky Mountain News* that Keystone was the "biggest-selling new product in beer industry history." I felt no sense of joy at having sparked the idea behind the "biggest-selling" new beer product. Instead, I felt remorse that Keystone ultimately contributed to the decline of an American institution, in one of Madison Avenue's biggest con jobs.

Keystone Beer didn't alleviate Coors financial problems; it merely exacerbated them. Due to the popularity of the bargain-priced Keystone, total sales of Coors beer products surged 17 percent between 1988 and 1990, allowing the company to reach Project Ten's coveted 10 percent share of the domestic beer industry.

Unfortunately, many Keystone drinkers were formerly drinkers of Coors Original Draft (formerly Coors Banquet) or Coors Light. With the ski-resort name and mountain peaks on the beer can, Keystone was quite obviously a lower-priced version of Coors, reasoned many beer drinkers. However, Keystone was much less costly for beer drinkers than Coors or Coors Light. Beer drinkers' ability to pay less for the same Coors quality was tantamount to General Motors offering Cadillac quality to Chevrolet buyers, at Chevy prices, in Chevy cars.

While Coors sold millions of barrels of Keystone per year, sales of Original Coors dwindled (by about 30 percent between 1989 and 1991), and Coors profits all but evaporated. Keystone's bargain price, lost revenue from the dwindling sales of Original Coors, and the exorbitant costs of advertising and promoting Keystone nationally, drove Coors net income down to a paltry $13 million in 1989, providing shareholders with a scant 1.2 percent return on their investment in the company. The total net income at Coors in 1989 and 1990, Keystone's first two years, was just $51 million, about half of what the company had cleared in profits in 1983 alone, and far less than Coors had made in any other two-year stretch during the 1980s.

As I watched the Keystone ad, I mused that Keystone Beer, by itself, didn't bring down the Adolph Coors Company. As but one misstep in a series of marketing blunders, Keystone merely perpetuated Coors disastrous course in the 1980s. If the Cosmos project hadn't stumbled across "bottled beer taste in a canned beer," the VOX project likely would have moved forward using some other marketing strategy. *No, my marketing brainstorm didn't bring down the Coors brewing empire; at least, not by itself.*

Unfortunately, while watching the Keystone ad, I was unable to deny my feelings of culpability in the advertising hoax Keystone perpetuated on the American public. "Bottled beer taste in canned beer" promised beer drinkers a new, revolutionary product—a better-tasting canned beer. But if the rumors out of the brewery were on target, the aluminum beer can used for Keystone beer wasn't any different from other Coors beer cans. In all likelihood, Keystone beer wasn't like bottled beer, but like any other canned beer. Keystone's slogan was an empty, unfulfilled promise, an apparent con job on millions of American beer drinkers.

"Wouldn't it be great to get the great taste of bottled beer in a can?" the TV commercial announcer asked again.

"Nope. I don't think so," I replied out loud. But by this time, no one was listening to what I said.

12

The Death March

We all live under the same sky, but we don't
have the same horizon.

—Konrad Adenauer

By the time Keystone was intro-
duced, no one at Coors was listening to my advice because,
like millions of other white-collar warriors in the 1980s, I had
resigned my commission (in the Coors military) and moved on
to supposedly greener pastures.[1]

The lack of loyalty in the white-collar world since the early
1980s is by no means a one-way street. While hundreds of
thousands of white-collar workers are idled each year in layoffs,
restructurings, buyouts, and mergers, many more voluntarily
desert their employers; or, more accurately, are bribed into
desertion. For in an era dominated by greed, the inducement
to switch jobs is, appropriately, green—the color of money.

---

1 In July 1988 I resigned from Coors in order to accept an offer to
become a Market Research Manger for US WEST, a Denver-based tele-
communications company.

Carl Sagan once wrote that to bake an apple pie from scratch, one must first invent the universe.[2] I always suspected there was a business corollary to Sagan's thesis: namely, that for greed to predominate, money and profits must first be created. Job-hopping in contemporary business would never have taken root without a profit incentive. And the big money isn't cleared by the job-hoppers, but by headhunters.

Headhunters, officially known as executive recruiters, hunt for executive "heads" for companies like Coors, IBM, Ford, and thousands of other major corporations. Hired by these corporations to lure gainfully employed executives from other companies to fill the client's own vacancies, headhunters are paid hefty commissions (by the companies, not the recruits) ranging from 10 to 50 percent of the annual salaries paid to the executives they recruit.

As stockbrokers make a living from frequent stock trading, headhunters profit from constant job switching. The more frequently white-collar employees defect, creating vacancies at major corporations, the more likely headhunters are to collect their hefty commissions. For this reason, Big Tim called headhunters "vultures, because they're always circling whenever someone's career is in trouble, and a job's going to open up."

An economist's nightmare, good headhunters not only *supply* companies with executives, but also *create demand* for their services. It isn't uncommon for a headhunter to lure an executive away with an enticing employment opportunity, and then earn a hefty commission by supplying a different executive to fill the vacancy the headhunter helped to create.

Of course, headhunters couldn't collect their substantial fees without the cooperation, even eager participation, of American workers. White-collar executives listen to headhunters' enticing offers when they aren't fully satisfied with their current employment situations. For this reason, discovering why an em-

---

2 This thesis is advanced in Sagan's book *Cosmos*, and also appeared on the television show of the same name.

ployee isn't satisfied is often the key to a headhunter's success. Like a temptress adept at seducing monogamous husbands, headhunters try to identify *any* source of potential unhappiness among prospective recruits, and then exploit their opening.

The most obvious source of discontent is money. Headhunters have the amazing ability to convince white-collar managers that no matter how much money they are paid, it isn't enough, or certainly not as much as the manager is worth. "I think you can do better," a headhunter will almost always say to a potential recruit, whether the executive is being paid seventy thousand, or seven hundred thousand per year.

Even if headhunters know that an executive can't find another job that pays much more than his current salary, they'll still cajole the executive into looking for a better job. Knowing that an executive is making $50,000 a year, a headhunter will talk about a job that pays "up to $55,000 per year." Usually, the malcontent manager will only hear the top of the salary range, not the key qualifier "up to."

Major corporations are only too happy to lure executives with the promise of substantial salaries and perks—aided and abetted by the headhunters, of course. Since headhunters' commissions are based on the salary paid to the newly recruited executive, they'll often con a company into believing that "it'll take at least sixty thousand dollars per year to lure 'Employee X,' " when in fact, it will take only fifty thousand dollars per year. Most headhunters defend this bald-faced lying by claiming that they're just trying to maximize the earnings potential of their recruits; of course, the headhunter also stands to benefit (via increased commissions).

Sometimes, hunters must rely on more than just money in order to bag their quota of white-collar heads. One recruiting technique is maintaining a "malcontent" list. If a manager is called by a headhunter, but isn't interested in the job in question, the headhunter will ask, "Do you know of anyone else who's unhappy, or might be interested in a move?"

At Coors, supplying names to the malcontent list was often

an act of revenge. If a beer warrior wanted to tweak an inter-office enemy, he would simply give the name of the enemy, even if he knew the enemy would have no interest in the job. Once a name was added to the malcontent list, that person would be pestered for weeks by a zealous headhunter or two. Rod Sterling guessed that The General was prominent on such malcontent lists, "courtesy of all his good friends at Coors."

Being added to a headhunter's recruiting list usually meant dogging the headhunter's relentless pursuit. Like college football coaches recruiting star athletes, headhunters thought nothing of tracking down prospective recruits at home, on weekends, at bars and restaurants, and even on the road. Rod Sterling and I once checked into a hotel in Los Angeles, only to receive "urgent" messages at the front desk upon checking in; both messages were from headhunters.

When old-fashioned human greed and weeks of harassment fail, good headhunters rely on guilt. Headhunters often warn that a manager's career is "going to stall," or that a job is "a once-in-a-lifetime opportunity," or that if the executive refuses to interview for a position, he'll "regret it for the rest of [his] career."

Over the years, Big Tim and I learned that these dire warnings were usually far from the truth, nothing more than coercive exaggerations. So we began compiling our own version of the "headhunter dictionary."

EXCERPT FROM THE HEADHUNTER DICTIONARY

HEADHUNTER PHRASE	REALITY
"It'd be a great career move."	A dead-end job that no one in their right mind would be interested in taking.
"The opportunity of a lifetime."	You'll get a call, or two, next week about a similar job.
"You need to think about more than just salary."	Job doesn't pay squat; you'd probably have to take a pay cut.
"I think you'd be perfect for this job."	Couldn't think of anyone else to call; headhunter desperate.
"Work with me on this job."	Headhunter really needs the commission; doesn't care if you're right for the job.
"It's a great place to work."	If it's so great, how come they need a headhunter and have a job opening?

When the rumor mill indicates that a manager is pursuing job opportunities through a headhunter, he is described as being "in play." Given Coors dismal fortunes in The Beer Wars and Herr Rechholtz's management shake-up in 1987, which threatened job security at Central Command, it was hardly surprising that many of the Coors beer warriors were in play in 1987 and 1988.

The symptoms of "job-hopping syndrome" were easily diagnosed at Coors. Given the noisy cubicles at Central Command, in-play managers often engaged in hushed, muffled telephone conversations that ended with, "Can you call me later, at home?"

Another obvious sign was a newly found zest for, or dedication to, the job—or at least what appeared to be latent workaholism. Whenever a beer warrior arrived very early for work, or stayed later than usual, it was quite likely that he was waiting for a private phone call from a headhunter, if not a telephone job interview with a prospective new employer.

The most obvious signal that one of The Marketeers or members of The Force was playing "wheel of fortune" with a headhunter was the use of a conference room that was reserved for a conference of one. The in-play beer warrior would use the conference room for a private phone call with a headhunter, to avoid the din of the Central Command cubicles.

In 1988, Rod Sterling guessed that at least half the officers of Central Command were exploring new jobs. "Hell," he noted, "most of 'em aren't even trying to hide the fact that they're looking [for a new job]." Often this was true, as the mere rumor that someone was in play was enough to secure a raise, promotion, or both. But not in the Market Research Department, where Captain Kangaroo circulated a preemptive threat that "I'll never negotiate or make a counteroffer. Either you want to stay, or you want to go. You can make up your mind without my help." This warning failed to cool the ardor of many of my colleagues, who decided to investigate whether the grass really was greener outside of Coors.

Wee Willie spent a weekend in Dallas, where he was courted by a major snack-food company. "It's right up his alley," Big Tim noted sarcastically. "If they give free snack foods like we give free beer in the lunch room, he could eat a helluva lot of fringe benefits." Naturally, Wee Willie's evaluation of the new job opportunity centered on the quality of the restaurants in Dallas. "I think Dallas might work out okay. They've got some great European restaurants, and top-notch Tex-Mex," he claimed. Unfortunately, Wee Willie's potential suitor eventually offered the job to another candidate.

Rip, the flatulent researcher, caused a stir in the Research Department by discussing his job prospects openly with co-workers over the cubicle walls. His boss, Mumbles, caught wind of Rip's dealings, and warned him that, "I need . . . to know whether . . . part of this team . . . not out there . . . plan for next year . . . let me know." This warning was apparently as clear to Rip as it was to the rest of the department, as he resigned in the fall of 1987 and moved to a Denver-area high-technology company.

Cowboy also abandoned the Research Department in the summer of 1988, ruefully noting that it was "time to ride into the sunset." In the tradition of cowboy crooner Gene Autry, Cowboy's sunset lasted for months. He gave his notice in May, but didn't actually leave Coors until September 1988.

In 1988, nearly everyone else in the department was also in play—at least according to the rumor mill. Valley Girl, who often punctuated her presentations with the cryptic phrase, "Let's move on," was apparently thinking of doing so; supposedly she interviewed with the California Raisin Board. "You know, it's like, worth thinking about," she told me when I asked if the rumor were true. Mumbles reportedly was negotiating with Coors arch rival Anheuser–Busch. But Sterling claimed that this was no threat to Coors, as "they [Anheuser–Busch] won't understand anything he says, either." And Big Tim talked to another company about a senior-level marketing position. "It never hurts to talk," he told me.[3]

Across the fifth floor of the Central Command, many of The Marketeers and member of The Force were in play, too. Gary Truitt, then the vice president of sales, left Coors in June 1988 to join a training-seminar company. Igor and several other managers were being recruited by a prominent soft-drink company. The Silver Fox warned that he was likely to leave at any time, as "I'm already rich, and I don't need to take Rechholtz's shit any more." (Apparently he *was* rich, having invested in moun-

---

3 Big Tim and Valley Girl both resigned from Coors in 1989.

tain real estate in the 1960s. He left Coors in 1989.) Even Rod Sterling, who was called at least once a week by headhunters, admitted to being "mildly intrigued" by offers from a beverage company and an advertising agency in 1988.[4]

It was probably inevitable that, during the Coors summer of discontent (1988), I'd be in play, too. By then, I had forgotten my first, nightmarish experience with headhunters, a year earlier.

One cool summer morning in July 1987, my home phone rang shortly before 7 A.M. "Bob, I have a great job I want to tell you about," said the voice on the other end. This Chicago-based headhunter was a frequent and irritating caller. Almost intolerable at any hour of the day, her grating voice and persistent, demanding tone were especially hard to take before breakfast.

"I'm really not interested at this point in time. I'm happy with what I'm doing," I responded. *Plus, I'd like to take my morning shower.*

"But what does it hurt to listen?" she responded. "I haven't even told you how special this opportunity is. Couldn't you at least listen?"

Perhaps it was the early hour, or my recent disappointment at the demise of Crystal Springs Cooler. But in a moment of weakness, I blurted out, "I don't suppose it would hurt to listen." Telling a headhunter that you'd be willing to listen is roughly equivalent to inviting a vampire to a blood bank. Before I could even catch my breath, I'd been told the standard lines about this job being a "once-in-a-lifetime" opportunity with "unlimited rewards" and "great potential." A few days later, I was on a plane to Chicago, where I was whisked by limousine to my prospective new employer's corporate headquarters in suburban Chicago, and herded into the sterile, windowless conference room where I would be interviewed.

4 Rod Sterling resigned from Coors during the summer of 1989, to move to an executive position with another beverage company.

Though I had no interest in leaving Coors at that time, the promise of a pay raise, engaging work in the new-products arena for a major food manufacturer, and a promotion were seductive. As I passed each interview hurdle, I began to believe that maybe this new job *was* an offer I couldn't refuse. Then, in my last interview, with the company's vice president of marketing, my bubble burst, and I quickly learned the down side of being in play.

"What do you see yourself doing in the next ten years" the vice president asked in the typically direct manner of a former Harvard MBA who had quickly ascended in the management ranks. As if to communicate my relative unimportance in his high-powered corporate world, he refused to look at me as he asked the question, and instead doodled on a yellow legal pad.

Figuring that I needed to display a healthy level of ambition to catch the attention of this high achiever, I responded, matter-of-factly, "Well, in ten years, I'd probably want to have your job."

He immediately stopped doodling, and stared menacingly at me, his head shaking vigorously, as if enraged, surprised, or even appalled by my declaration of ambition. Judging by the look of utter contempt in his eyes, I thought maybe the words had come out wrong. For a brief moment, I wondered if maybe I'd mistakenly asked to wear his underwear, cohabitate with his wife, or even help myself to his new Porsche.

"Uh, I have a meeting I have to go to," he interjected, "so I think I need to cut our talk short. Good luck to you," he finished, as he abruptly walked out of the room.

If it wasn't already crystal clear that I was no longer in line for this opportunity of a lifetime, my limousine was replaced by a rickety Yellow Cab for the ride back to the airport. As I stared at the cabbie's dashboard picture of Iran's Ayatollah Khomeini, I reminded myself that careers sometimes took strange twists. "Where you go-eenk?" the cabbie asked in broken English, as we pulled away from the offices that I'd never call home.

"I'm going absolutely nowhere," I told him.

The cabbie chuckled briefly, politely, and then asked again, "Are you go-eenk to arrow-porty? Fly whirly plane?"

"Yeah, that's where I'm headed. A whirly plane back to my same old job."

Humbled by the reality that my career options weren't boundless, and chastened by the abrupt end to the job-courting process, I vowed to stay out of play indefinitely. I kept this vow for a year, until the summer of 1988, when the winds of change were unmistakably swirling around the beer warriors in Coors Central Command.

By this time, the crisis at Coors had intensified. No matter how committed we felt to the cause of reviving the moribund brewer, constant rumors of an impending sale, the company's acute cash crunch, and the lack of new, innovative marketing initiatives all cast dark shadows over Central Command. "I wouldn't plan on retiring here, unless it's involuntary retirement," Sterling warned, when discussing why he was talking to several headhunters. "This place might turn into a shopping mall sooner than we think if things don't improve."

The outlook for the company was compounded by equally dismal career-advancement opportunities. In response to the cash crunch, Coors instituted a salary and hiring freeze. The maximum annual merit-pay increase for Beer Wars veterans was a meager 3.5 percent, less than the country's rate of inflation. "Your standard of living falls just by staying here," Sterling noted with disgust at one point. "There's not much incentive to bust your ass for the company, is there?"

When I asked Captain Kangaroo in the spring of 1988 if he could help me assess my long-term career prospects at the company, he replied, "My hands are tied. I have no idea if any of us are going to be here, and I sure can't guarantee you a raise or promotion down the line. You're a valuable part of the department, and that's all I can tell you. If you want to stay [at Coors], it can't be because of any guarantees I've made. Stay because you want to."

This indifference to the need for security and career fulfillment in the workplace was hardly unique to Coors in the 1980s. The United States had thrived after World War II, in part because of the implicit agreement between companies and employees that hard work would be amply rewarded, with increasing salaries, promotions, stable benefits, and comfortable retirements. During the Gilded Age, this agreement was shattered at most companies, and Captain Kangaroo's quandary was reflective of the new reality. Whenever a company experienced hard times, through leveraged buyouts, mergers, or just plain bad management, employees would bear the brunt of the suffering, regardless of their value and their past contributions to the company. Employees sought the new vistas offered by headhunters because, at times, they felt as if they had little choice.

In the summer of 1988, I went back in play when I received an enticing offer from another Denver-based company. In addition to a 20 percent raise, a promotion, and superior benefits (especially the 10-K retirement plan), this new job offer was attractive because of the relative prosperity of the company; my new suitor was solidly profitable, with a track record of consistent earnings growth in the 1980s. Having witnessed the systematic destruction of the Coors brewing empire due to the company's unwillingness to invest for the long term, the financial health of my suitor appeared to indicate a company that could take risks, absorb losses when necessary, and invest for long-term prosperity. Therefore, I was leaning toward following some of my colleagues and resigning my commission in the Coors military.

Nevertheless, there were compelling reasons to remain at Coors. Having already invested three years of hard work, resigning would constitute an admission of failure; I didn't want to leave before finishing the job. Also, if we had been able to develop Crystal Springs Cooler, "bottled beer taste in a canned beer," and the idea of a full line of spring-water beverages, there still seemed to be a chance, though remote, that the company might pull out of its tailspin. Finally, I remembered that free beer was still available in the lunch room and Wellness Center, a fringe benefit that few other companies could match.

Early in the summer of 1988, my career dilemma still unresolved, I flew to New York to make a speech at an international marketing conference. In an attempt to escape the stress of the impending career decision, I decided to take in a baseball game at Yankee Stadium. As a long-time sports aficionado, I was excited about my first visit to "the house that Ruth built."

The night of June 28 was crisp and clear in the Bronx, a perfect summer night for baseball. As I got off the elevated train at the Yankee Stadium platform, I gazed upon the legendary edifice for the first time. With its famous white facade and scores of pennants flapping in the summer breeze, Yankee Stadium stood as a shrine to the game of baseball, having hosted more World Series games and more great players than any other ballpark. Babe Ruth, Lou Gehrig, Joe DiMaggio, Yogi Berra, and Reggie Jackson had all called Yankee Stadium home. The stadium, built in the 1920s, had been refurbished in 1973 and 1974, at a cost of more than $100 million.

But as I made my way to the upper deck, I couldn't help but notice the dilapidated condition of the "refurbished" shrine. Cement in the aisles was chipped and crumbling; the escalators to the upper deck were out of order; concession stands were small and antiquated; worst of all, my plastic seat, high over the right-field line, was broken.

Like Yankee Stadium, the Adolph Coors Company had flourished during the first half of the twentieth century. By 1985, when I joined Coors, the company was showing signs of wear and tear. After it was refurbished, Coors, like Yankee Stadium, was still crumbling.

Since my seat was broken, I moved down one chair in Box 635F in the upper deck, next to an old man, who also had come to the game by himself. From his wizened form, thinning hair, unsteady, liver-spotted hands, and thick, horn-rimmed glasses, I guessed that he was well past retirement age.

"Mind if I sit here?" I asked as the old man copied the lineup for the game into his scorecard.

"Hell no," he responded enthusiastically, adding, "that is, if you're a baseball fan."

"Yeah, I sure am. But it's my first visit to Yankee Stadium," I told him. "You know, the stadium doesn't appear in very good condition for a renovated, rebuilt park."

"Renovated? Rebuilt? You must be a college kid to use fancy words like that. No, they just patched over a stadium that was already falling down. They'd a been better off to tear the damn thing down and rebuild it from scratch, instead of just patching over this wreck."

Coors was refurbished by patching over the company's crumbling line of beer brands with the word "draft," which merely accelerated the company's decline. Instead, the High Command should have invested heavily in new products and new businesses, like Crystal Springs Cooler and the line of spring-water based beverages (the secret weapon of mass destruction), in order to fuel growth.

Alexander Graham Bell once observed that, in life, we are often so preoccupied with closed doors that we fail to take advantage of newly opened doors. Though he was a ninteenth-century inventor, Bell accurately summarized the frustrations of new products managers at twentieth-century Coors. Like the architects of the "refurbished" Yankee Stadium, the High Command tried, unsuccessfully, to preserve Coors past glory, and failed to capitalize on new doors that had so briefly opened.

By the third inning, the Minnesota Twins had jumped in front of the Yankees by a score of 3–0. "You know," I said to the old man, "I don't even know who most of these players are. This isn't like the old days, when the Yankees were the 'Bronx Bombers,' is it? According to the scoreboard, Mattingly leads the Yankees in homers, and he's hit only eight."

"Damn right this isn't like the old days," he replied. "In the old days, the Yankees had a simple, consistent formula for winning."

"What was that?" I asked.

"I thought you said you were a baseball fan," he said, looking up from his scorecard quizzically.

"I am, but the 'Bronx Bombers' were before my time," I responded, defensively.

"It was simple, kid," he said, sounding somewhat annoyed. "They had left-handed power hitters, like Ruth and Gehrig, or even Reggie Jackson, to hit homers over the short wall in right field. Strong left-handed pitchers, like Whitey Ford, forced the other team to hit fly balls into the deep power alley in left field."

"And they stuck with this formula for years?" I asked.

"Almost every year for fifty years," he replied with a hint of hometown fan pride.

"Boy, you can't argue with the results," I mused. "More than twenty world championships, and more than thirty World Series appearances. All of those Hall of Fame players. But why did they change? If they were so successful, why did they deviate from the formula?"

"Arrogance, stupidity . . . because they wanted to be like other teams, I guess. You know, keep up with the Joneses. Instead of power, this Yankee team is built for speed, like most other teams nowadays. But this is the wrong stadium to play in if you're built for speed. Just look at their record," he finished as the Yankees were retired in order in the fourth inning, a frequent occurrence in this dismal season.

Everyone complains that American businesses are no longer competitive in the world marketplace. The fact is, too many American companies have simply stopped making quality products. Unfortunately, quality and consistency are what brought American businesses to the pinnacle of success.

For generations, Coors brewed a lighter-tasting, refreshing beer using pure, Rocky Mountain spring water, and the highest quality ingredients. Coors earned its distinct reputation for quality and craftsmanship by brewing beer in limited quanitites from a single brewery nestled in the foothills of the Rockies. By the end of the 1980s, this success formula had long since been abandoned, much to the chagrin of American beer drinkers.

Coors Banquet was traditionally known as "America's Fine Light beer," until Miller Lite stole its thunder in the mid-1970s. A decade later, Mark Harmon was telling a nationwide audience of upscale drinkers that Coors Banquet wasn't light, but "the one," America's highest-quality, best-tasting premium beer. Before too long, Coors Banquet became the "original draft" beer, pitched to young adults as a party beer. Then, the High Command changed the name of Coors Banquet to Coors Original Draft, and changed the can and the label, too. Confused American beer drinkers abandoned Coors in droves.

Undaunted, the High Command continued to tinker with the Coors formula for success. For more than a generation, Coors convinced beer drinkers that Coors beer was better tasting because it was brewed, shipped, and stored chilled. Then, Mark Harmon inadvertently pitched Coors beer from a warm display.

Throughout the 1980s, the company continued to cut corners and search for a magic success formula. Coors Extra Gold was targeted at Bud drinkers, until it became a draft beer to compete against Miller's Genuine Draft. Coors touted its Rocky Mountain spring water, and then began bottling some beer with Virginia spring water. Coors promoted a campaign to purify America's waters, while simultaneously polluting streams.

A beer cooler made with pure Rocky Mountain spring water (Crystal Springs) . . . a line of nonalcoholic beverages, like a natural soda with spring water, and flavored sparkling water . . . a cool, refreshing malt liquor, brewed with menthol . . . These new opportunities would have continued the Coors tradition for quality mountain spring-water beverages.

But just as it had for the Yankees, when Coors abandoned its traditional success formula, the winning stopped.

"Get some hands," my erstwhile companion yelled after the Yankee shortstop made an error. "You bum," he added as an afterthought.

"You know, mister, I bet these modern ballplayers aren't as good as the old-time ballplayers from your time," I told him.

"For once, you're right, sonny," he quickly agreed. "And it wasn't just the great players who were better, like Ruth. *All* of the players were better, guys you've never even heard of."

"That must have been something," I allowed with a hint of envy.

"It was. You see, today, all the players care about is money. Meal money, bonuses, endorsements, arbitration. They don't care if they're good ballplayers. They just care if they're well paid. In the old days, ballplayers paid their dues, learned how to play the game, and figured the money would take care of itself, if they played the game well."

"But most of the players today are no better than average," I noted, "and they still average more than one million dollars per year."

"Yeah, they get paid a lot of money regardless of how well they play, just for being a big leaguer. You ever see a ballplayer give money back when he had a poor season?" the old man asked. "Hell, money's ruined the game," he finished, his voice trailing off.

Money has ruined many American businesses, too. Traditionally, senior managers and chief executives were content to manage a company for the long haul, and earn fair compensation for doing so. If the company prospered over time, the executives knew that they would, too.

Today's managers, though, aren't compensated based on their performance. In a capitalistic anachronism, ''captains of industry'' plunder companies for as much salary and as many bonuses and perks as they can rake in right now, regardless of how the company fares. At Coors, Herr Rechholtz collected a fat bonus in 1986, more than doubling his pay, even though Coors was far less profitable than when he had assumed the marketing reins.

With greed predominating, managers in the Gilded Age don't seem well versed in business fundamentals. Marketing budgets are slashed, employees are jettisoned, product quality is compromised, and new business opportunities are ignored, because executives aren't man-

aging to increase the value of a company, but to line their own pockets.

"It's kind of a sparse crowd tonight, isn't it?" I asked the old man.

" 'Bout average for this year. But not like the old days. Why, they'd pack 'em in, sixty thousand for the Red Sox games."

"How many would they draw this season?" I wondered.

"Maybe half that, if the weather was nice," the old man replied. "They're just living on their past laurels. You know, people come, just because they're the Yankees. Or for the exploding scoreboard, or to look at the pretty girls, or even for the hot dogs and beer. But in the old days, they'd come for the ballgame. That's why not so many come, anymore. The ballgame stinks," he finished, staring away from the field.

Price discounting is to Coors what the scoreboard and hot dogs are to Yankee Stadium. Price discounts provide an incentive for some drinkers to keep buying Coors, despite the declining quality of the company's product offerings.

Coors Banquet was once known as "America's Fine Light Beer," until Miller brewed a beer that not only tasted lighter, but had fewer calories, too. Coors eventually introduced Coors Light, but not until nearly every other major brewer had introduced a light beer. And though Coors had used the cold-filtered brewing process for more than a quarter century, Miller labeled its cold-filtered beer "draft," and, within two years, was outselling Coors Banquet/Original Draft. Coors, like the Yankees, had simply been outplayed by the competition.

John Paul Jones once said that, "He who does not risk, cannot win." It's not surprising that Coors hadn't won many battles in The Beer Wars. And if the only substantial idea to emerge out of Coors during the Age of Imitation was selling an economy beer, then can nickel hot dogs and an exploding scoreboard at Yankee Stadium be very far off?

"These guys [the Yankees] really are bums," the old man said to me as the Twins scored four more runs. "Of course, that's the owner's fault."

"George Steinbrenner?" I asked.

"Yeah, that's the guy," the old man responded while nodding

his head. "Steinbrenner isn't a baseball man. He's a rich owner, made his fortune building ships. But when his ego got in the way, and he started making baseball decisions, the Yankees went straight downhill. Steinbrenner should just sign the checks, and let the baseball people run the team. He casts a mighty big shadow."

But not as big a shadow as the Coors family casts. The values and beliefs of the Coors family have had a major, mostly negative, impact on the fortunes of the family's brewing empire.

Unions boycotted Coors for a decade because of the company's anti-union policies at the Golden brewery . . . African-Americans won't drink Coors because of Bill Coors's alleged racist remarks . . . Despite the popularity of the "green movement" in American business, Coors Brewing Company has an extensive record for environmental abuse . . . Coors employees were subjected to lie-detector tests delving into their personal backgrounds, until the practice was outlawed . . . Coors was ten years late into the bottled water business, because of unfounded fears of exhausting the company's supply of mountain spring water.

Even at major industrial corporations, the political beliefs and values of business owners and managers can have a major impact on the viability of the business. Socially responsible owners and managers aren't a luxury; they are essential for business survival.

"C'mon, you leaving too?" the old man asked, as he bolted from his seat after the third out in the bottom of the sixth.

"Leaving?" I asked incredulously. "There are three more innings left, and we haven't even seen the seventh inning stretch."

"How much more exciting do you think the final three innings are going to be? The Twins lead eleven to two. Why bother to watch this crap?"

The old man had a point. This was, without a doubt, the worst "big league" game I had ever witnessed.

"Besides, if we leave now," the old man allowed, "we'll beat the rush to the subway trains after the game."

Remembering that I had an 8 A.M. breakfast appointment

the next day, I decided to trail the old man to the train platform. Seventh inning or not, this game wasn't worth watching.

Minutes later, the train pulled into the station, and I followed the old man into an uncrowded car.

"See, I told you it would be worth your while," the old man shouted over the din of the train, with a wide grin. "Imagine how crowded this car would be when the game is over, with a few thousand people jamming the platform, all looking for seats. Not everyone would find one."

"I don't know," I reasoned, as the car gently rocked on the tracks. "It feels funny leaving the game early. Three more innings to go. They play nine for a reason, don't they?"

"Sure," he retorted, "and in the old days it was worth watching for nine, ten, eleven innings, however long it lasted. But this isn't the same game, anymore."

"Maybe not, but it's still the major leagues, the best baseball there is. Real baseball fans stay until the end," I argued.

"That's where you're wrong, sonny," the old man chided. "They call it the 'majors,' and the teams are famous the world over. But it's far from the best baseball. You say you're a fan," he taunted, "haven't you seen better games than the one we just saw at Little League, American Legion, or the minors?"

"Yeah, I'll grant you that," I answered.

"Grant you," he mocked. "There you go again sounding intellectual, like a freakin' college kid."

"That's because I am one, a college kid," I mumbled. "You're right, I've seen better Little League games than the one we just saw, but I still feel funny leaving early."

"Did it ever occur to you, college boy, that if more people left early, the games wouldn't be so crappy? Just get up and leave when the game turns to crap, and there'd never be a bad game. If no one came to these rotten games, they'd build a new stadium, field a competitive team, and the players would play harder, like in the old days, wouldn't they?"

"I suppose . . ."

"You suppose?" he cut me off. "You say you're a baseball

fan. Baseball is our national pastime, America's game. But they play it in other parts of the world now, probably better than we saw tonight. The beauty is in the game itself, whether it's the Yankees, or the Hoboken American Legion team, or Taiwan Little League. College boy, winning teams play the game the way it was meant to be played. Anything else is a travesty, and good baseball fans *should* leave a bad game early,'' he finished as the train pulled into a station.

A generation or two of American managers aren't playing the business ''game'' as it was meant to be played. Perks, power trips, promotions, and office politics all get in the way of designing, manufacturing, and selling quality products, the key to the ''game'' of business.

Instead of bemoaning the loss of American competitiveness, the decline of once-great business institutions, like Coors, and the debilitating effects of greed, from Wall Street to Main Street, we Americans need to rededicate ourselves to the realities of business success. Why is it that a generation that was enthralled by a movie about baseball's magical ''field of dreams'' doesn't believe that if we build them (our products) well, customers will come back to America, and we will win again?

Unfortunately, this generation of American managers believes that individuals don't matter, especially when it comes to business. Instead of criticizing, or refusing to be a part of the management malfeasance of the Gilded Age, we grouse that ''that's just the way business is,'' or ''I'm just one person out of thousands at our company,'' or even ''things will never change.'' But by refusing to take responsibility, however slight, for our role in the downward spiral of the economy, we are consigning ourselves, and perhaps future generations, to economic misery and uncertainty.

If America is to thrive again in the international ''game'' of business, then we have to focus on the way we, as individuals, play the game. We must do our part to avoid perpetuating the greed, instability, and management miscues that have plagued our economy since the early 1980s, and avoid being swept up in the rising tide of mismanagement when we say ''that's just the way business is.'' It shouldn't be that way, not if the game is being played the way it was meant to be played, and if businesses are playing to win. And if we can't play a quality game at the ''Major-League'' level, for once-great corporations that are now dying, then American workers must be willing to play the game, and play it well, in the minors, for smaller companies that now fuel growth in our economy.

My mind suddenly felt clear. *Leaving Coors to pursue other opportunities is no longer a difficult choice; it's probably the only choice I can make. After three years of fighting The Beer Wars, I know I can play the game, the way it was meant to be played. I have the feeling that so can many millions of other American workers. Now, it's time for us to play.*

"You know, I came to the game to forget my problems, but I think you helped me to solve them," I confessed, as I looked up and noticed that the old man was gone, probably having left the train at the previous stop, while I was deep in thought. Believing that he somehow could still hear me, I shouted, "See you at a ballpark someday!"

A young nurse, apparently returning from the swing shift at a hospital, frowned and demanded, "Who the *hell* are you talking to?"

"To another fan . . . you know, of the game," I answered with a smile, as the train rolled down the tracks.

Epilogue:
The Band Plays On

Where life is golden, [there is] sadness.

—Sean Connery, in the movie
Sword of the Valiant

Bankruptcies are to the business world what crashes are to the Indianapolis 500 auto race: spectacular, headline-grabbing events that are the exception, rather than the rule.

For every business that declares bankruptcy, hundreds more end the "MacArthurian" way: They don't die, but simply fade away into obscurity. Suffering from years of minimal earnings, or losses, a weakened competitive position, and few, if any avenues for growth, the MacArthurian companies merge with one another, are bought out, or simply grow weak and less competitive over time.

Since Coors didn't borrow money until 1990 (and then, only a paltry $100 million), and earned a profit each year during the 1980s, a spectacular bankruptcy was not possible. Instead, during the Gilded Age, Coors faded into obscurity.

My tenure at Coors, by happenstance, was a defining moment in the history of the Coors brewing empire. With a tradition for brewing quality beers in the West, and years of solid, though not spectacular earnings, the Coors Brewing Company was poised on the brink of future success. But as the preceding pages have shown, shortsightedness, greed, and the management miscues that have plagued many American companies during the past two decades, as well as the Coors family's conservative philosophy, combined to weaken the company.

Those of us who still have an affinity for the company's employees, or for its beer, wish that the late 1980s were merely an aberration in Coors eventual march to greatness, and triumph in The Beer Wars. Sadly, the events of the last five years—since I left the company—have merely been a continuation of the gradual decline of the Coors brewing empire.

1990

March 1990   Coors announces that net income for 1989 *fell* 72 percent, to just $13.1 million dollars. Still, the company points out that revenues increased by almost $240 million, primarily on the basis of surging sales of Keystone Beer.

1991

March 1991   Coors earnings for 1991 jumped by more than $25 million, to $38.9 million, according to the company's annual report. Still, the report notes that the company returned just 3.6 percent on shareholder equity, half as much as a decade earlier, and that the $38 million in earnings, while an improvement over 1990's total, is still less than the company earned in any single year in the 1980s.

April 1991   Coors announces that first-quarter earnings for

1991 are off nearly 18 percent from the company's dismal 1990 performance. In a puzzling analysis in a letter to shareholders, Chairman Bill Coors blames the dip on the Persian Gulf War, among other factors.

April 1991   More than two years after Coca-Cola first used dancing cans as a promotional tool, Coors announces that its July Fourth promotion will feature dancing beer cans.[1]

June 1991   Continuing a disturbing trend, Coors announces that second-quarter net income is down 36 percent from year-ago levels. According to *The Rocky Mountain News,* the company blames "competitive pressures and the cost of new facilities for the dip." (This time, Coors couldn't blame the Persian Gulf War, which lasted just forty days, and had long since ended.)[2]

While Coors struggles under the weight of war and competition, Anheuser–Busch announces that its second-quarter income is up more than 11 percent over year-ago levels.

July 1991   More than two years after Anheuser–Busch introduced Michelob Dry and Bud Dry, Coors announces that it will counter with its own dry beer, Coors Dry. Commenting on the introduction, analyst Bob Messengers claims that "the dry-beer craze in Japan seems to be petering out . . . The same fate, I predict, will overtake U.S. dry-beer marketers."[3]

July 1991   The attorney general of the state of New York charges that Coors Light ads, using the slogan, "There's no slowing down with the Silver Bullet," create "dangerous and misleading impressions" with beer drinkers, since the alcoholic

---

1 Cyndee Miller, "Can Can Dance," *Marketing News,* April 29, 1991, p. 17.

2 Steve Caulk, "Coors Quarterly Earnings Go Flat," *The Rocky Mountain News,* July 20, 1991, p. 43.

3 Steve Caulk, "Coors Adds Non-Alcoholic and Dry Beer to Its Lineup," *The Rocky Mountain News,* July 27, 1991, p. 48.

beverage *does* slow down reflexes. According to the Associated Press, Coors denies the allegation, despite a previous agreement with the Federal Trade Commission to stop using the slogan as of October 1991.

The Denver Post runs a front-page headline reading "Series of Snafus Plaguing Coors." The article details two ammonia leaks at the Coors brewery, which sent sixty-two tourists and workers to the hospital, as well as production shortfalls during the company's peak summer selling season.[4]

October 1991   The Environmental Protection Agency announces that Coors will be fined an additional $700,000 for disposing hazardous wastes and waiting nine years to inform the EPA of groundwater contamination. Total fines for polluting the creek are more than $1.86 million since 1990.[5]

1992

February 1992   Coors announces that total net income in 1991 dipped 34 percent, to just $25.5 million, after a steep fourth-quarter loss of $22 million.

March 1992   One year after Coca-Cola ran a summer promotion featuring randomly-inserted talking Coke cans with prizes, Coors announces that its summer promotion will feature talking Coors cans that offer consumers special prizes.[6]

Advertising Age magazines runs the headline, "Budget Curbs Coors." In the accompanying article, Herr Rechholtz admits

4   Jeffrey Lieb, "Series of Snafus Plaguing Coors," *The Denver Post,* July 13, 1991, p. 1.

5   Bill Scanlon, "EPA Fines Coors $700,000," *The Rocky Mountain News,* October 4, 1991, p. 6.

6   John Accola, "Coors Pops Top on 'Talking' Beer Cans," *The Rocky Mountain News,* March 17, 1992, p. 57.

that Coors can't afford to advertise Coors Extra Gold nationally because of "budget constraints."[7]

April 1992   *The Rocky Mountain News* reports that Coors is considering introducing a "beer cooler for women," more than five years after Crystal Springs Cooler was shelved.[8]

Coors announces that its first-quarter earnings declined 88 percent over 1991's weak performance, to just $762,000. In an apparent understatement, investment analyst Aaron Buckholtz of Century Management claims that, "We weren't excited about the report." Rod Sterling calls, after the earnings report is released, to tell me that most Major-League baseball players now earn more per quarter than Coors Brewing Company.[9]

May 1992   The Environmental Protection Agency announces that Coors was the largest industrial polluter in the state of Colorado in 1990 (the last year for which the agency has complete data), having emitted 583,000 pounds of toxic emissions.

Coors Brewing spokesperson Dave Dunnewald announces that Coors is planning a "small reduction in its work force."[10]

June 1992   Pete Coors steps down as chairman of Coors Brewing Company, and is replaced by Bill Coors, his uncle. Alan Kaplan of Merrill Lynch comments, "It's totally inconsequential as far as I'm concerned."[11]

Peter Coors is quoted in *Business Week* magazine as saying that the brewery's goal is to build "critical mass" by doubling

7 Ira Teinowitz, "Budget Curbs Coors," *Advertising Age,* p. 10.

8 John Accola, "Coors Reportedly Plans Beer Cooler for Women," *The Rocky Mountain News,* April 2, 1992, p. 57.

9 Steve Caulk, "Expansion Hits Coors Earnings, Not Stock," *The Rocky Mountain News,* April 23, 1992, p. 55.

10 "Coors Planning 'Small' Number of Workers Layoffs," *The Rocky Mountain News,* May 30, 1992, p. 66. (Compiled by *Rocky Mountain News* staff.)

11 John Accola, "Coors Shifts Its Management and Adds Three Key Positions," *The Rocky Mountain News,* June 5, 1992, p. 51.

the company's market share to 20 percent of the beer industry. "And to do that, we're going to have to sharpen our spears." The article also outlines the company's sagging profits under a graph titled "Trouble Brewing at Coors."[12]

Though profits continue to sag, the assets of the Coors Brewing Company, including real estate in Golden, are estimated to be worth between $500 million and $1 billion. As the day nears when the brewery will no longer be able to generate even minimal profits for the Coors family, these assets will probably be sold to another brewery, or liquidated, constituting Coors official surrender in The Beer Wars.

Rest in peace, Coors Brewing Company, in the corporate graveyard of the Gilded Age.

12 Ronald Grover, "Coors Is Thinking Suds 'R' Us," *Business Week,* June 8, 1992, p. 34.

Index